LOST MOUNT PENN

Wineries, Railroads and Resorts of Reading

Mike Madaio

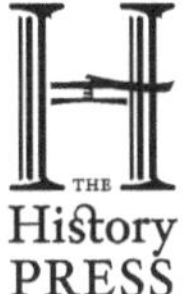

Published by The History Press
Charleston, SC
www.historypress.com

First published 2019

Manufactured in the United States

ISBN 9781467141147

Library of Congress Control Number: 2019948143

Notice: The information in this book is true and complete to the best of our knowledge. It is offered without guarantee on the part of the author or The History Press. The author and The History Press disclaim all liability in connection with the use of this book.

For Michael
I hope it inspires you someday.

CONTENTS

For bonus content, visit LostMountPenn.com

ACKNOWLEDGEMENTS

I could not have possibly completed this project without the generosity of both Joseph Webb and Charlie Adams, both of whom allowed me essentially unlimited usage of their vast collections of period artwork and photography. To both of you I am eternally grateful. Best to William Woys Weaver, for the initial inspiration as well as the photo to prove it. Also thanks to George M. Meiser IX, who shared several photographs from his wonderful series *The Passing Scene*. Thanks to Stephanie Frederick, for creating the Gravity Railroad map (and generally putting up with me). To the folks at the Berks History Center—especially Vicky and Alexis—I appreciate your help and encouragement. And of course thanks to Arcadia Publishing and The History Press, particularly Banks Smither, for giving me the opportunity, and all your help (to come, as of this writing) crossing the finish line.

Lastly, I'd like to appreciate, one last time, Jacob Louis Kuechler, for being a generally awesome dude.

INTRODUCTION

When I first started researching and writing about this topic, the Berks History Center invited me to present at one of its upcoming educational seminars. After accepting, I jumped on a phone call with communications director Alexis Campbell to work out some of the details.

"Are you from Reading?" she asked almost immediately. I replied that I was not. She then wondered if I had spent time in the area, or had family here, or something like that.

I again replied in the negative. "So," she continued, "why on earth are you interested in this?"

It's a fair question. And the answer is a great way to discuss why I wrote this book.

First, a little background. As a food and wine writer, I've long been fascinated by stories beyond flavor—the culture, the history, the impact that eating and drinking has on our lives, aside from simply sustenance. I've been lucky enough to travel around a bit, both for pleasure and as a writer. Wherever I go, I experience that place through food and drink first, expanding out from there.

One thing I have noticed, consistently, is how differently European countries treat alcohol compared with the United States. Here, many aren't exposed to drinking growing up. It's a kind of taboo in many families or communities. And there are countless rules and restrictions. It's no wonder kids take to binge drinking in high school and college, when they're first put in a situation with unfettered access. In Europe, wine (and beer, depending on location) is embedded in the fabric of society. And it is rarely taboo.

I can still remember, vividly, key experiences that highlighted this fact. Ordering a beer in a London pub during high school and being served without a second glance. (I was with my mom.) The revelation, in Paris, that one could buy beer or wine in a corner store and walk down the street, drinking it, without hassle or worry. Perhaps most strikingly, attending a harvest festival in Umbria, Italy, where the local wine was generously handed out, free, to anyone who wanted it. No IDs. No bracelets. No tents just for the drinkers. And there were no problems.

There's another story that a friend of mine—who happens to be one of the world's top wine critics—told me about Italy. It could've easily, however, happened in France, Germany or Spain. This guy, who is also a medical doctor, was working in the emergency room many years ago. A little old lady came in, and while initially examining her, he asked the typical questions. Do you smoke? No. Do you drink alcohol? Never. The latter gave him pause. An Italian lady, of a certain generation, who didn't drink wine, he thought… how could that be possible? "Not even wine?" he countered. "Of course I drink wine!" she responded, confused. "I drink wine every day!"

It's a funny story, and perhaps even apocryphal, but it also says a lot about the culture. Wine is not *alcohol*. It's food. It's part of everyday life. It's assumed. And, as well as the United States has treated me, this is one thing we most certainly get wrong.

(This is the type of stuff wine writers think about. A lot.)

THE PHOTO

As such, being this type of person, it's not particularly surprising that one day I found myself reading a book titled *As American as Shoofly Pie: The Foodlore and Fakelore of Pennsylvania Dutch Cuisine*, by food historian William Woys Weaver. It's an interesting book, mostly about how what we currently think of Pennsylvania Dutch culture is a lie, made up for tourists, and that there was actually once something great in this lie's place. But I bring it up for another reason.

As I was flipping through this book, a photo jumped out at me. It featured several men sitting around a table drinking wine. A good start from my perspective, though I was unprepared for what came next. Under the photo, the caption read: "Pennsylvania Dutchmen enjoying Mt. Penn wines at their

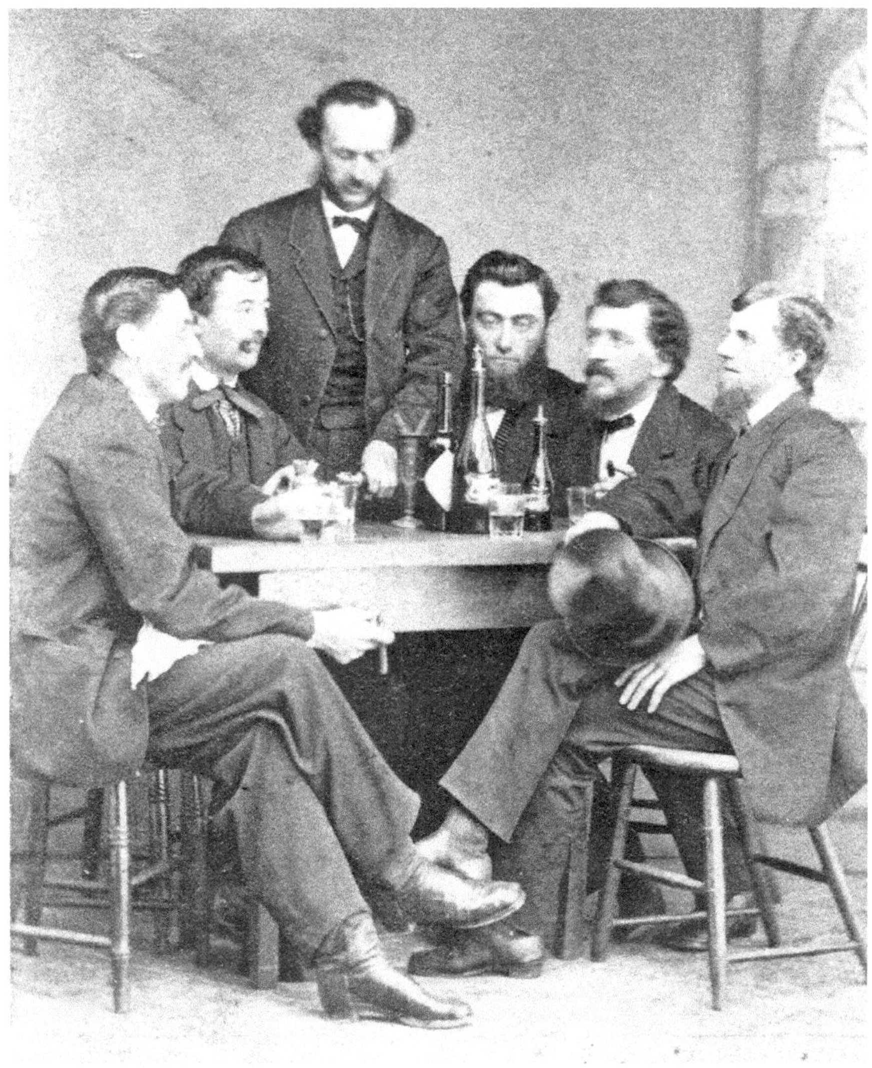

Reading men gathered around local wine in 1868. The photo that led me down this rabbit hole. *Roughwood Collection, Devon, Pennsylvania.*

Schtammtisch [regulars' table] in a Reading, PA wine saloon…1868." Hold on just a second, I thought. Local wines in a wine saloon? Yes, I get that…In *Vienna*. But Reading, Pennsylvania? Mount Penn wines? I was immediately transfixed. Spellbound.

On the opposing page, it spoke of "the famous meals served at Kuechler's Roost, one of the best-known of the Pennsylvania Dutch haute cuisine eateries of the late nineteenth and early 20th centuries." Whoa. Kuechler's Roost, the book continued, was the first of several Pennsylvania Dutch–style *wienstube* (wine bars), "where fine cooking and locally made wines went hand in hand with a style of cuisine that was European in tone yet thoroughly Pennsylvania Dutch in character."

As one is wont to do these days, I immediately headed to Google to find out more about these supposed Mount Penn wines and this so-called Kuechler's Roost. As my research continued to successfully probe the depths of the internet for more amazing details, I felt myself being pulled by an unstoppable force, deeper and deeper into the story. Day turned to night. After several hours, now sitting in a pitch-black room, save for the harsh light of the computer screen, I found myself shouting to my wife things like: "Hey! You're not going to believe what this Kuechler guy did in 1883!" (I couldn't see the eye roll, but I know it happened.)

"The Western slope of Mt. Penn has dignity; the Skyline has beauty; and the Eastern side, sociability," read one article I found that first day. "Here, for nearly forty years, flourished a Wine House, which was an ornament to the mountain, and an oasis of rest for congenial people. It was not started, established or founded, but created, and the creator was Jacob Louis Kuechler. His friends called him Ludwig, and said that 'None knew him but to love him; none named him but to praise.'"[1]

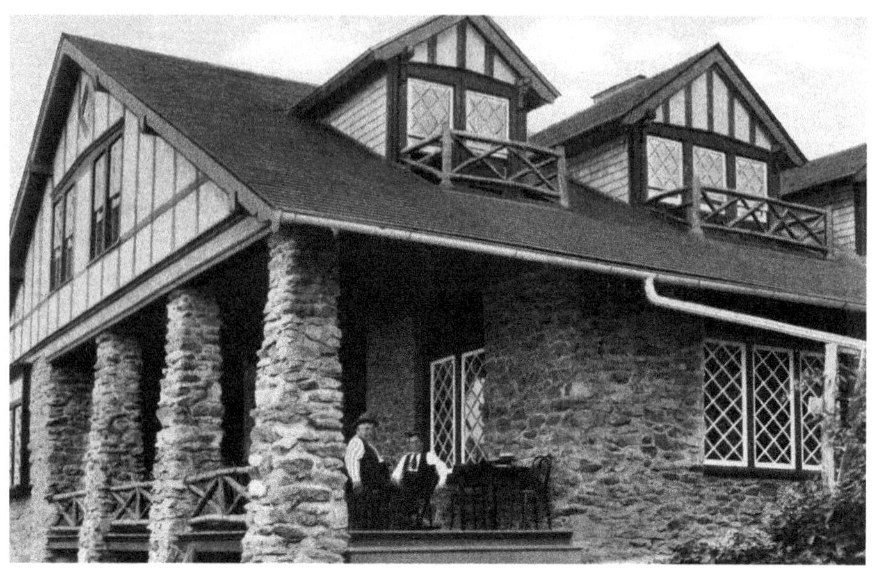

A postcard depicting Kuechler's Roost wine house in the early 1900s. *J. George Hintz.*

The more passages like this I read, the more hooked I became. And it wasn't just the fact that there was wine being made and consumed, in a previously unknown (by me) spot less than an hour from my house. It was the characters. The stories. The way people talked and wrote about them. Encountering them today, there's this still-beating heart, a zeal and zest for life that can't be contained by the fact that they no longer exist.

Thus, after a few twists and turns, here we are. I hope, to the best of my ability, through their own words and my own interpretation of them, that I can do justice to the citizens of Reading, Pennsylvania, during the wine house period in the text that follows. I believe wholeheartedly that their story is one more people need to know.

I

PENNSYLVANIA

Wine Land?

Though not a particularly well-known area for wine today—at least in comparison to California on the West Coast, and even the Finger Lakes of New York or emerging states like Virginia, origins of the American wine scene can be traced back to Eastern Pennsylvania. This legacy began when William Penn brought grapevines from Bordeaux to the continent on his trip to negotiate the purchase of land that would become Pennsylvania in 1682.

These plantings, which lived briefly in what is now Philadelphia's Fairmount Park, ultimately failed due to a lack of resistance to local pests and diseases. Of note, however, is how they—unknowingly at the time—cross-pollinated with some native grape plants to form the very first hybrid, or offspring of European grapes (*Vitis vinifera*) and native American varieties (*Vitis labrusca*). And while these hybrids could not match their foreign counterparts from a quality standpoint, they formed the backbone of the U.S. wine industry before modern technology allowed for the successful harvesting of imported vines.

Discovered around 1740 by James Alexander, gardener to one of William Penn's sons, this original hybrid—dubbed the Alexander grape, among other names—was the first colonial vinous success and quickly became planted widely across Pennsylvania as well as other eastern states, due to excellent vineyard performance and relative wine quality.[2]

Despite eventually giving way to more successful hybrids such as Isabella and Catawba, much of the early U.S. wine industry evolved out of this

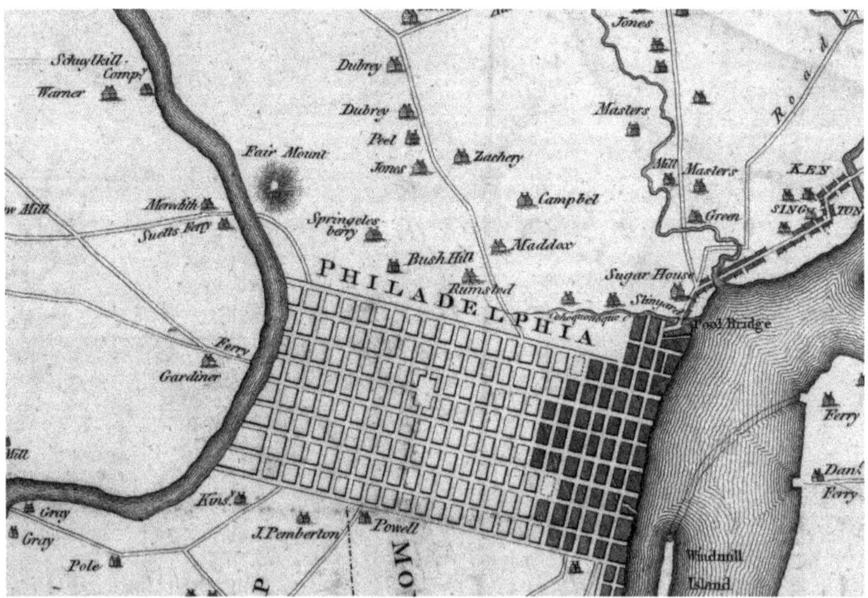

This map of Philadelphia shows Springelesberry, just northwest of the city limits, where the Alexander grape was discovered. *Library of Congress.*

original discovery. In his important 1908 book *The Grapes of New York*, U.P. Hedrick reported, for example, that Alexander was the principal grape grown in the York area—"one of the first, if not the first, extensive centers of native grape-growing in America"[3]—though originally it was known as York Madeira and rumored to have come from the famed Portuguese island. Other popular grapes grown here at the time, including York Claret and York Lisbon, are also believed to be subtypes of Alexander.

Hedrick spent considerable focus on this mostly forgotten grape (even by 1908), commenting on how it had become "a grape of the past, but no other of our American varieties better deserve[d] historical record."[4]

He went on to describe Alexander as "a coarse grape with so much foxiness of flavor that it did not please the early growers, who had been accustomed to European sorts, as a table-grape, but it made a very good wine of the claret type and was grown for this purpose until displaced by the Catawba. It was wine made from this variety that Thomas Jefferson pronounced 'worthy of the best vineyards of France.'"[5]

THE PENNSYLVANIA VINE COMPANY

Even before the aforementioned growth in York, a Frenchman named Pierre "Peter" Legaux founded the very first commercial winery in the United States, just outside of Philadelphia. Having in 1786 purchased a 206-acre property near Spring Mill—along the eastern banks of the Schuylkill River, about thirteen miles northwest of Center City—Legaux began experimenting with the cultivation of European grapes.

Unable to fund a truly commercial vineyard on his own, in 1793 Legaux successfully convinced the state legislature to pass an act that enabled "the Governor of this commonwealth to incorporate a Company for the purpose of promoting the cultivation of vines." In other words, to allow the public to invest in shares of his newly formed Pennsylvania Vine Company.

Despite heightened interest in producing wine in America during this period, Legaux had difficulty securing the necessary funding to make his business viable, requiring help a second time (in 1800) from the state government, which then allowed interested investors to pay the twenty-dollar share price in installments, with a down payment of just one dollar per share. Though that did encourage more investment, Legaux's insistence on succeeding with European *vinifera* grapes would be his downfall; in 1803 alone, he lost almost fourteen thousand vines to late spring frosts and hail.

Perhaps more noteworthy than Legaux's accomplishments (or lack thereof) as a winemaker was his controversial and unique personality. What remains lost to history is whether he was well intentioned or just a common-grade charlatan.

His main contribution to the wine industry was certainly that he was first to succeed with Alexander on a grand scale and helped spread the grape widely. It comes, however, with a caveat. He called this grape "Cape," claiming it came to him via the Cape of Good Hope and was in fact of the European *Vitis vinifera* variety. Whether Legaux intended to defraud potential investors—or mixed up the cuttings he had purchased and truly believed the grape came from South Africa—remains unknown. Documents do suggest that he stuck to his story when, as Hedrick put it, he was "reproached for his deception."[6]

Historian Thomas Pinney offered a possible reprieve:

> In defense of Legaux's good faith in calling a native *labrusca* a *vinifera*, it is important to note that the Alexander, unlike most pure natives, has a perfect (that is, self-pollinating) flower; every variety of unhybridized native vine bears either pistillate or staminate flowers that are, by

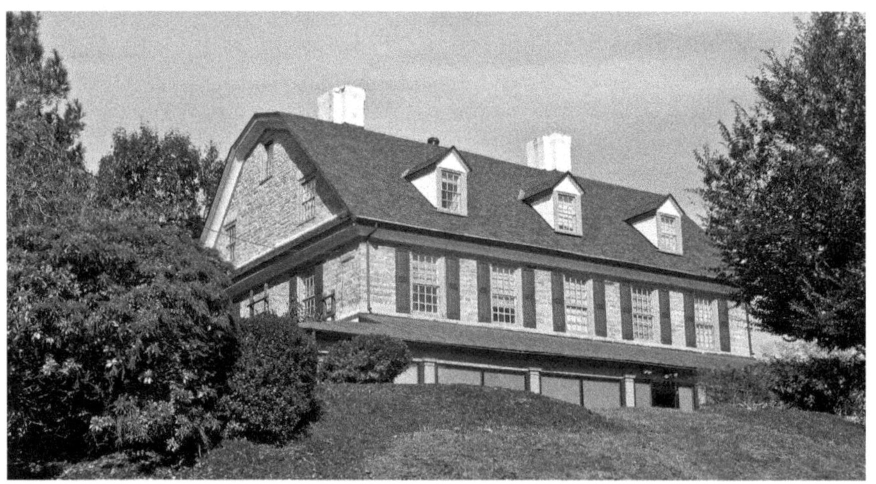

A modern-day view of Legaux's Spring Mill home, now a designated historical property. *Wikimedia Commons.*

> themselves, sterile. Dufour [another prominent winegrower of the time] himself was persuaded by this observation that the Cape was a genuine *vinifera*, and so he thought to the end, not knowing that the perfect-flowered characteristic is the effect of a dominant gene from *vinifera* that can enter into the genetic combination.[7]

Regardless, Hedrick astutely pointed out that

> Legaux's advertisement of this variety had the effect of making it known at least, and it is the opinion of writers of that day that many were induced to try this grape under the supposition that it was from the Cape of Good Hope who would have scorned it had they supposed it to be a native. It came to be considerably planted in all parts of the United States.[8]

The irony here is that the Pennsylvania Vine Company may have prospered if Legaux himself had put more faith in his so-called Cape grape.

Legaux's colorful lifestyle extended beyond his career as a farmer. Pinney noted that the Frenchman, who was a lawyer in his home country, was a

> remarkably difficult and litigious neighbor. When another...French traveler, the duc de la Rochefoucauld-Liancourt, was directed to Legaux's vineyard as one of the sights of the Philadelphia region in 1795, he took an instant dislike to Legaux—a man, he wrote, whose

> "whole physiognomy indicates cunning rather than goodness of heart." The duc was scandalized to learn that Legaux, in the nine years of his residence in Pennsylvania, had engaged in two hundred lawsuits, all of them unsuccessful![9]

Found among the papers of the Montgomery County Historical Society is yet more evidence to Legaux's impropriety: an account of one of his neighbors offering to pay for his beating and possible murder.

> When the name of Peter Legaux having been mentioned, the said Nicholas Dubey spoke very disrespectfully of [Legaux], saying that he was a very great rascal....Dubey proposed to the deponent to build him a house to live in...and to give him some dollars, provided he...would beat [Legaux], and hurt him as much as he could...that he would pay all costs and be his bail....Dubey added that if the deponent should kill [Legaux]...Dubey would be his bail and answer for all.[10]

Legaux certainly did, however, as Pinney put it, seem "to have had a genius for self-promotion." Consider, for one, his description of "the first vintage ever held in America" in 1793, an absurd claim to be making after nearly three hundred years of European settlement. Summing up the man's legacy, Hedrick wrote:

> Judging the man from his [writing] and from the words of his contemporaries, he was a capable, enthusiastic and intelligent grape-grower. His philanthropy is more doubtful. It is true that he distributed many grape plants but as he himself says to "fellow citizens possessing pecuniary means." That he practiced deceit in the matter of the introduction of the Alexander as the Cape is probable. However, his deceit, if such it were, may be forgotten and he should be remembered as the chief disseminator of the Alexander, the first distinctive American variety of commercial value.[11]

The Next Wave

Pursuant to the discovery of Alexander and, more importantly, the knowledge that hybrid grapes could be made to survive the native weather conditions

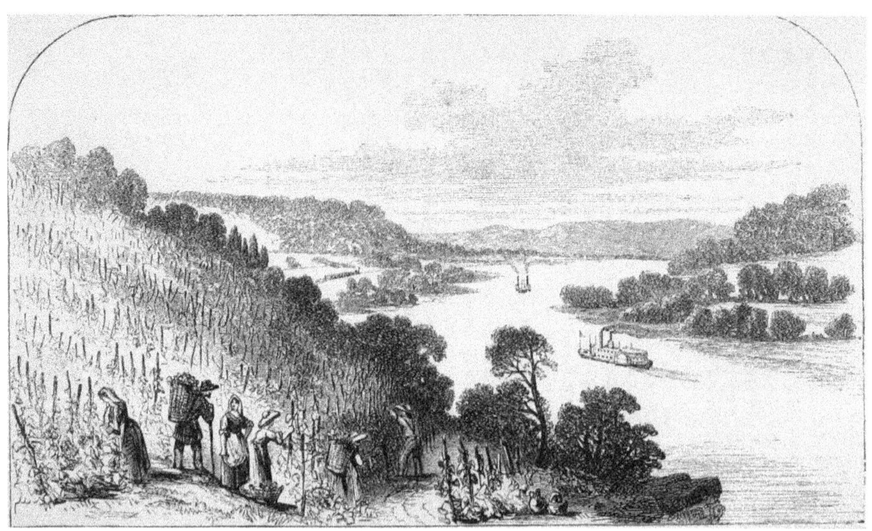

An 1859 drawing of Nicholas Longworth's vineyards along the Ohio River. *Wikimedia Commons.*

and produce palatable wine, a number of superior hybrids emerged over the next fifty years. Rumored but not proven to be from South Carolina, Isabella was first cultivated around 1816 on Long Island. Clinton followed in the 1830s, and Concord a decade later, the latter of which gained notoriety through its association with the Welch family of Erie.

The driving force behind industry growth in the early 1800s, however, was most definitely Catawba. In Cincinnati—a place not exactly associated with wine in the twenty-first century—a man named Nicholas Longworth established the nation's first commercially successful winery, along the banks of the Ohio River, with Catawba as his flagship grape. Though Longworth started his venture with the goal of producing a world-class dry wine, it was his off-dry sparkling Catawba rosé that propelled him to international acclaim, with one London writer even claiming, in 1850, that it "transcends the champagnes of France."[12]

By this point in history, the important centers of winemaking had moved away from southeastern Pennsylvania to places such as Ohio, New York and, of course, California, yet the development of this new wave of hybrid grapes such as Isabella, Catawba and Clinton would indeed be the foundation on which the German-immigrant farmers of Berks County would build their very own flourishing wine industry and culture.

2

VINOUS ORIGINS IN BERKS

The Stubborn Will of the Teuton

In most modern histories of American wine—even those focused exclusively on the East Coast or Pennsylvania specifically—the wine culture of Berks County in the 1800s is either relegated to footnote status or left out altogether. There exists, however, plenty of evidence that—at least during this period—the area's wine was highly regarded.

"In no county of Pennsylvania, it may be safely said, is the grape more extensively and successfully cultivated than in Berks," wrote the *Reading Times* in 1875. "Attention is paid to its cultivation on every farm, and in many sections of the county small vineyards have been established, which have proved a source of both pleasure and profit to the owner."

"No county in the State possess more favorable localities for grape culture," the article continued, gushingly. "The hillsides and vicinity of Reading are admirably adapted to vineyard culture, having situations properly exposed to the sun, a desirable soil, the hills in many respects resembling those in the most favored wine districts of the Rhine."

This was not lost on area residents, many of whom raised crops for personal consumption if not commercial purposes. "There is scarcely a farmer of the county, or the owner of a lot in Reading," the paper added, "who does not devote considerable attention to the subject of grape-culture." The article went on to list no fewer than thirty vintners in Reading proper and even more in the surrounding areas, with a final note that this incomplete list could be "indefinitely increased."[13]

It is of course fair to note that the biases of the *Reading Times* might move this hyperbolic praise into propaganda territory, but it was not only those of Reading who reported as such. In 1867, for example, speaking of the wines made from Clinton and Catawba by Reading vintner John Fehr, the *Lancaster Intelligencer* commented: "We doubt if they can be surpassed in purity and excellency by any others of the kind in this country."[14]

"Grape culture and the manufacture of wine in Eastern Pennsylvania have within the last fifteen years assumed an ominous importance," wrote the *Philadelphia Times* in 1887, when discussing the wines of Berks. "The time may come when instead of standing fifth on the list of production it may vie with California in this particular industry. It certainly is destined to become a vast source of national wealth."[15] (Ironically, Pennsylvania remains in this same fifth spot today, give or take.)

In 1890, Philly's *Times* added that "it is a fact not generally known that some of the best native wine in this country is made from grapes grown right on the side of Mount Penn, within fifty miles of Philadelphia."[16]

Vine Pioneering

According to legendary Reading brewer Frederick Lauer—whose family had a history in the wine business—when he came to Reading with his parents in 1823, grape-growing was already underway, led by three of the oldest settlers in the area: John Printz, Abraham Hoch and Jonathan Shearer.[17] In these early days, vineyards were located in town. Hoch lived on Penn Street at the corner of Eighth Street. Shearer's vineyard—established around 1820—stood near Seventh and Chestnut Streets, on a plot that later would house the Reading Railroad Company forge. (Shearer's family eventually became known for their winemaking in nearby Tuckerton.) These three vintners grew primarily the Schuylkill grape, another name for Alexander, whose thick skin was known for producing "foxy" wines, or wines with a distinctive (and generally off-putting) musk.

"The wine produced from it was of a bright red color, and was commonly called the 'Reading Red,'" wrote the *Reading Times*. "Germans who came here were very fond of it, and esteemed it highly as a table wine. It was relished by them all the more, because it reminded them very much of their native country and its fine wines."[18]

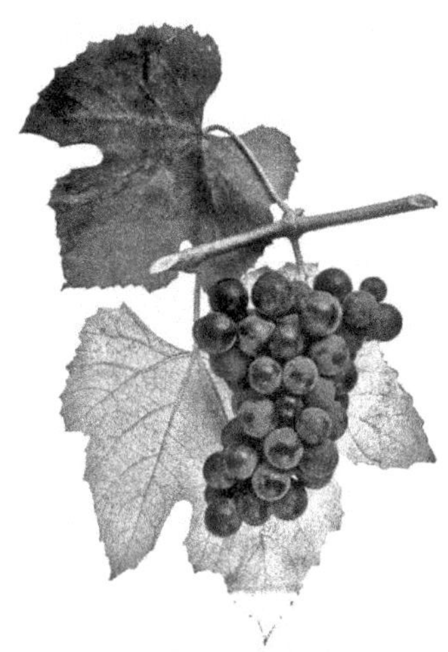

An illustration of the Catawba grape from U.P. Hedrick's *The Grapes of New York*. *Project Gutenberg*.

At this point, winemakers commonly sold "Reading Red" directly from their residences to willing private buyers, for no license was required for the sale of malt or vinous liquors, nor were these beverages subject to taxation. (Oh, how times have changed in Pennsylvania.)

In 1829, inspired by the industry's potential, Frederick Lauer's father, George, took it upon himself to import German vines—from his home region of Pfalz on the Rhine River—with the intent of cultivating European-style white wines. The elder Lauer paid $900 in gold for seventeen thousand vines of nine different varieties, which shipped in the spring. Unfortunately, a large number of these vines were "considerably sprouted"[19] upon arrival and thus were unable to adapt to a new climate. Some did, amazingly—considering the level of success with *vinifera* to this point in American history—prosper and bear fruit for several seasons. A severe winter a few years later, however, devastated the vast majority that still survived. By 1875, only a single vine of the original seventeen thousand imported remained in existence and could be seen on the lot at the northwest corner of Fifth and Cherry.

Yet Lauer was undaunted, continuing his search for a quality grape that would prove hardy enough to withstand Berks winters. Working with his friend and local grape expert George Zieber, he ordered the first area vines of both Isabella (in 1830) and Catawba (a year or two later), which they subsequently planted in Lauer's vineyard at the corner of Third and Chestnut Streets. According to the younger Lauer, "The vines grew vigorously, stood the winter well, and proved to be perfectly adapted to this climate."[20]

Zieber went on to create a vineyard on Third Street between Franklin and Chestnut, which came to be known as "Zieber's Garden" and served as a base for his business of raising Isabella and Catawba vines for general dissemination.

The Linchpin

George Lauer, for the reasons mentioned earlier, was one of two individuals in particular to which Berks County was "greatly indebted for the advancement it has made in grape culture,"[21] according to the *Reading Times*. John Fehr (occasionally written as "Fair"), a Swiss immigrant who arrived around 1830, was the other. Though originally employed as a shoemaker, and later a bottler, Fehr quickly befriended Lauer and Zieber and began experimenting in the vineyard.

In many ways, Fehr became the key link between the original attempts previously documented and the wine house culture that would thrive later in the nineteenth century. In particular, his determination through a variety of plagues to make winemaking in Reading a successful enterprise would have a lasting impact on the local industry. Early on, he faced a string of difficulties that, as the *Reading Times* described, would have been "sufficient to have discouraged the majority of men, but Mr. Fehr possessed a determination and courage that never failed him, and his resolute heart sustained him through every trial and adversity."[22]

In the 1830s, for example, winters were particularly severe in Berks, with many remembering in particular the season of 1836–37 for its extremely low temperatures (anecdotally, to negative twenty degrees Fahrenheit). As such, heavy frosts often destroyed any vines that were planted—even those hybrids that typically survived eastern winters—despite Fehr's furious efforts to protect them. As temperatures returned to normal in the 1840s, rosebugs and other pests attacked, all of which were native to the Americas and thus heretofore unknown in the vast European vine growing knowledgebase. During the 1850s, Fehr's troubles continued, as rot and mildew caused considerable destruction. Nevertheless, he persisted.

Though his first true success—which did not come until the early 1860s—featured Isabella, Catawba would launch his legend. "Soon his Catawba wine and Catawba brandy acquired a reputation which made 'Fehr's wines' known throughout the entire country," wrote the *Reading Times*, "and caused growers in other sections of the country to emulate his example, until the production of Catawba wine and brandy became an important industry of the country."[23] Fehr might have been following in Longworth's footsteps, but he was carving out a similar sphere of influence.

BIG STRAWBERRY

John Fehr, Esq, has sent us a strawberry, raised by himself, which measures four and a half inches in circumference. It don't take many of such fellows to make a quart.

—*Reading Times*, June 16, 1868

In 1863, Fehr began to work with Clinton, which the *Reading Times* described as "a small jet black grape, of pungent and aromatic flavor, producing a beautiful garnet colored wine, similar in appearance to claret, but much a superior even to that favorite French brand,"[24] and later as a grape that "recommended itself on account of its great productiveness, hardiness and excellent qualities for wine-making."[25]

The paper would also recall how "the superior judgement of Mr. Fehr did not mislead him," as well as how "the 'Clinton' ranks at the present day as the great American wine grape," with obvious implications to Fehr's influence on that fact. He "manufactured from it a rich garnet-colored wine, of sparkling appearance, and a real claret flavor, so that it soon acquired the name of 'American Claret,' and as such was highly esteemed by all connoisseurs."[26]

In addition to the ascendency of Clinton, Fehr is noted for bringing in and experimenting with newly popular hybrids such as the highly regarded Ives Seedling ("an excellent wine grape"[27]), Taylor (which produced a "pale, golden-colored" white[28]) and of course Concord, which was preferred for table use.

Perhaps Fehr's key legacy, however, was his realization that planting vineyards on east- or south-facing slopes, emulating the finest vineyards of Europe, would produce superior wine. Of this idea's importance, the *Philadelphia Times* commented:

> It was at first thought by wine producers that the vine would best grow on level river bottoms and on wide plains, where artificial irrigation could take place. But the far-seeing German of Berks has taken lessons of Germany and France, and has utilized the slopes of hills beautifully sheltered against the winds. The once barren flanks of mountains and hills heretofore looked upon as irredeemable waste, have yielded to the stubborn will of the Teuton, and everywhere are teeming with vineyards and flowing with the red wine.[29]

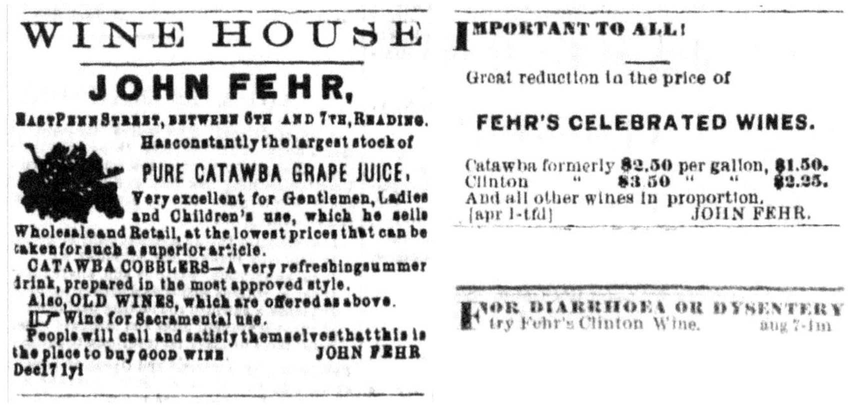

Ads in the *Reading Times* for John Fehr's wine business, 1865, 1870. *Newspapers.com.*

Fehr established two main vineyards on graded land just outside of town, near the Mineral Spring Hotel. The first, known as the "Big Vineyard," lived on the southeastern side of Mount Washington and housed nine acres of vines as part of thirty-three total acres of orchards and farmland. The second, or "Mineral Spring Vineyard," contained three acres of vines (out of seven and a half total land) on the 300 block of Friedensburg Road, along the eastern slope of Mount Penn.[30]

After Fehr's death in 1871, his son, also John Fehr, inherited the Big Vineyard. Though he turned over the maintenance of (and eventually sold) it to his father-in-law, Eberhard Barth—who himself would attain vinous success over the next several decades—he continued to make and sell wine throughout the 1870s, producing as much as 4,500 gallons in his best year. Building on his father's well-known brand, he developed markets in Philadelphia, New York and throughout the rest of the country,[31] selling both wine and unfermented grape juice (a product that grew in stature as the temperance movement swelled). He also ran a successful wine house and saloon in town—at 305 Eighth Street—before selling that business in 1883.

The Mineral Spring Vineyard passed to Fehr's daughter, Millie Schoener of New York City, but remained in operation under the watch of Fehr's longtime right-hand man, Jacob Roth.[32] In 1881, Schoener sold off her vast wine cellar on Penn Street and leased the vineyard to Max Schneider/Snyder,[33] so she could, as the *Reading Times* so eloquently put it, "no longer pay any attention to the wine business."[34] Theodore Benz purchased the vineyard outright in 1885.

Speaking of the elder Fehr's legacy several years after he'd passed, the *Reading Times* remarked that "during his life-time he did much to foster and encourage grape-culture in this country, and to bring about the consumption of native wines, in preference to foreign importations which are frequently adulterated and deleterious. In this, as well as in other respects, Mr. Fehr was a protectionist."[35]

3

WINE INDUSTRY GROWTH

1860s–1880s

Reading's wine industry did not flourish in earnest until after the Civil War, yet there was some critical activity in the early 1860s that helped establish a foundation to build on for the next several decades. Of course, the aforementioned and long-awaited success of John Fehr's enterprise led that charge. But others who came into prominence around the same time and developed the industry through the 1880s—especially those who contributed significantly—also deserve acknowledgement.

Wine houses in town were quite popular at this time. One in particular, the Rustic Retreat, opened by John Barth prior to the Civil War on the 300 block of Eighth Street, featured a large lawn area where patrons gathered during nicer weather to enjoy generous portions of homemade wine and cheese, as well as a bowling alley.[36]

In the early 1860s, fruit farmer William Young opened his own wine house on his nearly two-acre vineyard and farm at the corner of North Twelfth and Walnut Streets. Having purchased the property in 1847, Young had run a fruit store on Penn Street for about fifteen years, where he sold a wide variety of items, including apples, pears, plums, berries, cherries and grapes, before moving his entire operation to 205–7 North Twelfth. This spot quickly became a "popular place of resort for his wide circle of friends and customers,"[37] helped, perhaps, by Young's affinity for flowers, which beautifully adorned any space on his property that wasn't dedicated to growing fruit.

Beyond the usual suspects, Young experimented with a variety of obscure grapes, having as many as forty different varieties at any given time.[38] These included Eumelan, Delaware, Diana, Iona, Israelia, Hartford Prolific, Allen's Hybrid, Salem and others,[39] though many were intended for table use. At its most prolific, the farm could produce up to four tons of grapes in a season.

Just east of Young's land, Augustus Vollmer—who became well known as one of Reading's most successful vintners[40]—oversaw a vineyard and winery on three and a half acres along Thirteenth Street near Elm, Walnut and Birch Streets, which he started in the mid-1850s. This lot grew, a few years later, when Vollmer purchased some of Young's tract for himself. The property included a two-story brick dwelling with verandas, a summer kitchen and two cellars, the lower of which contained a spring of cold water. In addition to the vineyard and wine press, the grounds also featured stables, a large flower and vegetable garden and an extensive system for the manufacture of vinegar, including copper boilers, tanks and vats, all housed in satellite frame buildings.[41]

Of Vollmer's property, which sat at the intersection of Mount Penn's western edge and the city's urban center, the *Reading Times* noted that "it

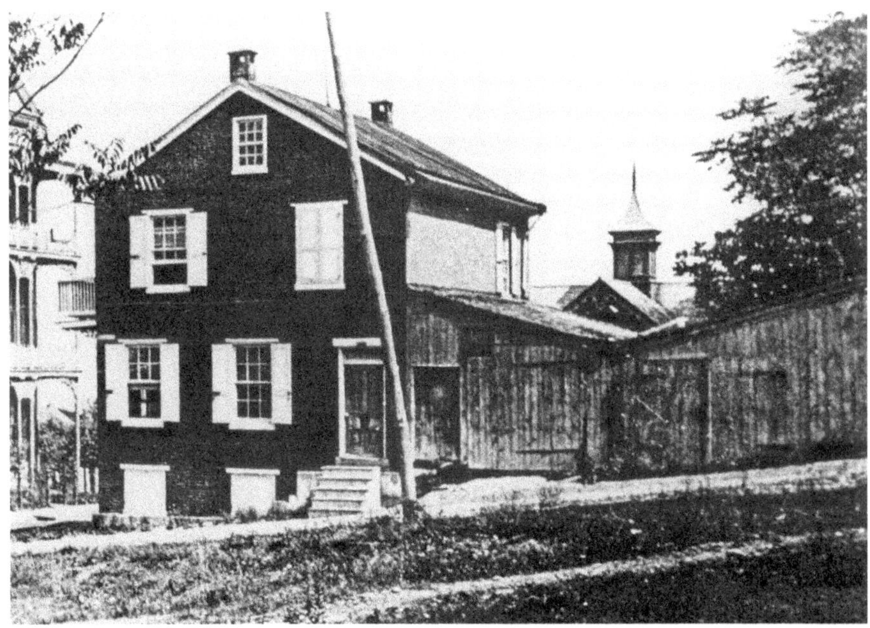

Augustus Vollmer's house; note the outbuilding to the right, where wine was made. *Joseph A. Webb Collection.*

commands one of the finest views in the vicinity of Reading…is convenient to the business part of the city, and possesses unsurpassed advantages in every respect.…Attached to the premises [is] an excellent vineyard and choice fruit and shade trees, which could be laid out into beautiful lawns and pleasure grounds."[42]

An active member of local society (especially within the Republicans of Reading organization), Vollmer earned praise similar to that of Fehr in the *Reading Times*, which once suggested that the choicest wines in *the country*[43] were made by these two men. Another *Times* piece said this of Vollmer:

> A gentleman of taste and judgment, whose attention was early attracted to the business, and who is now to Reading what Nicholas Longworth is to Cincinnati and the West. With proper encouragement he will soon succeed in making the Reading Wine ("Reading Red" as it was formerly called) as famous as the Johannisberger, of which (and of its imitations) so many thousand bottles are yearly consumed in this country.…His Reading Wines consist of three Vintages, viz: 1859, 1860 and 1861, and are especially worthy of attention.[44]

Vollmer also ran a popular wine and liquor store on Penn Street during the 1860s and early '70s, first in the cellar under Eben's City Hall German Theater, between Sixth and Seventh Streets, and later at the corner of Eighth, where he became one of the first tenants in the newly constructed Breneiser's Hall in 1869.[45]

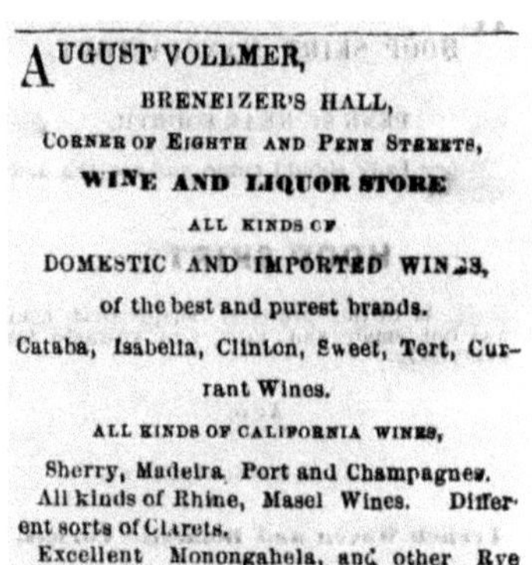
AUGUST VOLLMER,
BRENEIZER'S HALL,
CORNER OF EIGHTH AND PENN STREETS,
WINE AND LIQUOR STORE
ALL KINDS OF
DOMESTIC AND IMPORTED WINES,
of the best and purest brands.
Catuba, Isabella, Clinton, Sweet, Tert, Currant Wines.
ALL KINDS OF CALIFORNIA WINES,
Sherry, Madeira, Port and Champagnes.
All kinds of Rhine, Masel Wines. Different sorts of Clarets.
Excellent Monongahela, and other Rye Whiskey's, Brandy and Bitters. [ap6-6m

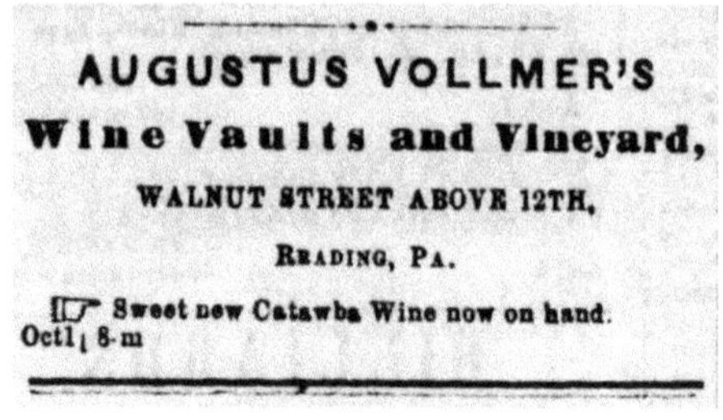
AUGUSTUS VOLLMER'S
Wine Vaults and Vineyard,
WALNUT STREET ABOVE 12TH,
READING, PA.
☞ Sweet new Catawba Wine now on hand.
Oct1 | 8-m

Ads in the *Reading Times* for Augustus Vollmer's wine business, 1869, 1863. *Newspapers.com.*

In 1872, after selling off his vineyard and the contents of his liquor store, Vollmer moved to Philadelphia, where he lived until 1886. On July 13 of that year, he passed away due to complications from an accident where a wagon ran over his leg and amputation was required. He was "about 70 years of age."[46]

Though the *Reading Times* showed foresight when commenting that Vollmer's Thirteenth Street property "affords a rare opportunity to establish a first-class summer resort, that would not fail to secure from the start a liberal patronage and support,"[47] the actual buyer was Father Bornemann of the St. Paul's Catholic Church (for a price of $10,000). Shortly thereafter, St. Joseph's Hospital opened, using Vollmer's original home until a new and improved structure was constructed in 1885. Interestingly enough, the vineyard remained an ongoing source of hospital revenue for many years.

The St. Joseph's name is still very much a fixture in the city, today as part of the Penn State Health system. The original property—on which the hospital resided until 1926—was donated to the Reading school district in 2007 and now houses Reading Intermediate High School. Some parts of the 1885 building, including the old chapel, remain.

"THE MOST FAMOUS VINEYARD IN BERKS"

George Leonard Reiniger arrived in the Reading area around 1858 as an experienced winemaker, having run the village co-op's winery in his hometown of Württemberg, Germany, where he was born in 1814 to another winemaker and his wife.[48] Life was not exactly easy for the Reinigers; George spoke of gaining his livelihood cutting wood in the forests of Germany's Hartz Mountains, and that, at times, food was so scarce that he would fill his stomach with water to drive away the pangs of hunger. As such, with work ethic and marketable skills in tow, it is little surprise that he answered America's beckoning call.

In Pennsylvania, he initially worked as an assistant to John Fehr, first at the Mineral Spring Vineyard and later at the Big Vineyard. In 1863, either dissatisfied with his pay or intent on embarking on his own project (or perhaps both), Reiniger purchased a small farm also on the eastern slope of Mount Penn—which bore close resemblance to the hillside vineyards of his native Germany[49]—and began what would become the most famous and long-lived winery in Berks County.

Reiniger followed in Fehr's footsteps by selecting land often described as stony and barren and turning it into a fertile and productive winery. He would discover, as had so many Europeans before him, that these seemingly useless and forsaken spots often produce the very best wines.

This battle with nature created a certain camaraderie among the area farmers, highlighted in the following passage from the 1878 *Reading Times*:

> Perhaps few of our readers are aware of what is meant by a "stone match." The term is undoubtedly familiar to people living in mountainous districts, and, briefly stated, may be defined thus: Clearing land of stones for tillable purposes by a friendly gathering of neighbors, who volunteer their personal services, their horses and sleds and wagons....Thus it was that several acres of mountain land in Alsace township, owned by George Reiniger, vintner, were cleared on Saturday last. Neighbors and friends to the number of fifty, with sixteen head of horses and a number of sleds and wagons, congregated in a six-acre field literally covered with stones, which were picked and thrown into heaps and then hauled to the eastern and southern boundaries of the field, where they were made into a substantial fence. The work of clearing the land was vigorously pushed until dark when the entire party repaired to Mr. Reiniger's new mansion, where a bountiful supper had been prepared.[50]

Reiniger slowly but steadily built both his reputation as a winemaker and the footprint of his farm, to the point that, by the mid-1880s, he oversaw more than eighty acres of vines[51] yet still needed to buy grapes from other farmers to meet demand for his wine.[52] In fact, his customers came from diverse locales, including, of course, Philadelphia but also New Jersey, New York, Baltimore, Washington, D.C., and even cities farther west.[53]

Later in his life, his journey was described as such:

> Some 18 or 20 years ago [Reiniger] purchased a little pocket in the side of the hill for a song. Its chief production was water, rocks and wild vines, and people charitably said he would not find enough dirt to bury himself in when he starved to death. But he and his boys went to work upon the rocks. They dug them up, they rolled them up in rows, buried them, and got rid of them in every way possible. By these means they disclosed a portion of the soil, terraced the hillside, planted vines, grains

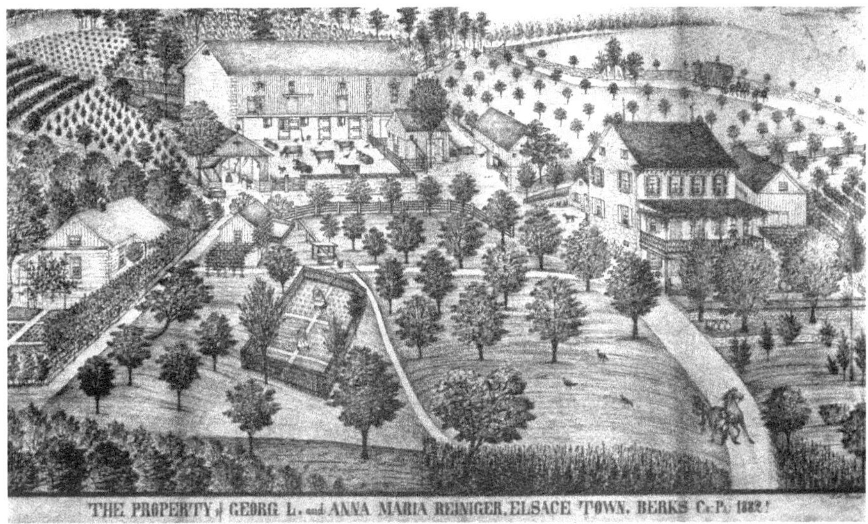

Ferdinand A. Brader drawing of the Reiniger Farm, circa 1880. *Center for the Study of Art in Rural America.*

> and vegetables, and toiled on, clearing away more rocks. They trained the water to run where they wanted it, pastured cows among the bushes and in the woods, and managed to live in spite of predictions to the contrary. It was slow work, but their toil told. By and by the vines began to bear, constant tillage enriched the soil, and carefully planted fruit trees began to yield a return; there began to be a surplus of vegetables to sell; people tasted the wine made from the grapes and pronounced it good, and the little pocket of rocks began to be a mine of wealth yielding a big income. Now the little log house which was the original home is cast in the shade by two big new houses flanked by a big, prosperous-looking barn, and all around are vineyards and orchards and vegetable gardens. It is a sight that delights the eye of everyone who looks upon it. The little pocket of rocks in the hills has become probably the most productive bit of ground in all of Berks county.[54]

Reiniger had become the largest vintner in the county, presiding over a picturesque farm that included, according to the *Philadelphia Times*, "a perfect little village" as well as wheat, corn, vegetables and berries. More importantly, he produced at least five thousand gallons of wine yearly, for which—in 1886 at least—he received $1.25 per gallon.[55]

After Reiniger died in 1892, his son Daniel J. and grandson George H. Reiniger (whose story is continued in chapter 8) carried on the family business for many years. The *Reading Times* lamented the patriarch's passing thusly:

> He was scrupulously exact in his methods of farming; painstaking in putting them into successful execution; shirking nothing that was necessary; sparing neither muscle nor means in keeping up his "place" to the highest possible standard of cultivation. The result was that through sheer force of these methods, thrifty, persistent and well directed industry, and a wise economy in the management of his farm, a barren hillside upon which his predecessors eked out a miserable existence became transformed into a veritable garden of beauty, fertility and profit. If more men of Mr. Reiniger's tact and industry could be induced to settle along the slopes of our mountain sides, Berks county would be an immense gainer and the revenues for farming be vastly increased.[56]

4

VIRTUAL TASTING

It is surely difficult to read about, think about and study these winemakers and their fascinating culture without spending considerable time wondering what the wine actually tasted like. Was it similar to what is drunk today or completely different?

Unfortunately for both amateur and professional historians, descriptions of wine from yesteryear were typically vague when compared to the tasting notes popular in today's society. Far before Robert Parker or *Wine Spectator*, in other words, there were no effusive recalls of obscure flavors such as quince paste, forest floor or Maduro tobacco, to name just a few. As over-the-top and subjective as our notes are, at least they'll give future generations usable detail about what we were tasting (if they can get over our pretentiousness).

Writers of the nineteenth century, while regularly proffering the type of generic praise that clearly indicated said wine was enjoyed, rarely offered any detail beyond that basic fact. To wit, a few telling examples:

"A pure and very superior wine is manufactured here. The grapes produced are heavier and of a finer flavor than those growing in the valleys and open plains."[57]

"Excellent and lucious [*sic*]...on first tasting we believed we were imbibing some choice old wine, not dreaming that a wine so rare, pure and delicious could be raised in this country."[58]

Of John Fehr's wines, "their qualities are too well known to the public to need any elaborate puff from us."[59] and have "every year increased in reputation at home and abroad."[60] Also, "unsurpassed for the delicacy of [their] bouquet and the elegance of [their] flavor."[61]

Vollmer's wine, by contrast, had a "rich garnet color [and] very superior flavor."[62]

Of Eberhard Barth's white wine from the Taylor grape, it "makes an excellent pale-colored wine."[63]

A few sources can be found to discuss these eastern wines in general, though not specifically that of any Berks producer. Of Clinton, for example, one writer noted that "it makes a good dark and heavy wine, with a most delightful wintergreen flavor, if used in a well-ripened state."[64]

Catawba, on the other hand, has been described as "yielding a white juice which is definitely foxy, after the nature of its *labrusca* parent, but which may be transformed into a still white wine that [is]...dry to the point of austerity and [has] a very clean flavor and a curious, special, spicy aroma."[65] (Catawba is a red grape, but was often made into white or rosé wines.)

Though tasting notes were sparse, writers of the time did often like to compare native wines to those famous European varieties known to

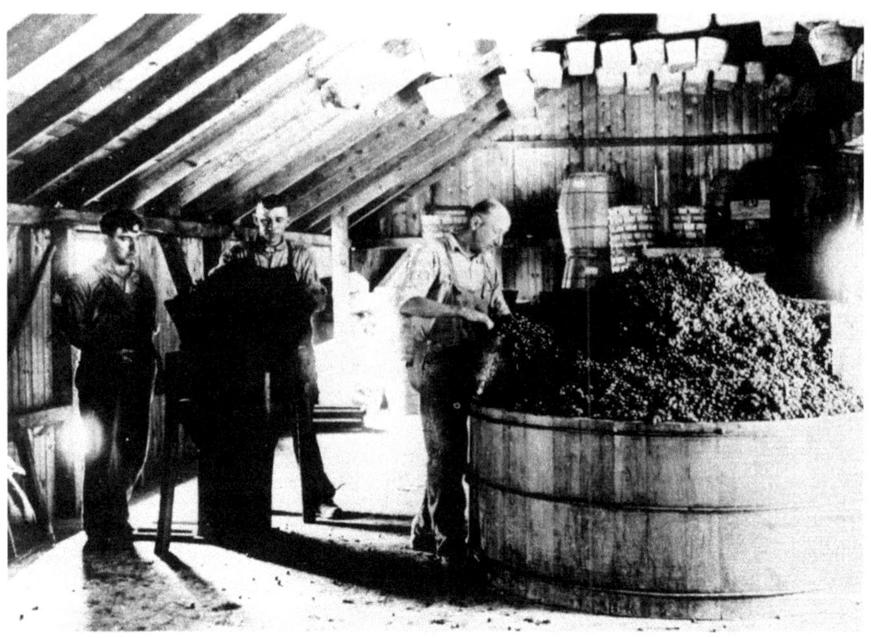

George Reiniger readies his grapes for winemaking. *Courtesy of Geo. M. Meiser IX from* The Passing Scene *series.*

any wine drinker, especially immigrants from those areas. Again, a few examples:

"John Fehr, wine merchant, No. 655 Penn street, has some of the choicest wines ever drunk in any land, whether it lies on the Rhine, or elsewhere. As a sample we quote that made from the Clinton grape. There never was any finer wine drank in America. Unbelievers will do well to give it a trial."[66]

"The Catawba is, as yet, the best grape we have....It is of two kinds—the still and the sparkling Catawba. The first resembles Hock, or Moselle; the latter, Champagne, or rather St. Peray."[67]

And lastly, a little closer to home: "The Reading Wines were superior, in purity and flavor, to those of Cincinnati, Missouri, or California, which are held in high esteem by wine drinkers. This is saying a great deal for our Berks county wine growers."[68]

NATIVE VS. *VINIFERA*

Why, one might ask—if these grapes were so capable and fared so well when compared to wines of the world's great regions—did the Pennsylvania wine industry turn its focus to *Vitis vinifera* once it was finally understood how to grow those grapes successfully (in the twentieth century)? The answer is simple, of course: when grown properly, the European varieties make better wine.

As Pinney put, rather succinctly, "the fruit that [native grapes] produce is often deficient in sugar, or high in acid, and sometimes full of strange flavors, so that the wine pressed from it is thin, unstable, sharp, and unpleasing—if drinkable at all. Wine from the unadulterated native grape is not wine at all by the standards of *Vitis vinifera*."[69]

Despite the often effusive descriptions from local journalists, there's plenty to suggest this other reality. Even the revered Nicholas Longworth of Cincinnati, for example, faced fierce judgment. Frances Trollope, mother of well-known novelist Anthony, wrote what was perhaps the very first published criticism of Longworth's wines in her *Domestic Manners of the Americans* (1832):

> During my residence in America, I repeatedly tasted native wine from vineyards carefully cultivated, and on the fabrication of which a considerable degree of imported science had been bestowed; but the very best of it was miserable stuff. It should seem that Nature herself requires some centuries of schooling before she becomes perfectly accomplished

> in ministering to the luxuries of man, and, perhaps as there is no lack of sunshine, the champagne and Bordeaux of the Union may appear simultaneously with a Shakespeare, a Raphael, and a Mozart.[70]

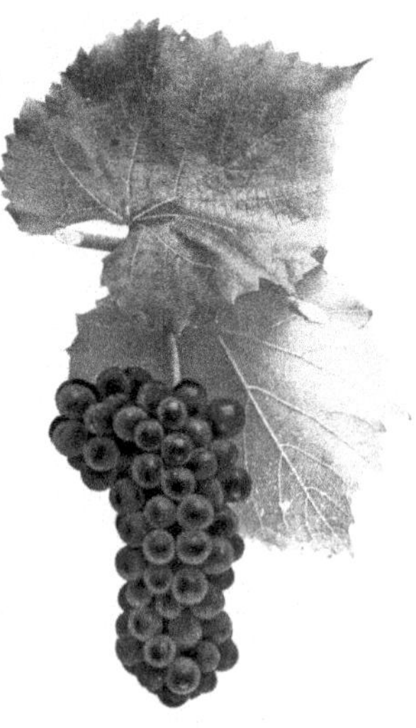

An illustration of the Clinton grape from U.P. Hedrick's *The Grapes of New York*. *Project Gutenberg*.

An Englishwoman and artist named Isabella Trotter noted that the Ohioans "beloved Catawba champagne…tastes, to our uninitiated palates, little better than cider,"[71] yet added that it improved when served in a mixed drink called the Catawba Cobbler, which was also popular in Berks. The *Reading Times* once wrote, in fact, that "in this weather, a Catawba or Clinton wine cobbler is about the very nicest and palatable drink that can be ordered at our hotels."[72]

Catawba is still grown widely in the northeastern United States, and thus relatively easy to find, typically as a sweet rosé. When compared to *vinifera* wines, it tends to be excessively grapey in both aroma and flavor, similar to what one might encounter in Welch's grape juice (which is primarily made with Concord). It's interesting how *vinifera* wines rarely smell or taste like grapes—compounds created during fermentation are more likely to suggest cherries, berries or plums (in red wine), for example—yet hybrids such as Catawba, Concord, Niagara and others are firmly grape-flavored, which comes across as simple and primary, thus less compelling.

YIELDING FLAVOR?

Another fascinating aspect of wine coverage in media was the focus on quantity of grapes. The more fruit, and the larger the fruit, in other words, the more impressive the harvest. By contrast, today it is widely accepted by most fine winemakers that controlling yields is crucial to intensifying flavor of individual grapes and thus producing more complex, deeply flavored wine.

"The canes are loaded with large clusters of grapes," wrote the *Reading Times* glowingly of William Young's vineyard in 1874, "and so great is the weight of the canes upon the trellis, that last Sunday, during the prevalence of a wind from the west, a number of the trellises gave way and fell to the ground."[73]

Another passage, speaking of Fehr's Vineyard, noted that "it was a rare treat to walk through the green avenues and see heavy clusters of fruit peering out on every hand. One single stalk—the 'father' as Mr. Fehr says of all the Clinton vines he has ever cultivated or sold—was estimated to contain from *eight to ten bushels of heavy bunches of grapes*."[74]

Fehr himself told the *Reading Times* in 1869 that "in all his experience he has never known a season that promises a more abundant or a better crop. His vines of Clinton, Catawba and Isabella...are literally covered with healthy young fruit, and should no blight occur, his vintage will be the finest he has ever had."[75]

It is difficult to come to definitive conclusions based on these comments, but it seems safe to suggest that the perceived value in producing as much fruit as possible must have had some effect on the intensity and concentration of these wines, meaning they would have been milder or less flavorful than today's versions. (Which, considering the lesser-quality grapes used, may have in fact been a good thing.)

SWEET OR DRY?

It is often assumed that native wine made during this period was primarily sweet, as opposed to the modern, dry style where most or all of the sugar has been converted to alcohol during fermentation. There certainly was evidence that American palates trended toward sweeter stuff. "The dry white catawba that Longworth succeeded in making," Pinney noted, "was unappreciated by Americans used to sweeter and more potent confections." In fact, Longworth liked to point out that even the finest German wines could be mistaken by American tasters for cider or even vinegar.[76]

On the other hand, immigrants who were accustomed to European traditions were more likely to appreciate wines that harkened back to the old country. "The Germans," Pinney continued, "were better instructed, and for many years, Longworth wrote, 'all the wine made at my vineyards, has been sold out at our German coffee-houses, and drank in our city.'"[77]

Another auxiliary character in this story—Alfred Speer, a notable New Jersey producer of both grape and elderberry wines—brings further evidence of dry winemaking in the East. Speer was most successful with his sweet "Port" wine, made without the addition of spirits, but instead by leaving grapes on the vine until they began to raisin (a technique that today would likely be called "late harvest"). Elderberry juice—a classic adjunct ingredient used in Portugal to provide color, strength and sweetness—may have also been utilized to some extent, even in the so-called grape wines. Speer did, however, produce several dry wines, including a "Burgundy," which he marketed as a "dark rich medium dry wine used by the wealthy classes as a table or dinner wine," and a "Claret," described as a "dry table wine especially suited for dinner use."[78]

As for Reading, there is compelling evidence that dry winemaking practices were observed to at least some extent. The most detailed description of both wine flavor and the process to achieve it from a Berks winemaker comes from a particularly comprehensive 1901 interview with Christopher Shearer—father of the well-known artist of the same name and son of Reading wine founding father Jonathan Shearer—who ran a fruit farm and winery in Tuckerton. (The full article—which gives fascinating insight into a process that was rarely documented to this level at the time—is reproduced in appendix A.)

"Good wine," said Shearer,

> should...be a deep madder. The scintillating lights playing in the wine glass must appear light and dark crimson, sometimes verging to the purples and deep, rich reds....The flavor must be agreeable and very grapy [sic]. The more pronounced the grape flavor, the better the wine....It should not be over much intoxicating and it must be extra dry. When being served, an excellent wine will fill the room with the odor of grapes.[79]

Of his process for producing quality wine, Shearer talked of making three grades from the same fruit. While this may seem peculiar to those familiar with modern winemaking, it is not that unique or significant in the continuum of worldwide history. In a time when, as mentioned above, quantity was often valued over quality, it was a common technique.

His first two wines—C.H. Shearer's X Pure Grape Juice and C.H. Shearer's XX Pure Grape Juice—similar to what today's vintners might call "free-run" and "pressed" juice, were vinified in a dry style with no additives. This was, it should also be noted, long after the heyday of Fehr and Longworth, yet remained true to the European tradition passed down by direct immigrants.

WINES ! WINES !

Dry Catawba Wine, Sweet Catawba Wine, Clinton Wine,

At 40c per bottle.

PORT WINE, CLARET WINE (St. Julien) at 50c per bottle.
SHERRY WINE (Grand Duchess) SHERRY WINE (Old Amontillado), at $1 and $1.25 per bottle
LAUBER'S CELEBRATED BOHEMIAN BEER, 80c per dozen. Bottles to be returned.
POTTSVILLE PORTER at 70c per dozen.
ROCK CANDY (Sirop di Gomnas).
RASPBERRY SYRUP, 36° gravity.
SPARKLING MONSTERRAT at $1.25 per dozen.
AROMATIQUE at $1.25 per bottle.
HAND CORKERS, GUM CORKS, &c., at lowest cash prices.

FRED. W. LAUER.

4-24 1y NO. 29 NORTH FIFTH ST.

Note the mention of both dry and sweet wines in this 1884 ad from Fred Lauer in the *Reading Times*. *Newspapers.com.*

Shearer's third wine, C.H. Shearer's Light Table Wine, which would be considered a "second press" wine today, was created by mixing the leftover pomace from the first two runs with sugar and water, after which a new ferment took place. This might not seem all that appealing to lovers of fine wine, but it is actually something that home winemakers still practice regularly.

What is noteworthy as part of a discussion of dry versus sweet wine, of course, is the addition of sugar, and the impact this did or did not have on the sweetness of the final product. Shearer noted that "the chemical composition of the last wine is about the same as that recommended by Dr. L. Gall, whose system is practiced throughout the entire civilized world, which is in consistency a little more than one-third grape juice, a trifle less than two-thirds water and about two pounds of sugar to the gallon."[80]

This referred to Dr. Ludwig Gall, of the Mosel region of Germany, a renowned wine scientist best known for his recommendation to add sugar to grape must to increase the alcohol (and thus ripeness) of wines when the fruit did not produce enough sugar on its own. Though this technique has actually been around since Roman times, it was French chemist Jean-Antoine Chaptal who brought it to the mainstream in the early 1800s—hence the modern name "chaptalization"—and Gall who evangelized the technique in Germany shortly thereafter.

Gall's method—which drastically changed the fortunes of the famed Mosel region in particular (and thus was likely well known by the German immigrants of Berks)—"involved adding a carefully calibrated solution of sugar and water to the must before fermentation. This did not increase the sweetness of the wine but diluted the acidity, thus giving the perception of sweetness and riper grapes."[81]

This latter point is crucial. The addition of sugar does not necessarily indicate further sweetness in the final wine. In fact, regardless of whether the sugar comes from ripe grapes or is added to the must, it will be converted by yeast to alcohol during fermentation. As such, it is both possible and common to encounter fully dry wines that have undergone chaptalization. It's also worth remembering that native grapes tended to be higher in acidity than *Vitis vinifera*, suggesting this process might have been even more important in the United States.

Not surprisingly, following Chaptal and Gall's advice was commonplace among Berks winemakers. A detailed example of this comes from well-known Mount Penn vintner Fred Kiedeisch, whose process was recalled by daughter Rose Schlappig in 1957. (Also note the Reiniger mention.)

> [Kiedeisch's] most popular wine was a clear red vintage made from Clinton and Concord grapes—a wine neither bitter nor sharp like Dago Red, nor heavy and sweet; somewhat like Claret, it was light but a good deal sweeter....The grapes were harvested in the fall, when they were ripe. After the juice had been pressed, it was put in 100 gallon (or even larger) barrels with sugar and water...The mixing formula called for one gallon of pure grape juice, one gallon of water and two pounds of sugar. Generally the same formula was used for white and red wines. Both wines were somewhere between sweet and sour....The Kiedeisch and Reiniger processes differ considerably from that used today by Italian-American vintners, who use primarily the Zinfandel grape and generally add neither water nor sugar.[82]

As this passage suggests, it is likely that much of the wine made during this period might be classified as "off-dry" today, or somewhere between sweet and dry. The German wine regions whence many of these immigrants hailed have long been known for this style of wine, particularly those made from Riesling. Especially considering the frequent comparisons to "Hock," a British nickname for German wine (especially Riesling-based whites from the Rhine region), it's not a stretch to imagine these displaced Teutons emulating the same.

Another likely possibility is that fermentation was not as controlled as it is today. Kiedeisch, for example, was also known for a Champagne Cider made from his own apples. He stated, amusingly yet tellingly, that "'it got harder, the older it got!' The only way this would be possible, of course, is if fermentation continued as the cider aged, and it also got dryer, the older it got. If this was true for Kiedeisch's cider, why not also for his wine?

All that said, this was still America, and, especially as Mount Penn became a bona fide tourist destination, it is safe to assume that plenty of actual sweet wine was also produced. Though this cavity-inducing example, found in the *Germantown Telegraph* circa 1880, is intended for home winemakers, it gives a good sense of how others might've approached the process:

> Grape Wine. As this is the season for making grape wine, I send you the following receipt, which is so simple and produces such excellent wine, that I hope every one having grapes will try it:
> *Five Gallons Wine.* Express the juice from twenty pounds grapes, rinse the pulp and skins in as much water as will cover them, mash them

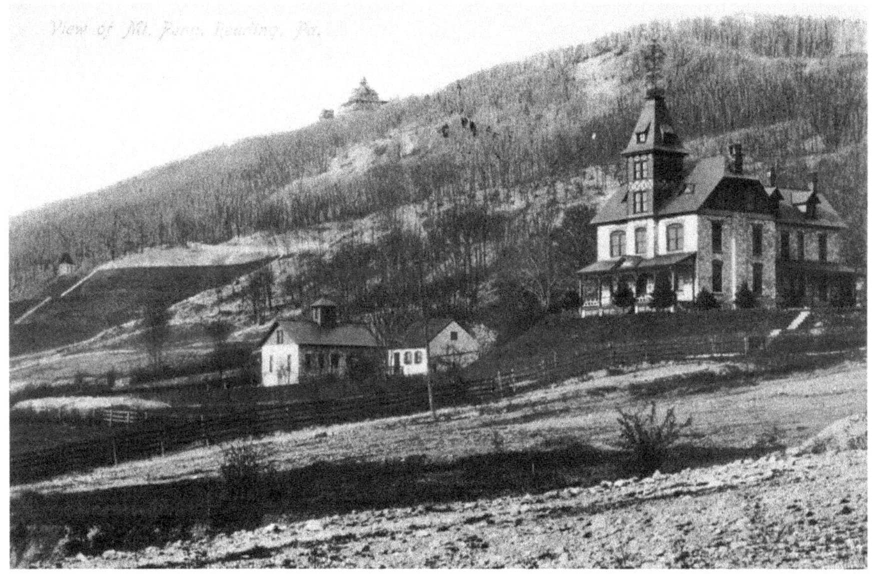

The grape-friendly Mount Penn, with Wanner Mansion in the foreground and the Summit House at the top. *Joseph A. Webb Collection.*

> and strain through a coarse cloth, add this to the juice and put in two pounds of brown sugar to each gallon ; when the sugar is dissolved, pour the whole into a keg, leaving the bung open, and let it stand where the temperature will be about 70° until *fermentation ceases*; then bung tight, and let it rest for a month to settle, when it should be drawn on quietly, the keg well washed, and the wine returned to it, adding one pound good raisins; and if the wine does not seem sweet enough two pounds sugar may be added to the whole. The necessity of doing this depends on the kind and quality of the grapes. The wine should remain until the keg is wanted the next season, when it may be bottled for use.[83]

Lastly, an interesting anecdote about the addition of sugar in winemaking, resulting from rations of the First World War. Berks winemakers "were dealt a solar plexus blow when Berks Food Administrator Charles T. Davies came out with an announcement that the use of sugar for wine making [was] prohibited," according to the *Philadelphia Inquirer*. The paper went on to report "at least three large wine manufacturers in this county [who] had laid in large stocks of sugar in anticipation of a busy season, the grape crop being very prolific. Mr. Davies ordered them to hold their sugar stocks for the present, with the understanding that if the sugar situation tightens the supplies of the winemakers will be confiscated."[84]

PURE, NATURAL

Purity of wine was another obsession of the time, a somewhat ironic viewpoint considering the regular addition of sugar. Although Gall himself, defending this very point, "insisted that his method was 'improvement' not 'falsification' because it did not add to the wine anything not already naturally there."[85]

Many did hold the common perception that imported wines available in this country were more grossly adulterated, beyond just the addition of sugar. "We have been too long palled by the villainous trash sold as pure wine,"[86] wrote the *Independent Phoenix* in 1865, as one example. Going even further, the *Philadelphia Times* published the following rant in 1884:

> It's almost impossible to get a pure imported wine of any kind. In fact, they have carried adulteration so far, especially in France, that the people of this country are fast dropping imported wines and using the native

> vintage instead. Our native wines are so cheap that it wouldn't pay to adulterate them. Flat? Not a bit of it. They have the pure flavor of the grape and that may be an unusual flavor to palates that are used to the "doctored" imported stuff. Why, nearly all the wines imported from France are American wines manipulated by French houses and sent back here to be sold at enormous prices. The French are the most expert "wine doctors" in the world.[87]

As such, similar sources were likely to discuss the benefits of their favorite wines by calling out their purity and, comically in retrospect, their medical benefits. Of Fehr's wines, for example, it was written that their reputation, "for their medicinal qualities and purity, [is] well known."[88] In addition, they were "celebrated among medical gentlemen"[89] and often recommended by physicians, especially "to weak and sickly ladies [for their] purity, non-intoxicating qualities and tonic and restorative properties."[90]

Augustus Vollmer's wine was another that "may be confidently recommended as the pure juice of the grape," and "those in want of a pure native wine" were advised to seek him out.[91]

So...How Did It Taste?

Having gone through all this detail, the question may rightfully be raised: are we any closer to understanding how these wines tasted? Well, it does seem safe to say a wide variety of wines were produced, just as today, including dry, off-dry, sweet and fortified. Considering, however, that winemakers from Pennsylvania who make fine wine now use *Vitis vinifera* almost exclusively, and having tasted a considerable amount of native and hybrid wines from more recent vintages, it seems unlikely any of these wines could have possibly measured up to what we would today consider high quality. Even so, it was likely palatable and enjoyable, especially when imbibed as part of a happy, healthy lifestyle. And it's hard not to admire the effort and commitment to make the best of resources available at the time and to further traditions imported from the homeland.

5

THE HERMIT OF MOUNT PENN

While George Reiniger certainly became the most famous and productive winemaker during the industry's heyday, he could never be called its most important personage. That honor instead goes to a man whose legend not only stemmed from his winemaking but also from his unique and colorful personality: the one and only Jacob Louis Kuechler.

Discovering Herr Kuechler—who might also be called Louis, Lewis, Ludwig, Father Kuechler, Mein Host, the Old Man of the Mountain, the Big Bearded Santa Claus of the Hills and, of course, the Hermit of Mount Penn—is akin to first encountering a particularly memorable character in a classic work of fiction. Considered handsome, he was tall for the time (five feet, ten inches), with a ruddy complexion, a long, scraggly beard and what was said to be the heaviest moustache in the city. Though born with a wealth of golden curls, baldness in middle age led him to regularly don a black velvet beret, which was as familiar a companion to those who knew him as was his trademark long-stemmed pipe.

The prototypical old-timey barkeep, he played confidant, sounding board and partner-in-crime, forming immediate and deep relationships with his patrons and friends, building camaraderie and lifelong bonds wherever he spent his time or plied his trade. He was what we might call an introvert today, seemingly shy and reserved—especially with people he didn't know—yet possessed an ineffable ability to forge a deep connection with those who walked through his door.

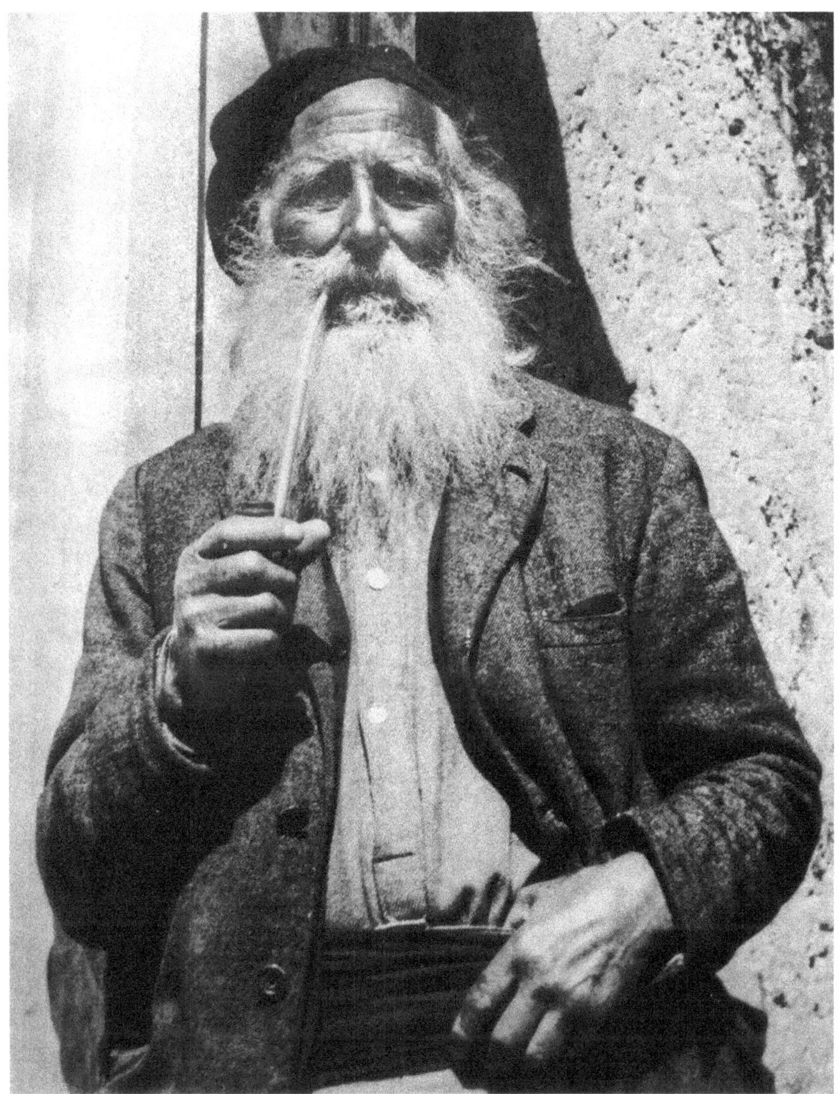

This mesmerizing photo of an older Jacob Louis Kuechler shows off the hermit's trademark beard and beret. *Courtesy of Geo. M. Meiser IX, from* The Passing Scene *series.*

Once a man-about-town, especially in his younger years, it was an isolated mountaintop home that would become Kuechler's enduring legacy, prompting even the most prosaic of men to wax poetic about beauty and fulfillment. "Though but a shanty, rudely improvised," it was described at the time, his home on Mount Penn "takes somewhat of the air of a Swiss

Inn. Its elevated seclusion, buried in the wild growth of a mountain top, gives it the misanthropic appearance of a hermitage. But upon a near approach it disenthralles the world-burdened soul and causes it to revel in the atmosphere of peace and contentment."[92]

BEFORE THE MOUNTAIN

Born in Michelstadt, Hesse, Germany, on October 26, 1830, Kuechler was well educated and enlisted into the local carving trade, quickly becoming a popular figure in his hometown, a precursor for things to come. He married his childhood sweetheart, Henrietta Lisberger, and the two made for the United States shortly thereafter, in August 1854.

Having grown up as a hunter in middle Germany, roaming an open mountain plateau 2,500 feet above the sea and even guiding noblemen on hunting adventures, it's no surprise Kuechler's stay in New York City was short or that he and his wife found a more apt home in Reading less than a year after arrival on U.S. shores. The landscape and hills around Reading particularly appealed to Louis, with their similarity to the Odenwald back home.

Upon arriving in Berks, the young family quickly grew, welcoming three daughters and two sons between 1855 and 1866. Kuechler put his carving expertise—of which he was said to have been "highly skilled in real artistic workmanship"[93]—to use at the Mellert Foundry at Second and Chestnut, working as a pattern maker. After a stint as foreman of the E.J. Obert Boiler Shop on South Ninth Street, he eventually would open his own wood carving and pattern making business. Of note was his woodwork for the Reading Academy of Music, on the 500 block of Penn Street, constructed in 1872. (Sadly, the academy burned down in 1917.)

He was an active member of Reading society, holding positions in the Teutonia Lodge, the Maennerchor and the Berks County Poultry Association, establishing himself as a popular figure in town, especially within the large German expat community.

The following text appears in the Reading City Directory, circa 1870:

J. Louis Kuechler, Architect, Designer, Carver, Pattern-maker. House and Furniture Carvings constantly on hand. Cigar Boxes Made to Order. No. 50 Lemon Street.*

*Fryer, "Kuechler's Roost," 15–18

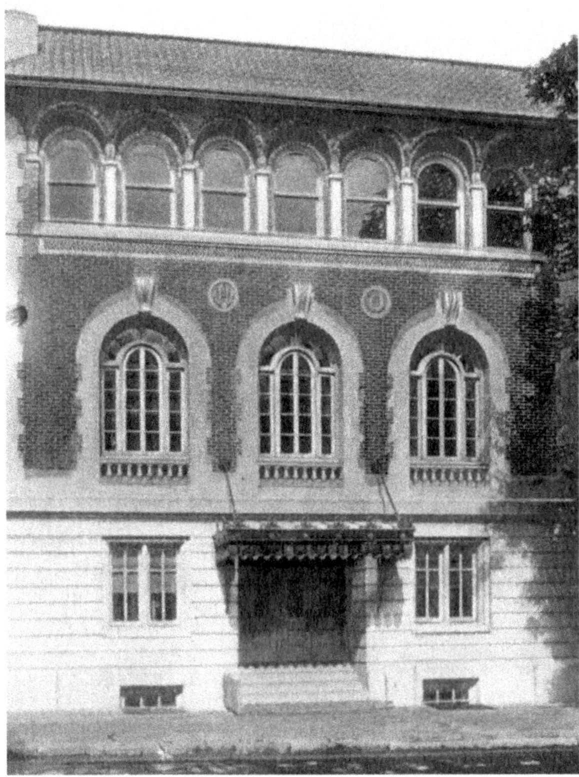

The Harmonie Mannerchor society, of which Kuechler was a prominent member, moved into this building—on North Sixth Street, between Washington and Walnut—in 1874. *Charles J. Adams III Collection.*

As Kuechler entered middle age, his vision began to deteriorate, forcing him to seek a new profession beyond the intricacies of wood carving.[94] Having long had an interest in the wine business,[95] he became proprietor at Triangle Hall, at Seventh and Cherry Streets, in 1875. Even as a newcomer to salooning, it's illustrative of Kuechler's stature in the community that many city officials and other prominent citizens frequented his establishment.[96]

Though he was generally a quiet and studious fellow, others were particularly drawn to Kuechler, and presiding over a popular watering hole was the perfect way to capitalize on that. Celebrating his fiftieth birthday in 1880—which, hilariously, he also did the year before, when he turned forty-nine—the *Reading Times* described him as such:

> Mr. Kuechler is, moreover, a gentleman who possesses literary acquirements of a high order. In years gone by he wooed the muses with good effect, as many of his German poetical efforts, which his

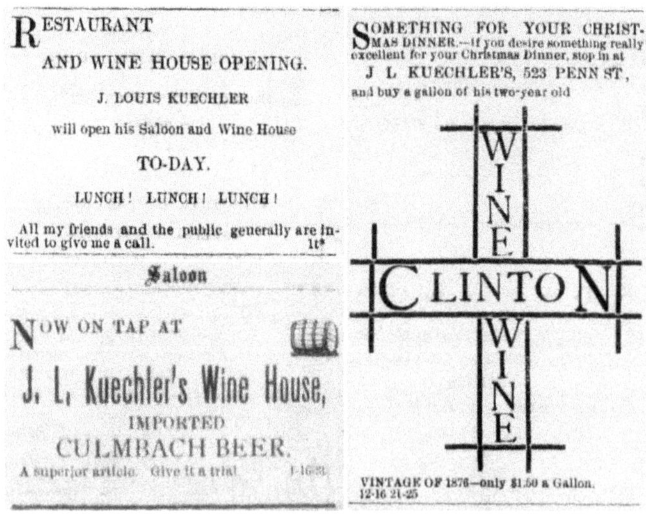

RESTAURANT
AND WINE HOUSE OPENING.
J. LOUIS KUECHLER
will open his Saloon and Wine House
TO-DAY.
LUNCH! LUNCH! LUNCH!
All my friends and the public generally are invited to give me a call. 1t*

Saloon

NOW ON TAP AT
J. L. Kuechler's Wine House,
IMPORTED
CULMBACH BEER.
A superior article. Give it a trial.

SOMETHING FOR YOUR CHRISTMAS DINNER.—If you desire something really excellent for your Christmas Dinner, stop in at
J L KUECHLER'S, 523 PENN ST,
and buy a gallon of his two-year old
WINE
CLINTON
WINE
VINTAGE OF 1876—only $1.50 a Gallon.
12-16 21-25

Several ads for Kuechler's Penn Street saloon: one from 1876, two from 1878. *Newspapers.com.*

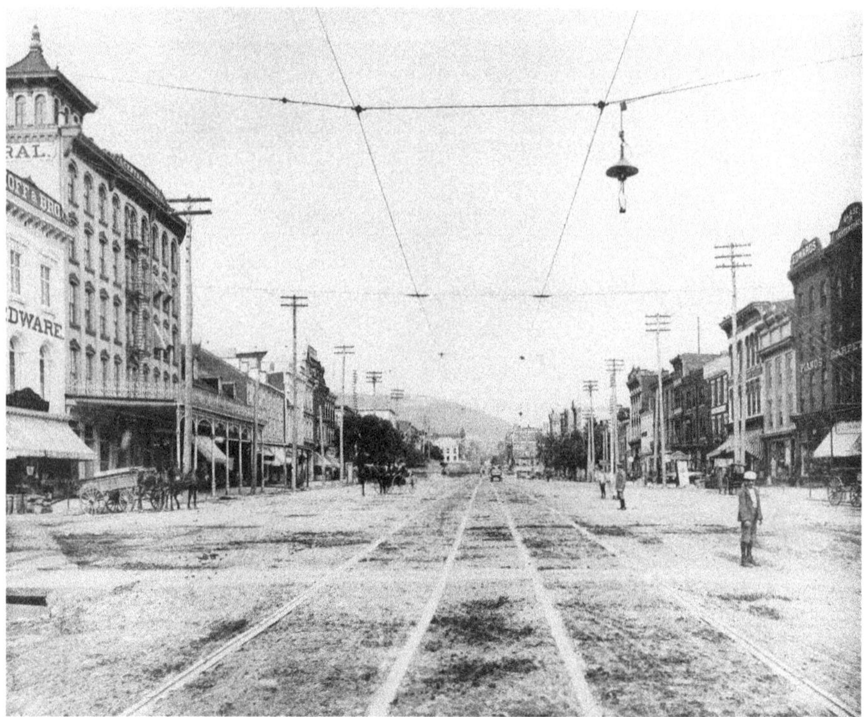

This undated shot of Penn Street, looking east from Fourth, was published in 1897. Kuechler's saloon would've been in this general area. *Joseph A. Webb Collection.*

> intimate friends are sometimes permitted to see, abundantly prove. He is an ardent lover of the beautiful in creative literature, and is also a close observer of all the good things afloat in current German publications. Agreeable in manner and entertaining in conversation, he is deservedly one of the most popular men in the community.[97]

After a short stint manning Triangle Hall, on April 22, 1876, he opened a new restaurant and wine house at 523 Penn Street, which was considered "very attractive and cosy,"[98] as well as a "gathering-place of some of Reading's leading business and professional men, [where] close friendships were formed."[99]

The saloon would quickly become known as one of the best places in town to procure high-quality local wine, made often from Clinton grapes.[100] Kuechler began, actually, sourcing his fruit from a vineyard in Allentown,[101] but it is unclear whether he owned said vineyard or was merely purchasing the juice for winemaking.

THE MOUNTAIN CALLS

Even while Kuechler's saloon was one of the most popular in the city, his eyes and heart were elsewhere—specifically on the woody forest and craggy rocks that lined the slopes of Mount Penn. "He knew every path, glen and beauty spot," it was said. "It was there he took his exercise. While not building castles in the air, he frequently imagined a home on the hill."[102]

In 1878, he took his first step toward that reality, leasing a "commanding eminence in Alsace township, overlooking the Olinger and Oley valleys,"[103] just west of George Reiniger's farm, where the Antietam Club House would later be located. A large number of Kuechler's friends (presumably frequent patrons of his bar) helped clear rocks from a portion of the property—a "stone match" of his own—to make room for a rustic villa and pavilion to be enjoyed during pleasant weather. "The situation is one of the finest in the county for such a purpose," recounted the *Reading Times*, "being of unusual high altitude and embowered among a grove of forest trees. The peculiar formation of the rocks (many of which are of immense size, weighing several tons apiece,) will give the proprietor a natural dining-room, kitchen, hall, etc., thus adding much to the attractiveness of an already charming spot."[104]

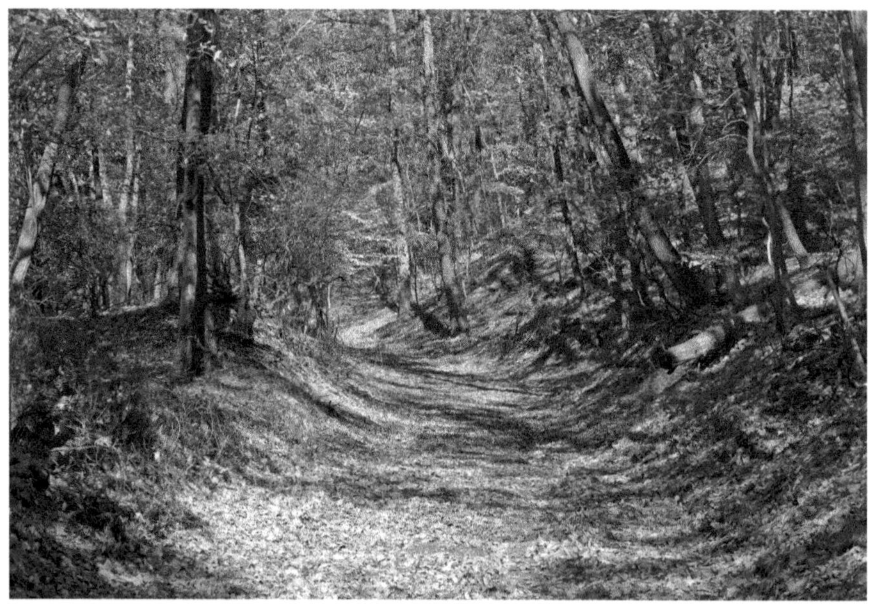

A hiking trail on Mount Penn, modern day. *Author photo.*

The place's iconic name would emanate, shortly thereafter, from the mind of Colonel Tom Zimmerman, editor of the *Reading Times*, unofficial documentarian of Kuechler's exploits, and perhaps his closest friend. Christening a pile of rocks just outside the retreat, the story goes, with a bottle of wine that surely came from the saloon's own stash, he proclaimed, for the ages: "Let this hereafter be known as Kuechler's Roost!"[105]

The original building, if it should even be called that, consisted of four posts, a floor and a few benches. It didn't even have walls or a roof. But this "mere skeleton" was "all right for Mr. Kuechler and his friends when the weather was pleasant."[106]

In 1882, Kuechler expanded his mountain presence, completing "a purchase important to pleasure seekers"[107] by acquiring a new Mount Penn property—twenty-four acres situated on the road between Miller's Spring and Antietam Lake, in an area known as the "Alsace Rocks"—with the intention of constructing a summer resort. Seven acres were designated for farming, the local newspaper reported, while the rest was earmarked as a park for the pursuit of leisure.

As it was surrounded by successful vintners—including Reiniger, Steigerwald, Martin and Reich—this *new* Roost was considered a great spot for winemaking. After reserving four acres for viticulture, Kuechler acquired

REBECCA WINE.—The finest native wine sold in Reading. Try it. $2.00 per gallon; 50 cent a bottle. Sold by J. L. KUECHLER,
4-15 2t 523 Penn Street.

REBECCA WINE.—The finest native wine sold in Reading. Try it. $2.00 per gallon; 50 cents a bottle. Sold by J. L. KUECHLER.
4-15 2t 523 Penn Street.

REBECCA WINE.—The finest native wine sold in Reading. Try it. $2.00 per gallon; 50 cents a bottle. Sold by J. L. KUECHLER,
4-15 2t 523 Penn Street.

REBECCA WINE.—The finest native wine sold in Reading. Try it. $2.00 per gallon; 50 cents a bottle. Sold by J. L. KUECHLER,
4-15 2t 523 Penn Street.

REBECCA WINE.—The finest native wine sold in Reading. Try it. $2.00 per gallon; 50 cents a bottle. Sold by J. L. KUECHLER,
4-15 2t 523 Penn Street.

REBECCA WINE.—The finest native wine sold in Reading. Try it. $2.00 per gallon; 50 cents a bottle. Sold by J. L. KUECHLER.
4-15 2t 523 Penn Staeet.

REBECCA WINE.—The finest native wine sold in Reading. Try it. $2.00 per gallon; 50 cents a bottle. Sold by J. L. KUECHLER,
4-15 2t 523 Penn Street.

REBECCA WINE.—The finest native wine sold in Reading. Try it. $2.00 per gallon; 50 cents a bottle. Sold by J. L. KUECHLER,
4-15-2t 523 Penn Street.

An ad (eight of them, actually) for Kuechler's Rebecca wine. *Newspapers.com.*

two thousand grapevines of Clinton, Concord, Ives Seedling and Martha grapes, as well as eight hundred cuttings of Rebecca, from Ohio, "from which Mr. Kuechler's popular and delicious white wine [was] made."[108]

The location's breathtaking outlook was another compelling feature. "A splendid view of the surrounding country for a distance of 20 miles toward the north, east and south is commanded from this place," reported the *Reading Times*. "The Chester Hills are to be seen, and on a clear day Birdsboro, Monocacy and the Perkiomen Railroad."[109]

Kuechler also brought his Aeolian harp (or wind harp)—imported from Germany in 1880 and first installed at the original Roost—to his new place. The unique, funnel-shaped design of this instrument allowed it to catch the wind from every direction, and to provide a persistently eerie soundtrack for the property.[110]

Though his initial intention appeared to be the enjoyment of this elevated land during the summer, Kuechler would not long be able to resist his dream of living along the ridge, with the solitude and pure mountain air it offered. In the spring of 1883, he sold his saloon and relocated to his Roost permanently, first residing in a simple frame building, with the plan, according to the *Reading Times*, of erecting, that first year, "a stone octagonal building, with embrasures, so as to resemble a castle," as well as a windmill for pumping water out of the well on the premises.[111] (Looking back, the "simple frame building" lasted much longer than originally planned.)

FAR FROM PEDESTRIAN

As interesting a character as Kuechler was, this story would not be complete without his loyal friends. Seeking conversation, camaraderie and, of course, wine, these former saloon patrons began regularly hiking up the mountain to visit their pal. Led by Zimmerman, as well as U.S. Congressman Daniel Ermentrout, they dubbed themselves the "Foosgangers" (also written Fuszgangers, Foozgangers, Foosgaengers, Fooszgangers, Fooßgängers or Fussgängers, literally foot-goers, or, in modern German, pedestrians) and included a wide variety of influential members of Reading society, including judges, authors, editors, clergymen, professors, lawyers, doctors, artists, newspaper correspondents, prominent politicians and the like.

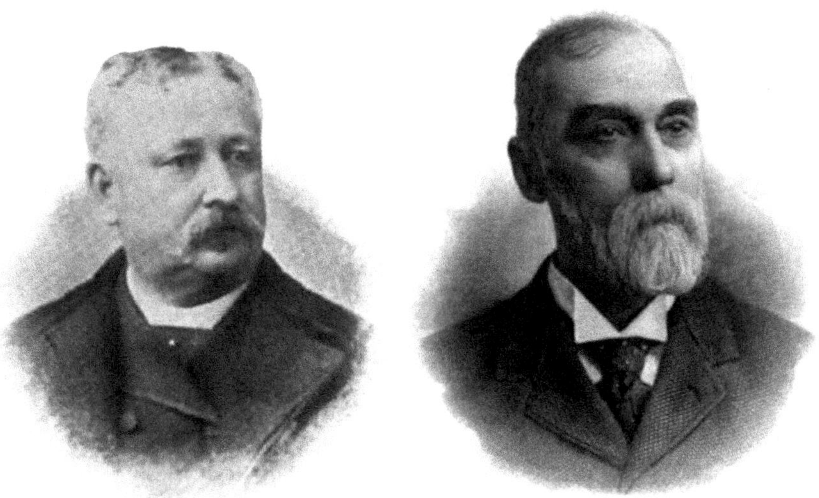

Prominent Foosgangers: To the left, Colonel Tom Zimmerman. On the right, Congressman Daniel Ermentrout. *Wikimedia Commons.*

In those days, there was no Skyline Drive, no Gravity Railroad, no Pagoda. Getting to the place was difficult, as charmingly illustrated by the *Philadelphia Times*:

> The climb afoot to the eerie-roost is four miles long, and by no well-trodden path. The mountain vales hither are thick with the foliage of aged oaks, jagged rocks project here and there in half-frightened attitudes, angled roots bend in weird, spectre-like shapes, and the terminus of the march is rugged and wild to first view. But no sooner there, you ascend the rustic observatory, carelessly constructed by the hermit, and from between the dense forest you have a panoramic sweep of landscape view down the Schuylkill valley, such as seldom found anywhere in the country.[112]

While the Foosgangers did claim to enjoy the hiking aspect of their little club, the joke of the day was that every Mount Penn path led to the Roost, where there were, of course, copious amounts of food and drink to be consumed. Usually, they started out at Mineral Spring Park, where, wrote former *Reading Times* editor Benjamin Fryer in his *Berks County Historical Review* profile of Kuechler, "they cast away their work-a-day cares and were ready to wine and dine with the Hermit, as they termed their host."[113]

"He was host, waiter and, often, cook," Fryer continued. "There was no bar, with the usual brass rail. The shrill blatant bell of the cash register was never heard. The early patrons were not customers, but friends. Companionship, not commercialism, was the keynote."[114]

"Ludwig's visitors were friends, not customers," wrote Ray Koehler in a mid-twentieth-century *Reading Times* profile. "Wine, mingled with song and talk, fostered good fellowship. Fragrant cigars lent bouquet to the rustic inn. There were no cigarettes. Highballs and cocktails were strangers. The patrons didn't drink. They sipped and talked—sipped and joked."

This can be further illustrated with the following—perhaps apocryphal, but no less relevant—tale:

> An intruder to the sanctum once asked for a mint julep.
>
> Kuechler, his ever-present pipe in mouth, eyed the man narrowly—and kept on smoking.
>
> "I ordered a julep," the stranger repeated impatiently.
>
> The innkeeper slowly released a cloud of Turkish blend. "Then stop at Mineral Spring Hotel on your way to town," he grunted. "William Behm will be glad to serve you."[115]

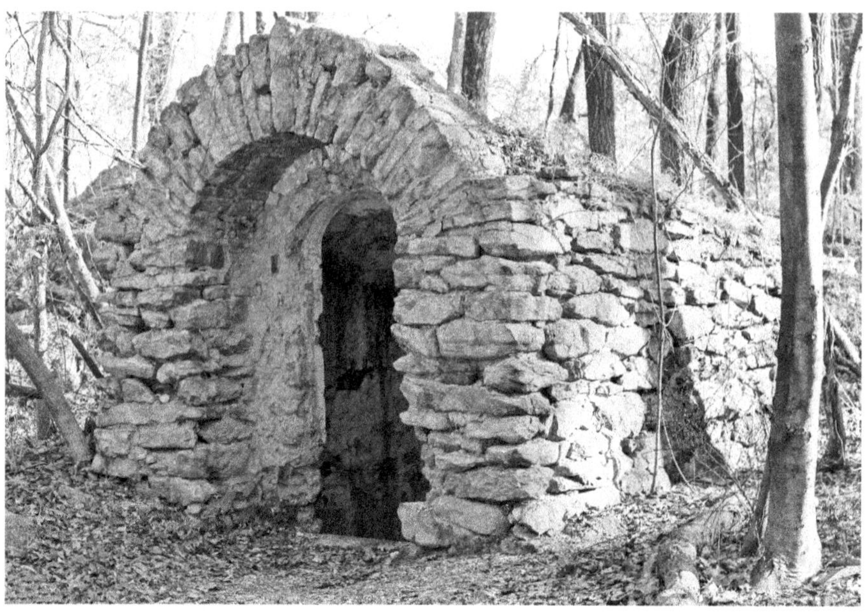

What remains of the Kuechler's Roost wine cellar, 2018. *Author photo.*

Though smaller in production than some of his neighbors, Kuechler's wine still earned a massive reputation. "Ludwig's artistry as a maker of fine wines dispensed in Kuechler's Roost," described the *Reading Times*, "lingers in the memory of the community's senior connoisseurs."

"Perhaps no better sample of stubborn tenacity in the sphere of grape culture in Eastern Pennsylvania can be cited than Kuechler's Roost of the Alsace Heights in Berks county," another newspaperman wrote in the late 1880s. "[Kuechler] speaks with pride how, by an indomitable will, he nursed his little vineyard into life, and proved to the world how Pennsylvania soil can produce the best wine made in this country. He has a modest little vault hid in a rocky cellar, from which he taps a wine that vies with the best brands of Southern California."[116]

THE CHEF OF MOUNT PENN

At first, Kuechler would prepare simple fare for his visitors to nibble while imbibing, such as rye bread and cheese, or ham, eggs and German pancakes.[117] As time wore on, more elaborate choices surfaced, mostly during banquets and special events.

The hermit became known in particular for hasenpfeffer, a sweet-and-sour rabbit stew quite popular at the time that has all but died out in favor of more modern preparations. (And rabbit is not exactly commonplace in Pennsylvania as of this writing.) The 1935 book *Pennsylvania Dutch and Their Cookery* contains several recipes for the preserved rabbit dish, one of which happens to be attributed to Tom Zimmerman. Perhaps it was in fact inspired by his pal Kuechler? (Recipe available in appendix G.)

If notices in the *Reading Times* were any indication, a common affair at the Roost during this period was the "Potato Roast," an event that earned renown in the region and often attracted visitors from Philadelphia, Wilmington and beyond. One announcement in the *Times*, from the 1890s, read like so:

> At Kuechler's Roost, there will be a potato roast today. It will be one of those events that have made this place famous and, as Herr Kuechler has invited all of his friends to be present, there will be a large gathering of those who know a good thing when they see it.[118]

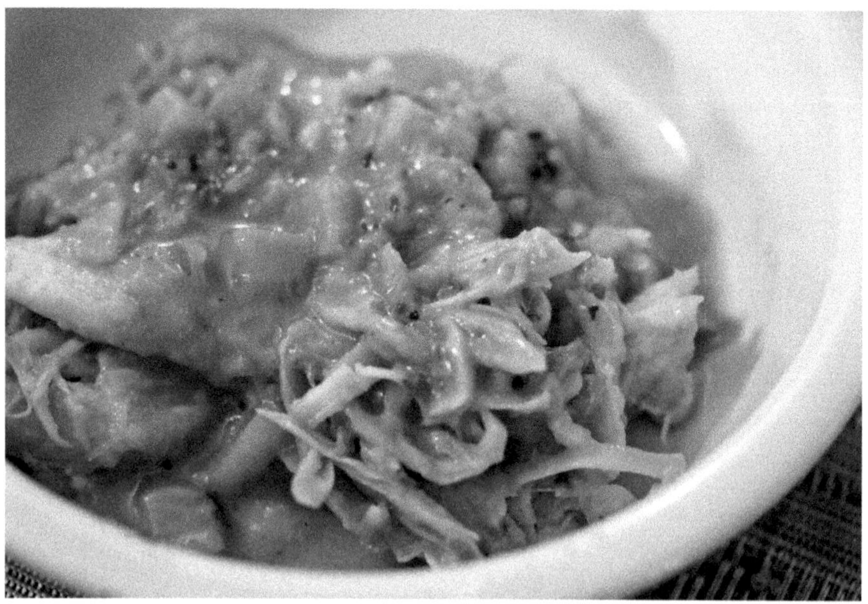

One of Kuechler's specialties was hasenpfeffer, the sweet-and-sour rabbit dish that has all but disappeared from modern menus. It tastes better than it looks (maybe). Recipe in appendix G. *Author photo.*

As early as the mid-1880s, the Roost also became a popular choice to host to a variety of dinners and banquets, usually with more elaborate food preparations. For example, on one occasion, Norman Wiard—a colonel and prominent Foosganger himself—held "a sumptuous dinner" in honor of Congressman Ermentrout, featuring, but not limited to, soup, canvasback ducks, lobster salad, potato salad, "Roost punch" and coffee.[119] After several passes of wine, "Ermentrout grew eloquent over the beautiful scenery surrounding him and proudly claimed that no other Congressman was the proprietor of so much magnificence."[120]

Another time, the clerks in the offices of Scott Works partook in a chicken and waffle supper, featuring another of Kuechler's specialties. This meal would have showcased stewed chicken in the Pennsylvania German style, however, not the fried soul food that has recently come into prominence in food trucks and comfort food restaurants across the country.

Kuechler's pièce de résistance was his pig roast, which acquired mythical status among Roost devotees. "It is a whole pig," one account read, "of tender age and well-rounded proportions, brought entire and steaming with savory fume from the stove to the table. It is served on slices cut straight around and with dripping zestiness is eaten from large plates."

A PIG ROAST UNDER THE TREES

Perhaps the definitive occurrence of said pig roast was the first annual dinner of the "Alsace Pedestrian's Club" (a.k.a. the Foosgangers), which took place in October 1884. The bill of fare, "handsomely printed on tinted bristol board" in German, not only showcased Kuechler's culinary stylings but also his wit.

A translated version:

First Round
Noodle Soup
Celery
Tomato salad
A little wine

Second Round
Suckling Pig, filled with Chestnuts
(Chestnuts, if Kuechler can buy them. If not, then perhaps bread or potato stuffing—not quite, but almost as good)
Apple sauce
Other things
A little more wine

Third Round
Sauerkraut (Berks County style)
Mashed potatoes
And still more wine

Fourth Round
Steamed rooster, with wine broth
And still celery
Potato salad
Red beets
Baked potatoes
To health!

Erschtie Round.
Noodle Soup Tselerich
Tomat Salawdt Bissel Wei
Tswetti Round.
Schpuseily, g'filled mit Keshta*
Eppel Sass Onner Schtuft
Bissel Meh Wei
Drittie Round.
Sauer Kraut G'maschte Grumbeera
(Berks County Style)
Als Noch Meh Wei
Fiertie Round.
G'demte Hahne, mit Wei Bree
Als Noch Tselerich
Grumbeera Salawdt Rote-Reeva
G'roschte Grumbeera
"G'sundheit!"
Finft Round.
Koocha mit Gravy Drauva
Als noch meh Wei, ovver bissel schporsomlich
Sexht und Letchtie Round.
Coffee, Elsasser Wei, Kronthal Wasser, Roost Champagne, Roost Punch, und Brunna-Wasser, wie mer's gleicht!

*Keshta wann der Kuechler sie kaufa kann. Wann net, donn gebts ferleigcht Brodt odder Grumbeera shtuffing—net gons, ovver doch sheergohr, so gute.

The menu for the Foosgangers first annual banquet, in the original German. *Newspapers.com.*

Fifth Round
Cake, with gravy
Grapes
Still more wine, but a little more saving

Sixth and Best Round
Coffee, Alsace wine, Kronthal spring water, Roost champagne, Roost punch, as we like it![121]

After the event, Zimmerman contributed the following recap:

> The dinner was served up under the trees, and although the old custom in kitchen and hall of summoning the servants by a thwacking sound produced by the cook's striking the rolling-pin upon the dresser, was not observed, yet did the host bring on the savory meats—the pig with its traditional embellishments—until the table was fairly loaded with good cheer.

Dire was the clang of plates, of knife and fork,
That merciless fell like tomahawks to work

There was no display of plate such as the voluptuous Belshazzar was wont to parade before the eyes of his guests when he brought forth the vessels or the temple: "flagons, cans, cups, beakers, goblets, basins, and ewers"; no sumptuously-lined sideboards, no rare prints, no vessels of curious workmanship, no harper twanging his instrument—none of these, but surroundings far more grateful and attractive. What are these surroundings, do you ask? They are the vine-clad hills of our own Alsace, which, like Italia's land of summer days, constitute that fair portion of Berks where, when the vintage sun has done its work and the grapes are gathered, the very air is "odorous with the dew which sweet grapes weep."[122]

THE HERMIT?

At this point, it would be perfectly natural to be wondering: if Kuechler had so many friends and was running such a popular and successful wine house—why on earth did he become a hermit? The truth is somewhat gray. Did he move from the middle of the city into a relatively isolated home on the mountainside? Yes. Was he a true recluse, in the sense that he completely removed himself from society? No.

Certainly, there was a romanticism of the hermetic lifestyle at this point in history. Combing through papers of the time—beyond just Reading—the discussion of hermits and their eccentric behavior was surprisingly popular, which in turn led to fascination with a figure like Kuechler. (It was, perhaps, a natural precursor to our current obsession with reality TV.)

The following, as a telling example, was once overheard—or so it was said—on Mount Penn: "In there, among the trees, lives a Hermit. He is an old man with long white whiskers. For years he has been digging a deep cave which is to be his grave. When the end is near he will enter, and die. It may be a long time before his body is found. Perhaps never." This type of gossip provided Kuechler with much amusement.[123]

It's also worth considering that Kuechler's friends—those who still saw him on a relatively regular basis, even after his Alsace relocation—were responsible for his moniker. Taking into account the evident humor among this group, the

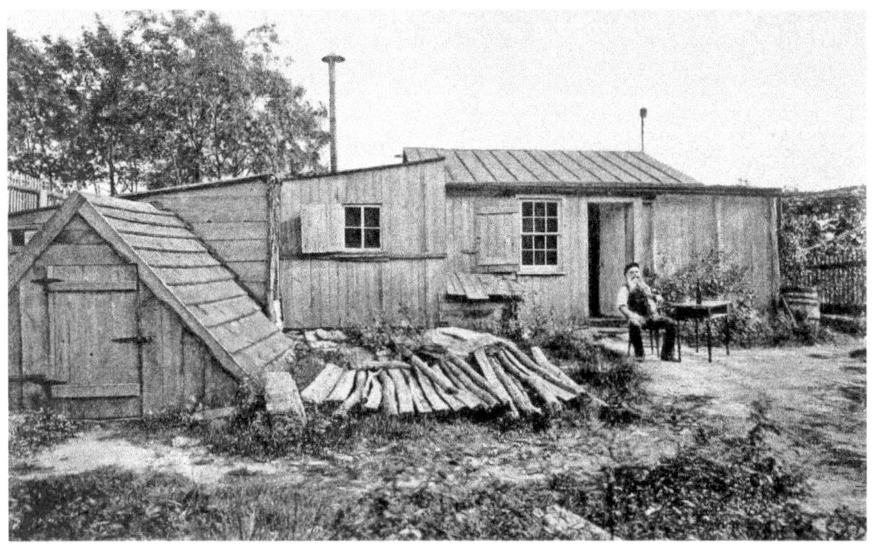

A great shot of Kuechler, sitting with a bottle of wine behind the Roost. *Lincoln Financial Foundation Collection/Internet Archive.*

nickname was surely at least somewhat tongue-in-cheek. On the other hand, those who knew him best, knew, as Zimmerman once noted, that he "for 30 years waited patiently to buy this mountain-top, and at last secured it."[124]

Richmond Jones, another friend, had the following to say about his hermetic lifestyle:

> It was from the social life that Kuechler fled. It was his antithesis. So long as he lived among men he was lost in the mass, but when he quit their haunts and habits and perched upon the mountain top, a hermit, he became picturesque and beautiful. There he sits! "See what a grace is seated on his brow, a front like Jove himself, an eye like Mars, to threaten and command, a station like the herald Mercury new—lighted on a heaven kissing hill."
>
> Serene and happy in the peace and quiet that surrounded him, "far from the madding crowd's ignoble strife" he contemplates at his feet the busy world from which he has withdrawn.[125]

It is thus clear Kuechler loved the solitary, quiet life of the Roost and had dreamed of this situation for many years. Why he decided to close his saloon in 1883 specifically is less obvious, though perhaps not particularly important to the overall story. It has been occasionally reported that some sort of family bereavement forced Kuechler to retire to the mountain; nevertheless, no specific evidence of this exists, at least among the obvious sources.

It is, however, noteworthy that there is no record of Kuechler's wife, Henrietta, ever having lived at the Roost, even though she did not pass away until 1890. Fryer mentioned briefly that she did not approve of the liquor trade but offered no further detail. According to the Reading City Directory, Henrietta was living separately from Louis as early as 1879: she at 1136 Elm, he at 523 Penn, with his mother, Catherine, as well as his son, Julius, who was listed as a bartender. (It has also been suggested that Kuechler's wife and mother did not get along.) This went on for several years, until Louis was listed as back at 1136 Elm in 1882–83, only to return to 523 Penn in 1883–84, during which time we know he moved up to the Roost. The next mention of Henrietta in the city directory was 1888, which put her at 41 North Third Street. All this detail, of course, does not provide much in terms of definitive evidence. Yet with rumors of her not approving of the trade, and no mention of having even appeared at the Roost, it's likely some sort of separation must have occurred. Regardless, Henrietta Kuechler is buried beside her husband in Charles Evans Cemetery.

As for the rest of his family, it appears that Kuechler remained relatively close. His daughters—all adults by the time he moved to the mountain—forged a constant battle with their father about whether he would spend the winter on his ridge or at their more safely located homes. (He always won.) Kuechler's mother actually lived on the mountain property with her son from 1883 until her death (unknown date) and was described as the "Countess of the Roost," having herself made considerable improvements to the place.

Of no dispute is that Kuechler could be cut off from society for weeks at a time during the winter months, especially when there was heavy snow. The Foosgangers, however, would attempt to check on their hermit anytime the weather was particularly bad. One winter, for example, a devastating deluge of snowfall encouraged a group to form a rescue party:

> The young men composing the party waded through deep snow drifts, and after enduring great hardships, owing to the bitter cold, they finally reached his one-story cabin, several miles from that city. Their shouts brought the grizzled old man to the door. He received his visitors hospitably, but refused to abandon his mountain resort. His faithless dog deserted him early in the winter, and Kuechler has since been entirely alone in the solitude of the snow-covered mountain.[126]

Another amusing anecdote, which follows, came from Edward J. Deninger, a Reading reporter at the turn of the century:

> "Some of the boys were sitting around the editorial room one afternoon. Outside, a blizzard was pelting the city and piling up record drifts. John Missimer, our managing editor, asked for a volunteer to hike up Mt. Penn and check on the hermit.
>
> I thought it would make a good yarn so I started out with two buddies. When we got to the house we had icicles hanging from our hats to our chins."
>
> When no one answered their original inquiries, Deninger, a short man, put a box under a window and peeked in.
>
> "I saw a form on the bed and figured Kuechler was asleep, so I slid my name card under the door."
>
> Sometime later, Kuechler stopped in at the newspaper office. He told Missimer the "form" the young reporter had seen was a sack of potatoes.
>
> "That reporter took a chance," he laughed. "I might have shot him for burglar."[127]

Aside from the obvious, this also reveals that Kuechler was not above coming into town for a variety of reasons, despite some more modern claims that he did not leave the mountainside for more than twenty years. Another classic episode further illustrates this fact:

> So closely did he resemble the accepted appearance of the patron-saint of Christmastide that one winter's day several years prior to his death he was nearly mobbed, by hundreds of children who saw him descending Penn's Mount near St. Joseph hospital on his way to town, believing him to be Santa Claus. And it was only by invoking the aid of the police to disperse the youngsters that he was able to escape from the clinging, clamoring crowd who had besieged him.[128]

Though the Roost was not considered a public wine house until 1890, from that point forward, its owner procured liquor licenses so that the public could indeed visit him and purchase wine and food. Upon Kuechler receiving his first license, the *Reading Times* reported that he "is of the opinion that after the Mt. Penn Gravity railroad is completed and in operation his many patrons will want to enjoy refreshments on the mountain." (Hardly the viewpoint of someone who wants to remove himself from civilization.)

A Hen with Twenty Chicks.

A hen, of the Plymouth Rock variety, belonging to Mr. J. L. Kuechler, on the Alsace hills, a day or two since hatched out twenty young chickens out of twenty-two eggs, which she herself had covertly laid in a snug nest in the rocks. This is an extraordinary large family, and the owner of the hen is quite proud of it. Mother and children were doing well at last accounts.

POTATO ROAST TODAY.

At Kuechler's Roost, there will be a potato roast today. It will be one of those events that have made this place famous and, as Herr Kuechler has invited all of his friends to be present, there will be a large gathering of those who know a good thing when they see it.

For Sale or For Rent.

DOGS FOR SALE.—For sale, a number of well-bred SHEPHERD PUPS—only a few days old. Apply to J. LOUIS KUECHLER, "Kuechler's Roost," Alsace township.

Several of Kuechler's *Reading Times* announcements, posted from the mountain. *Newspapers.com.*

In 1895, he secured a patent for a provision safe and held an event to showcase his work. (In fact, this was Kuechler's second patent, the first being for a type of stove in the 1870s.) He also regularly ran ads and announcements in the local paper—which of course could've been submitted via Zimmerman from the mount—that further illustrate his willingness to be an active participant in Reading life, albeit from a unique vantagepoint.

All that said, solitude may have indeed made the man a little batty. To wit, this story, from Zimmerman:

> In his inimitable way he loved, on occasion, to descant upon his mystical neighbors, who, he said, followed him from Odenwald, Germany, viz. "die Berge-Geist" (the spirits of the mountains), and who, he further said, appear about midnight in his bed-chamber seated on inverted beer-mugs, or on the tops of the bed-posts, holding sweet converse with him, and assuring him of their kindly offices and continued solicitude for his temporal and spiritual welfare. When the writer of this once asked his permission to publish some of these wonderful mythical legends, he was told by Mr. Kuechler that if he were to allow that, these good fairies would forever forsake him. In view of the threatened calamity to "mine host," the matter was pressed no further; Mr. Kuechler however, was wont to tell these stories with such earnestness and minuteness of detail that many an over-credulous listener was almost ready to believe them.[129]

In the end, it was by choice alone that Kuechler chose to live his life on the mountain, and whether hermit, recluse or something in between, he appears by all accounts to have been a contented man who continued to greatly influence local society from his beloved perch.

6

PROSE AND POETRY

"Kuechler's Roost!" A name to conjure with; a mountain-poem; a treasure-house for the lover of nature; a resort fragrant with delightful memories; a rendezvous for the pleasure-seeker; a rest for the brain-weary—such are some of the glories of this, the famous hermitage of the man who for 30 years waited patiently to buy this mountain-top, and at last secured it....

It is a favored spot in that it commands a wide sweep of charming landscape; and because of its great altitude and comparative seclusion.... The "Roost" enjoys more than a mere local celebrity for the good dinners that have been served here—for the exhilaration which attends the walker in his mountain climb; for the magnificent prospect, on every side, of superb mountain scenery.[130]

There's clearly some hyperbole in the previous passage, but this highlights an important factor in the development of Roost lore. The Foosgangers essentially consisted of a group of guys who liked to smoke cigars, drink wine, eat lots of food and have a good time. This became, surely, legendary to those who participated in it, but its appeal to outsiders would have been limited. These men, however, were quite literary and well educated, and the way they described their adventures at the Roost, as well as Kuechler himself, played a pivotal role in the place's ever-growing stature. This poetry about the place, both actual poems and lyrical prose, stokes the legends to this day.

A *Philadelphia Times* article from 1887 offered perhaps the definitive published description of the pre–Gravity Railroad Roost. (Even though

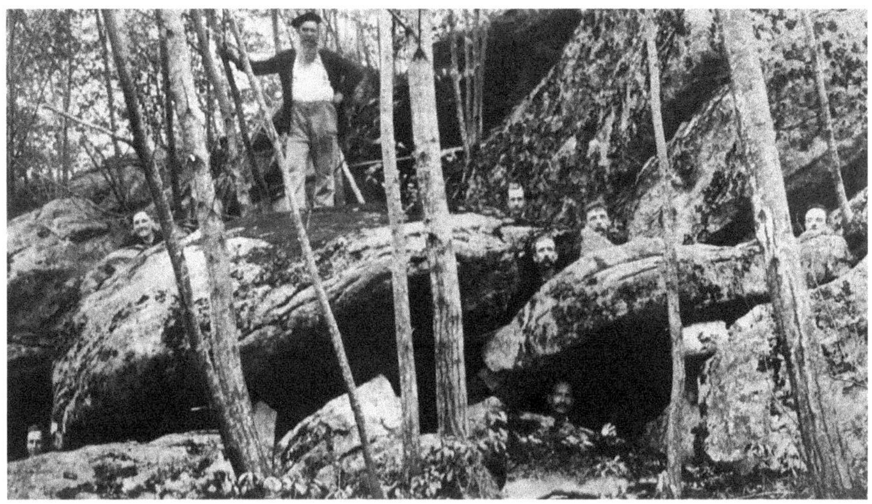

Kuechler and his Foosgangers, posing on the rocks near the Roost. Note the faces in each opening. *Courtesy of Geo. M. Meiser IX from* The Passing Scene *series.*

this was published first in Philadelphia, it has all the markings of a Tom Zimmerman work. The actual writer is not credited.)

> Aside of the fact that pure wine is manufactured here, a romance of life hangs around the spot that is extremely fascinating. It is dubbed a "roost" because of its eerie-perch and the siren magnetism it has to make weary pilgrims linger there. It is styled "Kuechler's Roost" after the name of the founder, who is altogether a most unique character....
>
> Therefore it has been sought out by those of a literary bias and those lured by the romantic and picturesque. It is the retreat to which the Hon. Daniel Ermentrout, Berks' stalwart Congressman, goes with lingering affection. Randall, Bayard and other dignitaries of the political world have visited it, and not any notable that falls to the hospitality of Reading citizens is allowed to depart ere he has folded his wings on Kuechler's Roost. Editors, whose brains reel by the hum of a busy world; lawyers, fagged out by the daily excitement of the bar; artists, business men and the leisure gentry of a select circle make their visits thither to gain a recreation of fresh spirits and new vigor....
>
> There is an occasional hilarity at Kuechler's roost that may break the spell of quiet that hangs around the place, but as a whole, in winter's snow and summer's heat, it is a charming panacea for burdened brains and disquieted souls.[131]

Whether Zimmerman did indeed pen the story or not, he would otherwise have his recognized turn at presenting elaborate, lovely prose to describe his friend's mountain retreat. One astonishingly vivid recollection reads as such:

> An Eastern fable tells us that when Paradise was fading from the earth, a single rose was saved and treasured by an angel, who gives to every mortal, sooner or later, in his life, one breath of fragrance from the immortal flower—one alone, but, according to the fable, it is worth a million ordinary breaths.
>
> There are some favored portions of our earth where one can almost persuade himself that he inhales this perfumed air of Paradise; and one of them surely, in a limited way it may be, is the wooded eminence [the Roost] whereon we are assembled tonight.
>
> I recall some of the beauties of this sylvan brotherhood as reflected in the sunny days of autumn, when the hills were aflame with color, and the air, brisk and bracing with autumn coolness, was redolent of spicy, balsamic odors and the sweet smell of autumn leaves. Maples, oaks and sumacs were already letting out the glowing secrets of the alchemist, whose frosty torch turned everything as by magic into pictures of vivid beauty. The mountain solitudes were gorgeous in their encrimsoned vestments.
>
> From a cluster of large rocks close by the hermitage, the views in all directions were charging to look upon. Turning toward the North, at the time of our visitation, there were faraway ranges of mountains, whose outlines were soft as swan's down fretted by the wind. Towards the South, peaceful valleys dotted all over with pleasant home, kissed the feet of half a dozen hills of real Alsatian beauty. A look Westward, and there, down behind the dark wood, was the sun garlanded like a king in robes of imperishable glory. Beneath us and around us, the glory of the woods. Above, "a canopy which love had spread to curtain her sleeping world."
>
> Surpassingly beautiful as are the surroundings here, in the autumn days, all the seasons are alike attractive.
>
> I recall another exceptional day when, in climbing to the "Roost," it was as if one had entered into the portals of a world of crystal, arched over by as clear a dome as ever spanned the skies; or like a veritable dreamland, painted in the imagination's most delicate tints "an endless phantasmagoria of sparkling color" surpassing anything that fancy

could conceive. The whole landscape seemed as if in a solar trance, with an opulence and splendor of winter sunshine that continued throughout the day.

The torpid touch of the Ice King's glazing breath—he who "with an un-scorched wing hurried on, where the fires of Hecla glow on the darkly beautiful sky above and the ancient ice below"—fell on the leafless trees, and soon the forest was transformed into, an object of glittering silver. Indeed, the whole scene, as it presented itself to the appreciative beholder, seemed like a bright vision from fairyland. Trunks of trees, bare and dark upon the one side were encased in crystal to their very tops on the ether.

[Poems referenced include "An Evening's Aurora" by Fridtjof Nansen and "The Frost Spirit" by John Greenleaf Whittier][132]

TALES FROM A MOUNTAIN LOG BOOK

A feature of the Roost that remains most interesting today—especially to those of us who seek to better understand the attitudes of the time—is the "Mountain Log Book," in which visitors would, from time to time, record passing sentiments, the very first bearing the date April 15, 1886. According to Zimmerman, it was "quite a treasure to the host and to his friends. Artists have decorated its pages; prose and poetry in pleasant alternation may be found on them, not only in English and German and Pennsylvania German, but in Latin, Portuguese, stenographic characters and in musical symbols."[133] After the wine had passed several times, according to legend, these poems often became songs.

On occasion, Zimmerman was wont to publish notable entries from said logbook in the *Reading Times*, which contributed much to the overall literary purview of the Roost. Some of the more interesting poems and passages are included here.

First, "an extract of some impromptu rhymes" added by Foosganger Norman Wiard, which "appears to be addressed to the inert who have not braved the morning air for health on foot."

Memorable Tramp Over the Mountains to Kuechler's Roost

by Norman Wiard

Weary of brain and tired of brawn,
You should have joined us at the dawn;
Braved with us the mountain steep,
Then taken 'round its top a sweep,
Passed down the slope on t'other side,
(The halt and maimed alone should ride),
And here we found—oh wondrous thing!—
And drank the waters of a spring.
'Twas such a fount and all so free,—
He loved his fellow-man, did he
Who walled it 'round, and roofed it o'er,
As ne'er did gracious man before.
'Tis granted few to own the ground
On which a spring like this is found;
And fewer springs that ever find
An owner of the land so kind.
And now we sit in "Kuechler's Roost,"
Let's drink to him a loving toast
"May he ne'er want for drink or food,
Or feel regret for doing good;
And when he's gone to lasting rest,
May his soul fore'er be blest."[134]

***

Next, this brief, yet poignant, anonymous verse, highlighting the spot's German influence.

A corner of the Fatherland
Set down in th' Alsace hills,
Where Kuechler serves with open hand,
A cure for all man's ills[135]

***

This note from C.N. Farr, dated December 10, 1893, offers a brief glimpse into a culture of inns that has long past:

> "Kuechler's Roost:" The last of the old nook-and-corner inns; the "Mermaid" of Ben Johnson and Shakespeare; the "Mitre" of Sam Johnson and Goldsmith, of which we can still say:
>
> Whoe'er has travelled Life's dull round,
> Whate'er his pleasures may have been;
> Must nigh to think, he still has found,
> His warmest welcome at an inn.[136]

***

This pretty sentiment from the pen of Edgar M. Levan bears the date May 18, 1880:

> Never, since the world dropped in beauty from the plastic touch of its Creator, has there been beheld by mortals fairer vision of landscape loveliness than that which dawns upon him from the "outlook" at "Kuechler's Roost."[137]

***

As Zimmerman noted, many poems found in the logbook were scribbled in German, Pennsylvania Dutch or some combination of the two. Henry Lee (H.L.) Fisher of York, a friend of Kuechler's and a Pennsylvania German writer of distinction who garnered acclaim for his translation of Edgar Allan Poe's "The Raven," was one such contributor. One of the "most singular of his poems," according to Woys Weaver, was a "four-page salutation devoted to Kuechler's Roost that was originally published as a holiday greeting for friends in December of 1884."[138] The epic "Kuechler's Rouscht" would eventually find its way into the logbook, and the original Pennsylvania German version is available, along with several other gems in that language, in appendix B.

LOGBOOK PROSE

Some authors chose to pen their sentiments in a lengthier format, but these passages are no less poetic. On July 11, 1893, for example, John Michler, a well-known local citizen known colloquially as "Uncle John," added the following classic entry:

> There are many famous and lovely summer resorts, but in the whole world there is only one "Kuechler's Roost," and Reading fortunately has it.
>
> Old and young, men and women—all are happy in paying tribute to this romantic mountain resort, surrounded as it is by scenery unsurpassed in loveliness and health-giving influence—with much in evidence everywhere about us to please the eye and enliven the heart, and when the natural demands of sustentation assert themselves, something besides, to moisten the lips, tickle the palate and bring comfort and digestion to an appetite waiting to be appeased.[139]

***

Also on July 11, 1893, coincidentally, James B. Shrigley, son of the one-time pastor of the Reading Universalist church, added this brief but telling sentiment: "After busie laboure cometh victorious reste," which Zimmerman called "as appropriate a motto for Kuechler's Roost as for the Royal tent on Field of the Cloth of Gold."[140]

***

This passage, which contains perhaps the definitive description of Kuechler's home from the period, came from the pen of a well-known Reading clergyman, who also contributed the article to his church paper. "The frequenter of the 'Roost,'" added Zimmerman, "will see in its poetic lines, not only a delightful appreciation of the singular beauties of this rugged eminence, but a faithful description of the 'Roost' itself." (Zimmerman would later borrow several phrases from this piece for his own work.)

> The "Roost" is a secluded spot hanging like a crested rook from yon mountain heights of our fair city. It is four miles up and no public thoroughfare leads to it. We were a company of ministers who upon

Monday meant to seek the hills to cool off the brains that were yet seething from the effects of Sunday evolutions in the pulpit.

Oh, the hills! The hills in Autumn! A lonely path of the hills, winding with a line of dignified clergymen is a novel sight, at least to the hill. Viewing the picture from behind one is amazed at the striking contrasts. The jagged rocks project in half-frightened attitudes from all sides, and wildly stare as if theology on the hills were something new. The rugged stones heave up and dart from under foot in throbbing fear sending the dominee reeling against the tree. And, then, the limbs above, bald as Methuselah, bend round and up in crouching fright and open, their dull knars, like eyes of owls, to solve the strange procession below. You need not wonder, for seldom does such measured dignity walk among the secluded hills.

What would you think if you were one of those frost-shorn trees away up in the mountain vales, which never felt anything smoother than a storm, and never saw anything slicker than a confused heap of moss-grown stones, were such a spectacle to confront you, with silk polished hats in a row, black coats buttoned to the neck and cut like a mould; immaculate ties setting to the chin like chiseled marble; silk handkerchiefs pressed to the sweaty brow with colored initials in the corner; gold-headed canes flourished in the accidental ray of sunlight; polished boots that mirrored the tufted grass beneath you; say, what would you think and do at the sight of such a dress-parade as this? You would crouch in awful respect and hide.

It is a luxury to wade through a heap of dried leaves in the forest; to press your foot in the hoof-marks of the mountain horse; to walk over the cushioned moss by the tree; to climb a weather-beaten rail fence; chase up a squirrel or bird from its retreat; look up through the stripped branches to the chasing clouds; inhale the bracing atmosphere impregnated with the balm of life, and labor on and up for miles in one pull to the cheering anticipation of such a place as Kuechler's Roost.

A roost, in the common acceptation of that term, is the perch of a fowl for sleep at night. Mr. Kuechler, a high-bred German, with the instinct of an eagle, spread his wings to soar aloft and build his eyrie here. It is a lofty perch—a little frame but built with hatchet and nail. Around it are rocks, but clearings here and there for garden and vines. Its outlook takes in the sweep of miles, which suddenly breaks upon you as you emerge from the dense forest.

What a glorious view! How it ravishes the soul! Down, away down in an undulating rise extends to the distant mountains the enrapturing scenery and in all that valley is the travail of toil, but up here is built a nest far removed from the follies of the world. So let us greet mine host under the door. A stalwart, rosy-cheeked fellow he is—good will in his eye and hospitality in his hand. "Welcome, shentlemans! Kom in!"

Upon the threshold you suddenly stop—you hear sweet strains or music, not from within, they are from without. Mountain nymphs!—goddesses of the forest-caves, perhaps! "It is not'ing but mine mountain harf!" says this freeman of the hills. Sure enough, there on the end or the low roof is fixed a tin funnel in the shape of a dice-box. Graded tongues of wire are arranged right in the neck of it, and when Aeolus lets out the winds from their prison, he stops here as he passes on his way to play a celestial tune upon that harp for the rugged mountaineer. Within, we sit. So must be those havens of rest on the Switzerland mountains where the traveler turns in to regale himself with hearty meal.

"Mine host, we want a mountain dinner!"—hardly seated, so we said. "We hab chickens und waffles, partridges und rabbits, beef und soups, schweitzer und everydings vat vos good." Then steams the pot and fills the room with the savory smell of a mountain dinner—German at that.

Very modest are our apartments, but that is an enjoyable feature of the feast. Let the host have time—our hungry stomachs must have patience for a little while. Look around: here is a bare floor; on the wall fanciful newspaper pictures; the ceiling is striped in fantastic colors—there in box-cages sing dozens of canary birds, and on the rickety tin of the roof and through the mechanical harp in the loft plays the howl of the outside storm. So, here the table is spread—we will spare you but a feast is fit for the gods.

You clergymen down there speak of "blue Monday"—no blue Monday up here. Eight miles of tramping up hill and down hill on Monday with six hours of lung exercise in the mountain air, and such a lunch between, laying the foundation for a good sermon next Sunday.[141]

***

Another of Reading's clergymen—or perhaps the very same; it is unclear—contributed this envy-inducing description of a visit to the mountaintop, which includes detailed descriptions of both Kuechler the man and Kuechler the winemaker:

It takes all kinds of people to make a world, but considerably more of some kind than others. The kind who live and conduct themselves as nearly as possible like their neighbors are a numerous kind. A much less numerous one is composed of those who strike out on original lines and carry out their own ideas regardless of what other people do or say.

I am led to make these reflections from the circumstance of having visited a place called Kuechler's Roost the other day. Here I found a man who had been bred among the mountains of the Vaterland, who lived in cities through youth and middle age, and who in the last quarter stretch of life, yearning for the mountains again, yielded to the feeling and planted himself upon the top of one of the highest mountains in Alsace township, where he could look down on all the rest of the world and have for his constant companions the clouds and the eternal hills. Here I found a man with a genuine love of the hills and the apparently inhospitable rocks. He does not stick to them because he knows of nothing else, for he has seen life on two continents, has looked upon the capitals of Europe as an artist of merit and skill, and is versed in many branches of the literature of his native tongue.

He came, as I said, to this rocky eminence; and with his own hands builded [sic] himself a house, or rather the house grew as he needed it; and afterwards, like Noah of old, he planted himself a vineyard. He has an idea that the rock and the nearness to Heaven will impart a superior flavor to the grape, which can be tasted in the wine, and is confidently waiting to see his belief vindicated. He expects to show a wine which shall reveal in every sip its lofty origin and its superiority to that produced from the stall-fed grapes of the valleys and lowlands. People said when he went there he would soon tire of his rocks and the unequal struggle against nature, but he sticks to them, and whoever wants to see a picture of a stalwart old man of the mountain can find it at the Roost any day in the person of its stalwart owner, whose magnificent beard and stately head would delight an artist. On the top of his house, over which an athlete might jump, is fixed an Aeolian harp, which breathes out a mysterious, far-away music all day and all night long. Near the house is a little garden dug out of the rocks, and a little farther away the vineyard, with rows of vines lifting their heads among the boulders, from whence the wonderful wine is to come.

It is a curious and quaint resort, and everybody who goes there is charmed and is divided between a sentiment of admiration of the panorama disclosed to the eye and of wonder at the perseverance of the owner in wrestling with the rocks and leading such a hermit-like existence in so isolated a spot. But, hermitage though it be, it is not so lonely as it seems. A great many people have penetrated the mystery of the labyrinthine ways that lead to it, and the rocks and the little room are familiar with the faces of many citizens of Reading and of the surrounding country.

The entertainment at the Roost is appreciated by a good many people whose appetites pretend to considerable culture. The bills of fare are not as a rule elaborate, or the viands rare or costly, but the music of the champagne corks is not an unknown sound there, and canvasback ducks have been known to come to their final account at the Roost board. Preachers are not averse to the place; editors take kindly to it; judges and lawyers have been known to unbend there; congressmen do not disdain its cheer, and many distinguished people from abroad are taken up there and shown the place as one of the side shows of Reading. So that the hermitage is by no means lonely nor a total stranger to the sounds of hilarity. During the coming cool, pleasant autumn days, it will be the objective point of many a pilgrimage on the part of those who love to wander in the mountain paths.[142]

LIGHTER FARE

Not everyone who scribbled in the logbook was so eloquent. A *Philadelphia Times* writer, for example, after attending a canvasback duck dinner, added:

Dere vas no bleasures ekval choost
Do eadin' Duck in Kuechler's Roost[143]

Zimmerman once described an encounter with H.L. Fisher, from which the following entry came—the first part written by Fisher, the second by the owner of the dog (Zimmerman):

DER MANN UN SEI HUND (THE MAN AND THE DOG)

Der Mann tringt Lager, (The man is drinking lager,)
Sei Hund isch mager; (The dog is lean;)
Der Mann isch fet, (The man is fat)
Der Hund isch net. (The dog is not.)

Brief though this be—
 A lawyer's brief at that;
It tells a lie, you see.
 About the lean and fat.[144]

On October 16, 1891, "Senator Magee"—presumably Christopher Magee of Pittsburgh—led the following toast, which was then recorded for posterity:

Here's to you as good as you are.
And here's to me as bad as I am;
And as good as you are,
And as bad as I am,
I am as good as you are.
If I am as bad as I am

Magee added the following stanza, later, on the same page:

The day was cold and blust'ry
And the wind was blowing hard
And when we got to Kuechler's Roost
The stove was in the yard![145]

A PENNY FOR HIS THOUGHTS

Speaking of politicians, a Pennsylvania governor faced widespread derision and ridicule for his contribution to the logbook in the early 1900s. Samuel Pennypacker, the state's twenty-third governor, initially took fierce criticism during the gubernatorial campaign of 1902 for acting as a puppet for then U.S. Senator Matthew Quay, who was the de facto boss of the state's Republican Party. Charles Nelan, a cartoonist for Philadelphia's *North American* newspaper, regularly depicted Pennypacker as a preening parrot.

Pennypacker won the election handily, but he did not forgive or forget Nelan. Shortly after becoming governor, he signed the Salus-Grady libel law, which became more widely known as the "anti-cartooning law." Absurdly, it banned "any cartoon or caricature or picture portraying, describing or

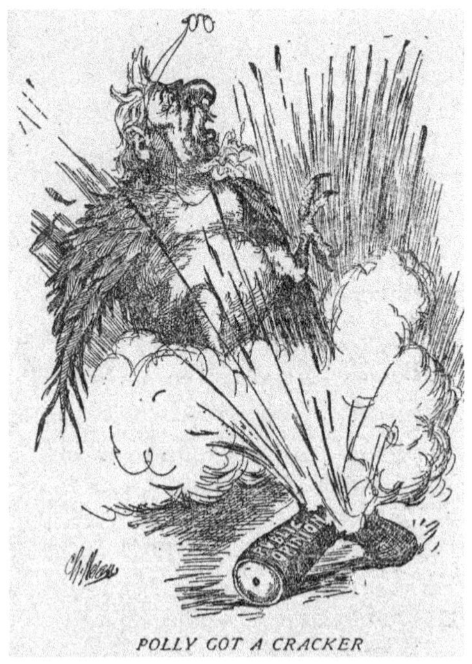

Left: Samuel Pennypacker, portrayed by Nelan as a parrot. *Wikimedia Commons.*

Below: Pennypacker as a beer stein, along with other hilarious depictions. *Wikimedia Commons.*

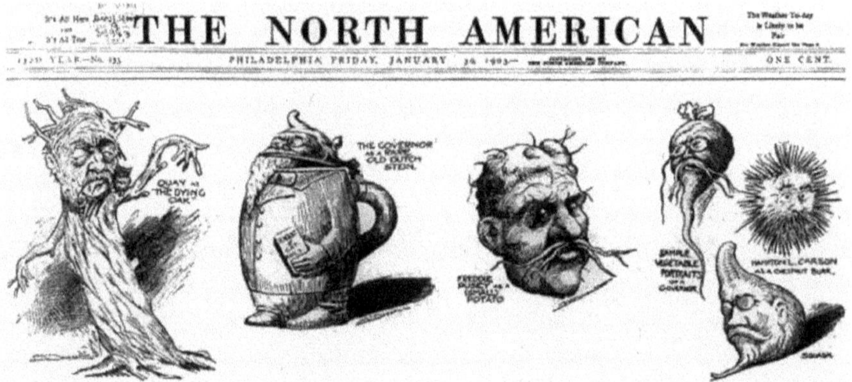

representing any person, either by distortion, innuendo or otherwise, in the form or likeness of beast, bird, fish, insect, or other unhuman animal, thereby tending to expose such person to public hatred, contempt, or ridicule."

As is not hard to imagine (and has rather amazing parallels to current events of the late 2010s), the press—both local and national—rebelled against Pennypacker and his odious law. Instead, the new governor was portrayed as a beer stein and other state officials who supported the law as oak trees, turnips, squash, chestnut burrs and other inanimate objects. The editors of the *North American* went on to suggest a new coat of arms for the state that "would include an impaled cartoonist's head, a 'gag,' a muzzle, a dwarf on a stool, a pussy cat, and a jackass in knee-high boots."[146]

At some point, the Philadelphia press discovered that Pennypacker had contributed a lighthearted verse to the Roost Log Book, and this amusing text was used against a man who was seen as lacking anything resembling a sense of humor. A St. Louis paper presented the following commentary on the incident:

> To a virtuous personage, lacking humor and oversensitive to criticism, it must be rather trying when half the current waggery in the world is aimed at him; and Governor Pennypacker of Pennsylvania seems to stand in need of sympathy. This excellent but splenetic, if not explosive, gentleman is so steeped in seriousness that he cannot relish caricatures and cartoons of himself. This being the case, of course, the cartoons multiplied.
>
> By way of punishing the offenders he fathered and effected the passage of a peculiar and somewhat absurd species of libel law—and was the first to break it, being one day unable to keep down his choler at the sight of a fresh caricature! While it is difficult to find it in the heart to blame the humorists for laughing, it is no less impossible to restrain a tear for the Governor.
>
> Especially so, considering the lengths to which fun leads his tormentors. Just now, for no reason other than to increase the sum total of gayety, they are digging up some of his poetry. It seems that in a resort half way up Mount Penn, which is called Kuechler's Roost, there is a book in which visitors inscribe more or less appropriate sentiments.[147]

The poetry in question, which was penned during Pennypacker's time as a judge in Philadelphia, reads as follows:

> Though steep the climb.
> Though road be lost
> The wine is good
> In Kuechler's Roost
>
> Some people think when wanting drink
> The crystal stream is fine
> But I care not for such as that
> Give me the sparkling wine

The sparkling glass for me when there
Is one who gazes in my eyes
With slender waist and face that's fair—
O wine that opest Paradise[148]

THE HOST'S MUSE

Kuechler himself penned the occasional poem, writing only in his native German. Originally part of a private letter from the hermit to Fisher, this particular composition was kindly translated by Zimmerman in order that the rest of us could enjoy it. (Several of Kuechler's other poems—available only in the original German—are reproduced in appendix C.)

SPRING DREAM IN WINTER

By JL Kuechler
Translated by Tom Zimmerman

I sing the praise
Of my Alsace here:
Prospects more fair
Than circling here
Cannot be seen
From anywhere.

Here, fields of corn
There meadows green
O'er azure wood.
The crows are seen.

And on this height
A garden fair.
And close in sight
My rest from care.

So name I this—
In words not sage
My dearly loved
Sweet hermitage.

In recluse joy
My life is led;
While, intertwining.
Vines, rank and climbing,
Make verdant spread.
In yon sweet vale, like a silver hand,
The Schuylkill flows thro' the beauteous land;
The iron horse attends the flowing tide,
Now here, now there, 'tis seen on either side.

In distant hills its smoke a trait doth leave
Like down on swans or wreaths of mist at eve.
Till, wafting upward in its veiled flight,
'Tis joined to ether and is lost to sight.

The early beam of day's awak'ning morn
Reminds me e'er of duty to perform.
In regal splendor, as he takes his way.
Comes forth in state the glorious King of Day.
And, laughing, greets me with his rosiest beam:
Dear brother! Hear me, this is joy supreme!

Life its light is pleasant all the while,
And toil is sweetened by its cheery smile.
It gives to labor an increase fine—
Imparts the fire to the sparkling wine,
Which grows so luscious on this lofty height
Hedged in by balmy woods of verdure bright
The fairest product of our rugged soil—
Reward the fullest for hard, honest toil.

The evening hour, ere the day doth die,
The smoke of furnaces against the sky:
These, with the moon's clear, silvery beams,
Invite to well-earned rest and dreams:

High up, upon the naked "Bank von Stein,"
With well filled pipe and glass of ruby wine,
When to the heart Aeolus whispers bland—
No, brother! this you cannot understand.

Thus freely I say.
And will never say nay.
Prospect, more fair
Than circling here
Cannot be seen
From anywhere.[149]

EVERYTHING IN ONE PIECE

The single greatest work created in the name of Kuechler's Roost is without a doubt a poem dubbed "A Foosganger's Evening," first published anonymously in the *Reading Times* in 1906 with the subhead "A mythical midnight feast at Kuechler's Roost as felicitously described in verse by a waggish local historian."[150] Said historian was later revealed—after his death in 1911—to be Garrett Stevens, father of Pulitzer Prize–winning poet Wallace Stevens and a founding member of the Foosgangers.

Though fictional, the entirety of the Roost experience is neatly summed up here, helping even a reader of the twenty-first century understand what it would've been like to encounter such a unique and fantastic locale (and its owner).

A FOOSGANGER'S EVENING
FELICITOUS DESCRIPTION IN VERSE, OF A MYTHICAL MIDNIGHT FEAST AT KUECHLER'S ROOST

by Garrett B. Stevens

The Judge and Tom, and Doc and I!
  We four afoot
For Kuechler's Roost one snowy day
  quite late set out.
The snow was deep the paths were
  hid, and only marks
We long had known on tree and stone
  made sure our route.
We struggled, hard and puffed and
  swore, while many a fall
Forced groan suppressed; and it was
  dark when round a turn

Of garden wall we struck a place well
known to all.
Leading to gate, always a-swing, to
Kuechler's own.
The Judge and Tom, and Doc, and
I.

"Ho, Kuechler! Ho," Loud we shouted.
Door we battered.
"Schlofsht du, Louis? Bisht du tod?" [Are you sleeping Louis? Are you dead?]
Low voice we heard,
And soon a shuffling sound, as snow
we scattered
And at the door the lantern lit, with-
out one word.
Like bear disturbed, old Kuechler
stood, and peering out
With hand 'bove eyes, with draggled
beard, wondering he
What fools these be, this time o'night,
to cause this rout.
And there we stood, a famished gang,
half shamed stood we—
The Judge and Tom, and Doc and
I.

"Guten Abend! Wass it? Ach Gott!
[Good evening! What is it? Oh God!]
Der Chudge und Dom,
[The Judge and Tom]
Und Doc and Du! Wass meant ihr
[And Doc and you! What do you guys mean?]
Kerls? Dis makes me proud.
Kommt g'raut herei! Ich hab juscht
[Come here! I'm sleeping.]
g'schloft. Ihr sind schpot. Warum?
[You are crazy! Why?]

Und ich hab yo nichts. Keh beer, keh
[And I have nothing to do. The beer, the]
fleisch, keh grout."
[meat, the kraut]
"Hast guter Wei Her Kuechler, mein?"
[Do you have good wine, my herr Kuechler?]
"Ya, dass hab' ich.
[Yes. I have that.]
"Dann bleibe mir do!" "Ich hab' noch
[Then stay with me! I still have]
Kaes und bissel Brod."
[cheese and a bit of bread]
"Don't worry, Louis," says genial Tom;
"im dissen Sack
[in this bag]
Sind vier Phesante, sheh g'dressed;
[Are four pheasants, dressed]
und alles gutes."—
[and everything good.]
Sly Judge and Tom, and Doc, and I.

The birds all trussed from basket came,
and lots of things
To kitchen went, and on his face there
showed a smile
That broader grew as jest went round.
Then Kuechler brings
From "Keller deef," something all
dust, and mused awhile
As though in doubt, and then he said,
"Here's something, Chudge,
I tink you'll like. Der Kaiser's own! I
have not mooch.
Zwei dutzen Flaschen, or so verleicht. [Two dozen bottles, or so lost.]
See the Doc, nudge
Slyly Tom, and Judge move foot gouty
under the couch.
Staunch Judge and Tom, and Doc,
and I.

The Judge with "specs" the label
reads and doubts his eyes.
But glasses clink and gurgling soon,
in each parched mouth
That sparkling wine, not Kaiser's
now, but our own prize.
Reaches the spot where spirits weak
grow quickly stout.
A flow of soul, each genial friend in
friend confides.
Tom recited then his choicest bits, and
Doc, he sang.
I stories told, and the Judge he well—
he moralized,
And sniffed the smell from kitchen door.
A jolly gang
This Judge and Tom, and Doc and I.

Outside the storm with fury raged, a
perfect gale;
The roof it shook with thund'rous
sound—an awful night!
But what cared we! This mountain
hut in sleet and hail
All cased and hid, the old Storm
King his worst defied.
Along the wall on wainscot shelf the
"empties" pile.
The Kaiser's good, the Roost is
warm, and we are there.
Kuechler beaming comes from kitch-
en with knowing smile,
Spreads the table with feckless cloth
and shining ware
For Judge and Tom, and Doc, and I.

Oh! those pheasants! I see them now,
with chestnuts stuffed
And browned just right, and juicy, too
not dry and tough.

The Judge—ah he! the connoisseur;
was strangely bluffed,
For no remark, as was his wont,
'gainst these made he,
But rising quick with glass held high,
this potentate,
To humble Louis, there still standing
proposed this toast:
"We drink best health to King of
Cooks Kuechler the Great.
The only man at midnight call, can
pheasants roast."
Brave Judge and Tom, and Doc, and
I.

"Wie schmachts by ihr" quoth rosy [How tired you are]
host: "Wie gleichsht der Wei?" [How about the wine?]
"The wine oh, yes! Kuechler, fill up
and join us now."
And then that king with us did sit and
sip his wine,
And stories told, and secrets gave, and
you'd never know
He gave one thought of our strange
trip, but in his home
As welcome guests he bid us stay as
long as he
Each joke and jest and rare retort enjoyed enjoyed as much
And did his share to entertain as well
as we—
The Judge and Tom, and Doc, and I.

"Boys, what hour is't?" the Judge now
asks, but Kuechler, he
Brings some glasses new, and quickly
Tom, whose nose is trained:
"The Royal Punch! Old Kuechler's
Best! By gum," says he;

"And that's the stuff for me, for me,"
we each exclaim:
And at that brew, this merry crew,
make fresh attack,
And things forgot are now brought
out, new stories rare.
'Till late we spy on kitchen floor,
chalked score on black,
A modest sum to such as we. We
chip our share—
The Judge and Tom, and Doc, and I.

We pass on out. "Good night, Kuech-
ler!" "Good night, all!"
The storm is spent, the stars are out;
but, oh, the snow
In drifts is piled, our tracks are gone.
"Who knows this wall?"
In single file with eyes half shut and
cheeks aglow.
This crowd at night past Spuhler's go,
facing sharp wind
On down the road and make each
turn, silently, true,
Till Mineral Spring is reached all
right, and there we find,
Banqueters late, dressed in state,
having good times, too.
Without Judge or Tom, or Doc and
I.

We trudge on home and parting late;
we're soon abed
With conscience clear, but feel well
fed, and soon we dream
Of kings and cooks in dingy nooks,
and visions red
Go through each head, and just as we
are getting there

"What's that rumpus? Why, can it
be? Not eight o'clock!
And breakfast waits, Ye gods!" we
say. Don't we feel sore?
But coffee strong, a roll or two, and
out we flock
And go to work and soon forget the
night before—
Stern Judge and Tom, and Doc
and I.

They tell us now, "Herr" Kuechler's
gone. New men abide,
In that old place we loved so well, and
spick and span
New buildings grow where we were
housed on mountain side,
And that a bar and a trap and a
younger man
Usurp the spot where oft we stayed
and had such fun.
Ah, well, 'tis done! The place is sad
with Kuechler gone.
A mem'ry sweet—a dream disturbed,
On Zion's crest,
In Ivory Tower, his spirit rests till we
are done
With earth and care, then joins us
all Foosgangers Blest—
The Judge and Tom, and Doc and I.

7
TOURISTS ARRIVE, VIA GRAVITY

Although the Foosgangers could claim at least partial domain over Mount Penn during the 1880s, that would all change—and drastically—in 1890. On March 25 of that year, the Mount Penn Gravity Railroad—a train that used engine power to climb the mountain, but only gravity to descend—officially opened, creating a major tourist destination for Reading. In the twenty-first century, it may be difficult to understand the power of a simple, primitive train to completely transform a community, to fathom that people would come from far and wide just to ride the rails and look out on the mountain. But transform the city it did. And come they did.

Modeled after (and often compared to, favorably) Lehigh Valley's Mauch Chunk Switchback railway, the Gravity, as it was commonly known, grew in popularity from 1890 through 1920, often finding visitors from Philadelphia, Wilmington and New York sharing a car on a weekend afternoon, all of whom had traveled to Reading specifically to ride the famed attraction.

"It is impossible for the young today to visualize that different world," wrote Beneval Weiss, who had ridden the Gravity in his youth, for the *Historical Review of Berks County* in 1952 (a time itself that has become difficult to visualize).

> When civilization lacked airplanes, radio, television and easy automobile travel....The Gravity gave our young people many of the pleasures that we now secure only from an electrical or automotive device. No one today could imagine that feeling resulting from being lifted out of the hot, dusty, summer city of Reading, through the cooling woods, to the Tower, there to dance between the city and the stars.[151]

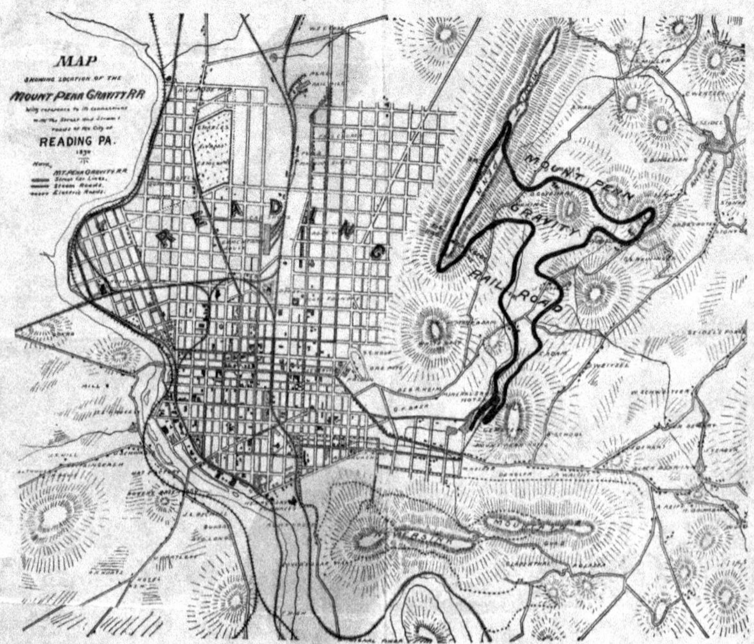

An early promotional map of the Mount Penn Gravity Railroad. *Library of Congress.*

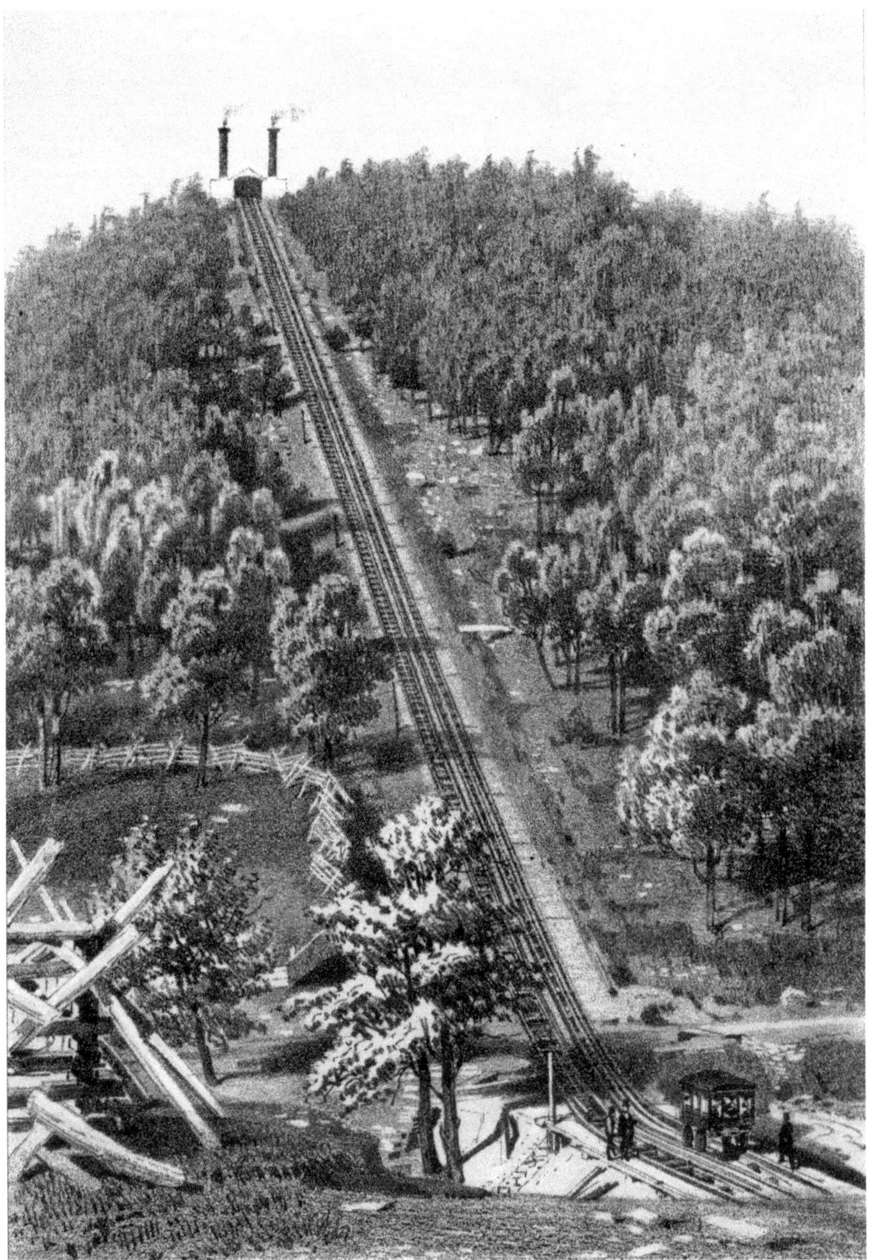

A view of the famed Mauch Chunk railroad in the Lehigh Valley, from which the Mount Penn Gravity Railroad was inspired. *Library of Congress.*

ROOTS

For years prior to the actual opening, there were numerous attempts to build a pleasure ride and/or leisure area on Mount Penn, surely spurred on by the expansion of farmers and vintners into Alsace Township, as well as the ridge's popularity with hikers and nature lovers like Kuechler and his Foosgangers.

In the mid-1860s, a city park was the hot topic, with a certain faction desiring it to be mountainous. "I think of having Penn's Mount and the Neversink em[b]raced in a Public Park, with serpentine walks, groves and grottos, and a first-class hotel on the top of each," read a letter to the editor in an 1866 issue of the *Reading Times*. "Posterity would doubtless erect a monument to the Councils who voted such a magnificent affair."[152]

The year 1870 brought a dream—from the minds of lawyers Eckert and Boyers—to begin "the construction of a pleasure drive along the crest of Penn's Mount, to extend about two miles northward from the White Spot, affording a carriage communication with that point." A firm of civil engineers—the Kendall Brothers—even conducted a survey of the proposed road, which would have reached almost nine hundred feet above the valley. But "the most picturesque and romantic drive in this vicinity"[153] never became reality, at least in this particular form.

The road and summit hotel idea resurfaced in 1881 with the creation of the Mount Penn Improvement Association, led by Alderman William Graul. More pertinently, this group was the first to officially propose the idea for a railroad up the mountain and, in fact, changed its name after just one meeting—at the suggestion of member John Michler—to the Mount Penn Incline Railroad Association. Yet, like those before it, the project stalled due to lack of funds.

The concept was revived at least once during the mid-1880s, but it was not until December 1888 when the committee that would finally see these ideas become reality established itself. Led by B.F. Owen, president of the City Passenger Railway Company; John Rick, board member for the Sixth Street Passenger Railroad Company; and engineer Calvin Dechant, they quickly secured close to $40,000 in stock options and, by May 1889, had raised that number to $65,000 and created a business charter.

Though additional investments (to reach the agreed-upon amount of $100,000) still needed to be gathered, and agreements with landowners all along the mountain were required, it was quickly clear that the long-considered project's luck had shifted, and everything fell into place relatively easily. Grading (preparing the roadbed for railroad tracks) began in July.

The construction crew consisted of ten gangs (of about twenty men each), most of which worked upward from the beginning of the line, but a few of which began near the Black Spot—the summit, so dubbed because of its appearance from afar—and worked down the mountain. Among other things, these gangs were in constant battle with local copperhead snakes, as it was not uncommon to kill as many as seventy-five in a single day or come across one that was five feet long.

As workers began to lay the actual track in September, excited locals would walk the line each weekend to observe progress and surely ponder their upcoming first ride on the novel attraction.

SETUP

When the railway began, steam engines pulled trolley cars to the top of the mountain. The first locomotive, dubbed the "William Penn," was a twenty-ton Baldwin similar to those used to haul lumber. It failed to prove itself in early runs, however, so it was replaced with two twenty-eight-ton Shay locomotives after less than a year in service.

The thirty-five-foot passenger cars, manufactured by Philadelphia's J.G. Brill & Company, were carried on double trucks of eight wheels. Measuring nearly ten feet in width and featuring an arched roof, they included twelve rows of seats, accommodating six persons per row, or seventy-two total per car.

"As to the Mt. Penn Gravity Railroad," read one account of the time, "there is nothing just like it in the world. Differing from other Mountain gravity lines, this is a solidly constructed, fully equipped, broad gauge railroad, laid with heavy steel rails on stone ballast and using locomotives instead of stationary engines for motive power."[154]

Starting at the depot in Mineral Spring Park (the current Pendora Park), the railroad loosely followed what is Glen Road today, climbing past the old Hessian Campgrounds, then Mineral Spring Hotel, through Egelman Park and up toward the northern part of Haag Rd., running parallel to Angora Road. From there, it veered sharply southwest, along the modern Spuhler Lane (today a private drive). It soon reached what is now Skyline Drive at the "South Turn" or "Schwartz's South Curve"—the first scenic overlook to gaze on the city of Reading, the Schuylkill and Lebanon Valleys and the distant ranges and peaks of the Blue Mountains—then made a virtual

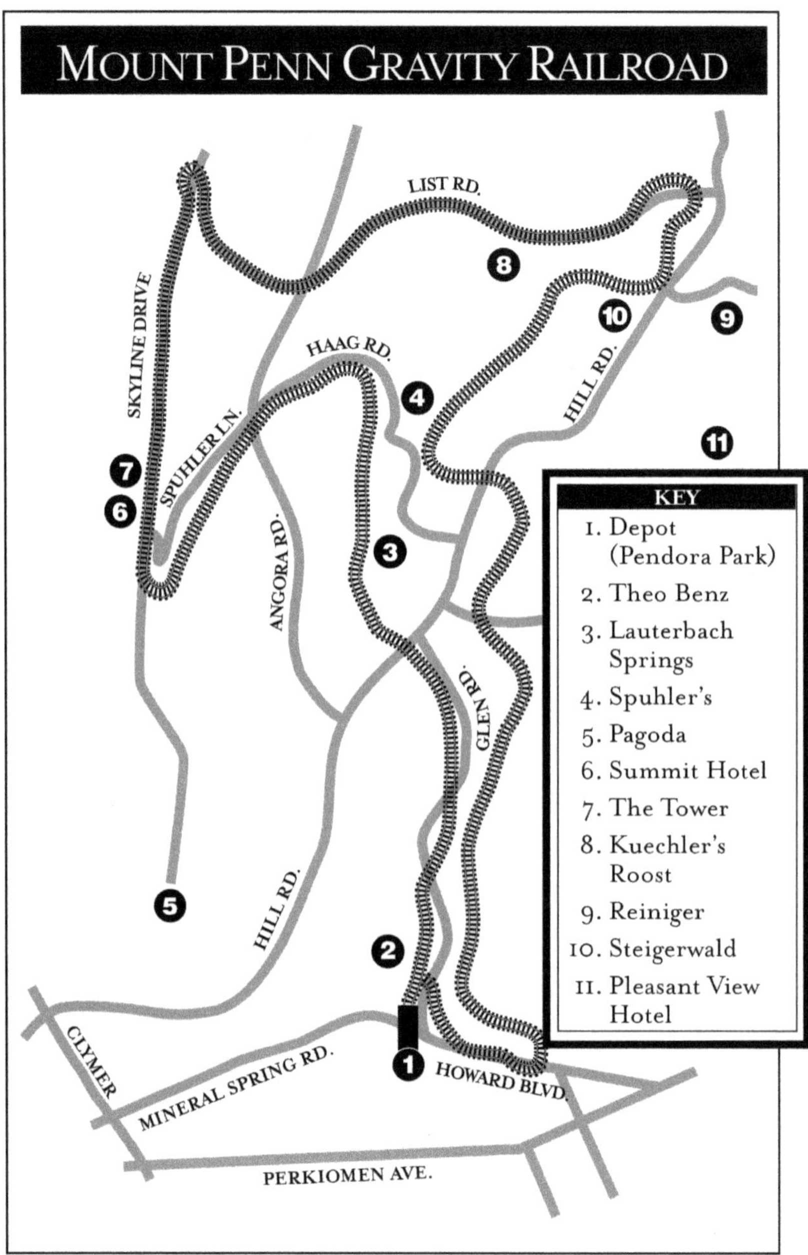

A map of the Mount Penn Gravity Railroad route, with notable highlights. *Illustration by Stephanie Frederick.*

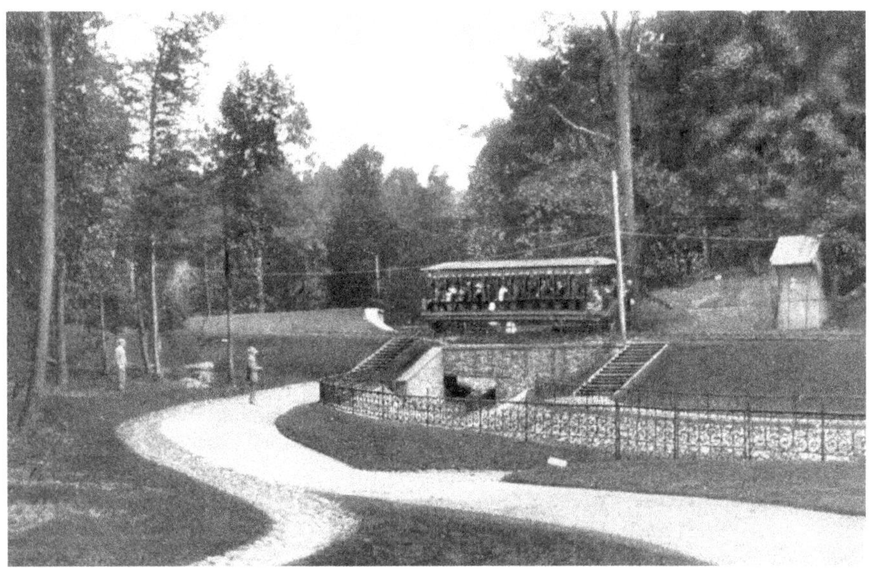

A postcard of a Gravity Railroad car at Egelman Park, 1911. *Charles Adams III Collection.*

U-turn onto what would become Skyline Drive and followed that to the summit, having traveled two and a half miles from the depot.

The five-mile descent, made only with gravity, followed today's List Road almost to Hill Road and then veered right to cut a meandering path south down a road of light grades—through groves, summer resorts, picnic grounds, vineyards and mountain farms—before finally returning to the depot. Most official sources suggested that the top descending speed was twelve miles an hour; at least one reporter, however, claimed it could reach upward of forty.[155]

"The car started so slowly," wrote Weiss of the ride's descent, "that you could walk beside it for the first hundred and fifty feet. You had the sensation that you feel when the train beside your train, in a great city terminal, pulls out and you think you are moving but are not. Down through the cool, quiet night the car traveled, the only sound of motion being a peculiar groaning of the wheel flanges on ungreased curves. Then came a straightaway through sleeping farmland, utter silence but for the laughter of young people and their singing of songs."

"This latter part of the trip is most enjoyable," wrote another journalist of the time, "the cars dashing, often at great speed, around the steep slopes in curves and bends which make one hold his breath with something akin to a pleasurable fear if such term can be rightly understood by the reader who has not had the thrilling experience."[156]

(Those interested in more technical details of the railroad should view appendix H.)

The First Runs

As construction continued throughout the late summer, palpable excitement grew among the citizenry. When a train whistle was heard from the mountain on Friday, September 27, 1889, the city was poised to explode. (It was only a construction train.)

The following morning, however, the railroad's officers and stockholders—as well as members of the city press—did indeed make the inaugural trip to the Black Spot, where they "were afforded one of the grandest views of the city and its surroundings that could be given." Since the line had only been constructed to that point, the car made its way back down, via gravity, on the same path.

Though only a portion of the road had been ballasted (packed with gravel for stability), the train "was drawn up the mountain side as smoothly as if it had been on the level." Passengers—who "were perfectly delighted with the trip through the romantic mountain glens and forests"—also reported the grade as being "scarcely perceptible."[157]

That afternoon, the *Reading Times* noted, "a number of Grand Army gentlemen from distant points were given a trip over the road, and they expressed the opinion that it was not only a wonderful achievement, but that it would make Reading one of the most popular resorts during the heated term."[158]

By Sunday morning of the same weekend, residents throughout the city had learned cars would be running that day; as such, thousands descended on Mineral Spring Park in hopes of being one of the first to experience the Gravity Railroad. "It was not the company's intention to open the road for business until it had been thoroughly equipped," reported the *Reading Times*, "but there was such a tremendous pressure brought upon the officers by those who wanted to go up the mountain that it was concluded to make a certain number of trips in order to accommodate the great desire of the people."[159]

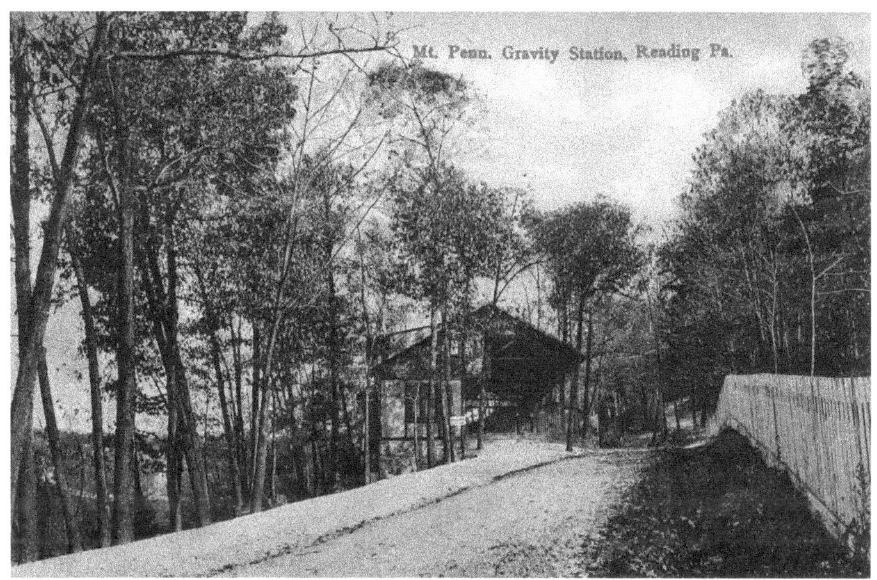

A postcard depicting a Gravity Railroad station. *Joseph A. Webb Collection.*

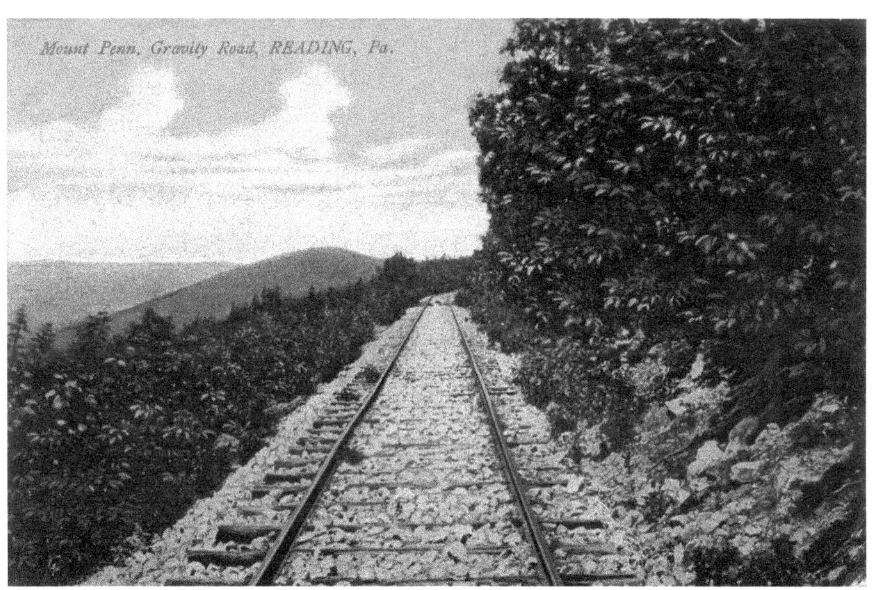

A postcard of the Gravity Railroad. *Joseph A. Webb Collection.*

With just one car in service—which could handle a mere seventy-two passengers concurrently—the company would manage only ten trips that day. As a result, an estimated 60 percent of the people who attempted to purchase a twenty-cent ticket were turned away. Some of those unable to score tickets instead celebrated the launch by walking the rails between the depot and summit. During the hike, they counted sills and reported a total of 4,365.[160]

At the end of that first Sunday, at around 8:00 p.m., officers and stockholders made the Gravity's first night trip, enjoying, it was recalled, a "grand sight"[161] as they looked down over the lighted streets of Reading.

Trains continued to run periodically until about Thanksgiving, when the line was shut down for the season. Construction on the remainder, however, continued through the winter with an eye on a spring unveiling to an eagerly awaiting public.

"Messrs Editors: Two gentlemen, standing on Black Spot, the present terminus of the Mt. Penn Gravity Railway, on a clear day—the one states that he can see fifty miles distant, while the other contends that no one can see more than ten miles with the naked eye. Now, how far can a man really see?"

—*Reading Times*, November 22, 1889

GRAND OPENING

The first complete trip over the full route—which again included officers and stockholders—took place on March 25, 1890. It being early spring in the mountains, the air was still raw, but that did not stop the splendor of Reading's new marquee attraction from displaying itself fully. The available views were, according to the *Reading Times*, "pronounced by all as excelling any in the State, the view of Reading and up the Lebanon and Schuylkill valleys being almost beyond description." It could be safely declared, the article continued, "that this mountain railway exceeds any other in this section of the country for grandeur of scenery, and cannot help but be the means of attracting thousands of visitors to Reading during the coming season, *and all future time*."[162] (Emphasis added, because, wow!)

Two days later, the general public received its opportunity, with four hourly trains starting at 1:00 p.m. In the early days, crowds were so thick

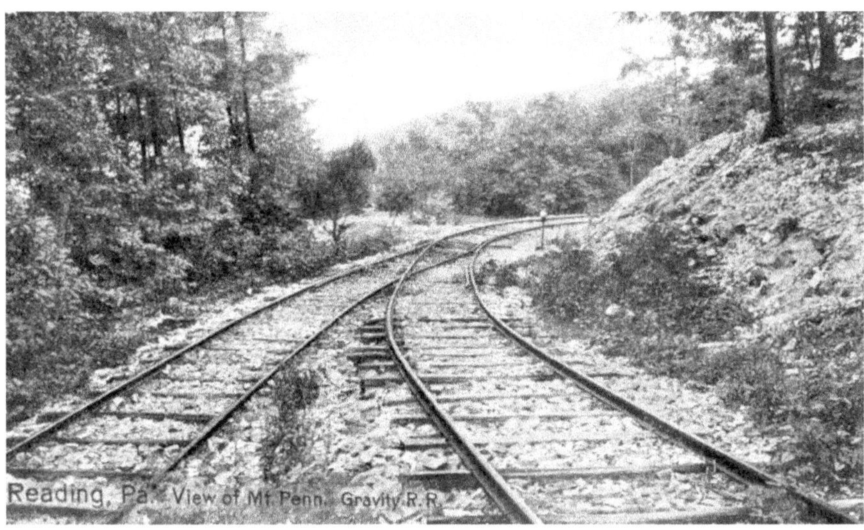

Another postcard of the Gravity Railroad. *Charles J. Adams Collection.*

that hopeful riders were forced to either endure long waits to secure a ride or miss out altogether. By May, however, the number of trains and cars had been increased, with trips beginning around 7:00 a.m. and running through 6:00 p.m. each day. Eventually, there were three engines and nine passenger cars (three closed, six open), allowing the company to take as many as one thousand passengers over the mountain in a single hour.[163]

The attraction quickly gained popularity not only in Reading and Berks County, but in surrounding counties and larger regional cities like Philadelphia and Wilmington. Shortly after launch, it was being referred to as "the famous Mount Penn Gravity Railroad"[164] and "the best trip of the season"[165] in nearby papers. Starting on May 1, excursion tickets were available via the Pennsylvania Railroad in Philadelphia and other principal Schuylkill Valley stations, and more than one hundred private excursions were booked that very first season.[166] All told, when the line shut down after Thanksgiving, about thirty-five thousand passengers had experienced the ride.

Early Hype

If some of the early press received is any indication, the Gravity Railway's officers showed a knack for marketing and self-promotion. Several groups of notable citizens—including, importantly, many members of the press—toured the town and reported back with glowing, lofty praise.

After visiting the city on May 13, 1890—a day that included a ceremonial opening of the Gravity as well as a visit from Forepaugh's famous circus and Wild West parade—the *Philadelphia Times* published a glowing, front-page recommendation for the railroad, titled "A Gala Day at Reading." Thousands from greater Berks, the article recalled, came dressed in holiday attire to enjoy a city most ready to accommodate their "charming life and color and animation."

Of the Gravity Railroad, the paper described an "incomparable mountain ride…one of the most interesting rides possible in this country," and declared there to be "no more varied and interesting panorama or more beautiful prospect in Pennsylvania." Finding comparison to the aforementioned Lehigh Valley counterpart, it went on to call Mount Penn's version so "accessible and possessed of so many charms that Mauch Chunk can no longer hold undisputed claim as 'the Switzerland of America.'"

The article's one notable lament was the inevitable effect this new line would have on Kuechler's Roost: "The railroad will doubtless in time change the wild and rustic character of this spot," it noted, "but at present it is charming and quite unlike anything close to civilization."

In June, a trip organized by the Philadelphia and Reading Railroad Company for journalists working all along its route brought over three hundred visitors to the slopes of Mount Penn. Arriving in "one of the prettiest inland cities in the country"[167]—as one of the writers described it—around 10:00 a.m., they were greeted at the train depot by officers of both the P&R and the Gravity, as well as the Germania Band. After marching via horse carriage to the depot at Ninth and Green Streets, they rode streetcars to Mineral Spring Park, with the band following the entire way.

After a ride up the mountain featuring plenty of time to be awed by the spectacular views, the party arrived at Wildwood Park, a designated picnic grove along the descent (located at the junction of List and Hill Roads today, near Antietam Lake). There they enjoyed a catered luncheon alongside yet another concert from the Germania Band, "its sweet cadence falling on the ear on those mountain heights like the song of the Syrens,"[168] as one journalist noted. It is certainly lucky they enjoyed the music, because one last concert would be performed when the group finally returned to Mineral Spring Park.

This outing's purpose was, of course, to generate publicity for excursions on the P&R Railroad to Reading, and not surprisingly it succeeded, with

Mt. Penn Gravity R. R.

Mt. Penn Gravity R. R.

MUSIC AT THE TOWER BY

GERMANIA ORCHESTRA

Every Monday, Tuesday, Wednesday, Thursday and Friday, from 2 p. m. to 10.30 p. m,

GRAND CONCERT BY

Full Germania Band

Every Saturday afternoon and evening. Trains every half hour.

ON WEEK DAYS

Every half hour from 10 a. m. to 10 p. m., and every hour from 7 a. m. to 10 p. m.

ON SUNDAYS

7 a. m. to 1 p. m. every 30 minutes.
1 p. m. " 5 " " 20 "
5 " " 9 " " 30 "

Grand and beautiful views, exhilarating air, shady stretches, delightful ride, for trifling expense.

Fare for round trip............} Adults, 25 cents; Children, 15 "

Good to stop off anywhere for any length of time.
C. M. DECHANT, Supt.

This ad promoted the very first concert at the Tower in 1890. *Newspapers.com.*

many effusive articles appearing over the next several weeks. What follows are some of the more noteworthy passages:

From Allentown's *Morning Call*:

> At the summit, after the 3-mile climb behind the ponderous and curiously constructed engine, a natural panorama of indescribable grandeur greets the eye. From an eyrie, 1200 feet above the sea level, the visitor looks out over 30 miles of magnificent landscape, while directly at his feet lies the city of Reading, its many dwellings, factories,

furnaces, railroads with moving trains, etc., looking like so many toys set out on the edge of an old fashioned "Christ putz." The Schuylkill and Lebanon valleys, bounded by the Lehigh and Blue Mountains, lie before you, dotted with streaks of silvery waters, farm houses, villages and so on, the whole relieved by the green hills and dales scattered over the landscape.[169]

***

From the *Easton Express*:

The Valley of the Schuylkill, whose loveliness has been sung by the poets of two continents; the broad and fertile Lebanon Valley; the purple peaks of the Lehigh and the bold outlines of the Blue Mountains; the mighty Appalachian Range, looming against the far northern horizon; the scores of cities, towns and hamlets; the distant railway trains flashing around mountain curves, and the lazy barges drifting down broad streams: the silver gleam of rivers and brooks; the sombre masses of ancient forest groves and the more vivid coloring of meadow and field—all these combine to form a panorama of superlative and surpassing beauty.[170]

***

From the *Easton Free Press*:

The scene is one of great beauty and has few equals anywhere....At an elevation of 1,149 feet above the sea, a wide view is obtained and the country for thirty miles around lies before the eye. The valley of the Schuylkill can be traced above and below Reading, the various lines of the Reading road radiating from their union depot wind off in all directions, while the splendid stretches of farming land, dotted here and there with evidences of mineral products, are only bounded by the limit of vision.[171]

***

From Pottsville's *Miner's Journal:*

> From the top of the mountain you look down upon the thousands of brick buildings below whose color blends so beautifully with the landscape that for the moment you are deceived into the belief that you are looking upon an autumnal forest skirted with the green of spring.... Some who had gone round the Switchback said it surpassed even that picturesque view, and Harry James, of the Ashland Local, said he saw nothing equal to it during his trip abroad.[172]

***

Finally, the *Lebanon Daily News*:

> At [the summit], there bursts a panoramic view that is grand beyond description, defying the pen of the writer or the brush of the artist to adequately portray. From an altitude of 1,200 feet we have the city of Reading at our feet, as it were; the thousands of brick houses; the streets

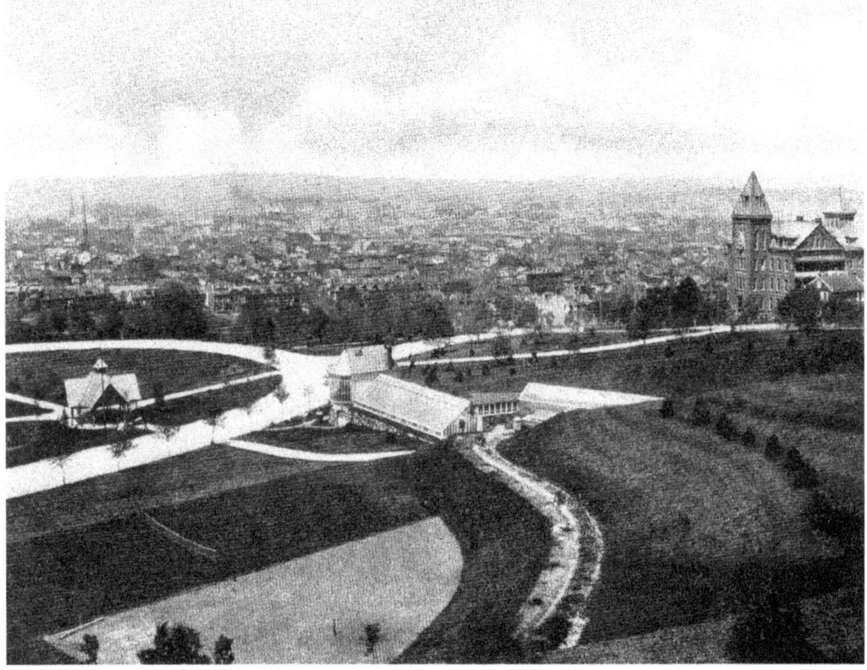

A view over Reading from Mount Penn, 1907. *Souvenir Post Card Company.*

> and squares outlined like a map; the black clouds of smoke which went floating into space, indicating the large industrial works, the towers shooting skyward, locating the churches; and far off in the north sweept [sic] the placid Schuylkill river in its serpentine course to mingle with the waters of the Delaware and thence into the sea. Although a city of 60,000 population, from this great height it resembles a city of toy houses, so small and dwarfed it appears, but its profile as distinctly revealed as the map of the engineer. The scenery presented is not as rugged as the picturesque Mt. Pisgah and other points of the Switchback at Mauch Chunk, but it is far more animated, as to the left lies the rich fertile fields of our own Lebanon Valley, to the centre and right the Schuylkill Valley, while on the south side Oley Valley is spread before the eye with Birdsboro dimly seen in the distance. On the Black Spot a stone tower 60 feet high has been built from which the tourist is given a beautiful bird's eye view of the city of Reading and the country for miles around, broken only by the ranges and peaks of the Blue Mountains.[173]

THE TOWER

As referenced in the last passage, the Mount Penn Gravity Railroad would not have been complete without its crown jewel, a four-story, fifty-foot stone entertainment center known simply as "The Tower," which opened in July 1890. Located on the Black Spot, 1,200 feet above sea level, it was, in its day, as iconic as the Reading Pagoda and the absolute must-see attraction for any Reading visitor.

From the third- and fourth-floor balconies of this splendid structure, as well as the magnificent rooftop designed to look like battlements, one could see in any direction for at least thirty miles, as so eloquently described earlier. Around the twenty-six-foot base was a pavilion seventeen feet wide on all sides but the south, where a twenty-four-by-sixty-foot dance floor was installed. Also, to the south were the restaurant and restrooms. In time, bowling alleys and additional space for dancing—to accommodate up to one thousand people—would be added.

On Wednesday, July 9, 1890, the Tower officially opened, celebrated by concerts from the Germania Orchestra, to which "quite a crowd rode to the top of the mountain to hear the music and enjoy the exhilarating breezes."[174] From that day forward, during the first season, the same orchestra would

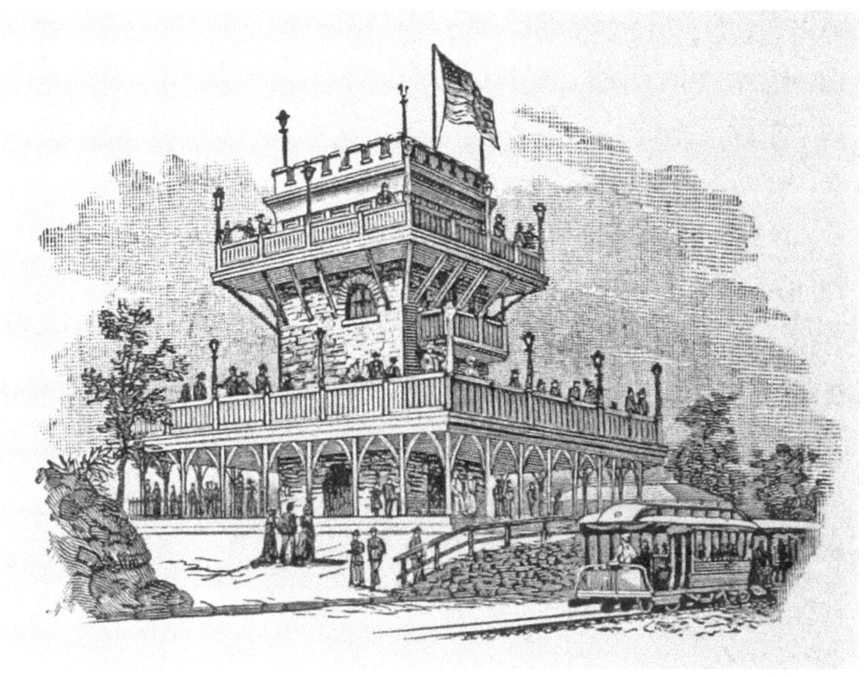

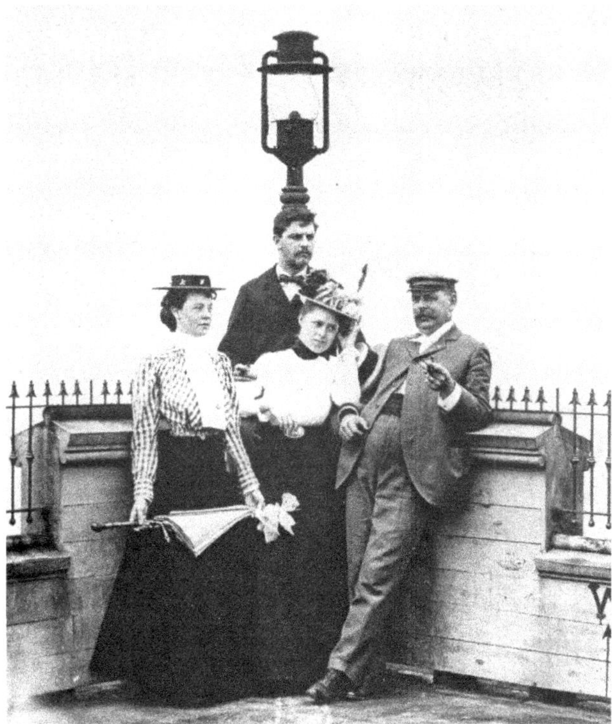

Above: An illustration of the Tower. *History of Reading, Pennsylvania, and the anniversary proceedings of the sesquicentennial, June 5–12, 1898/Internet Archive.*

Left: A group of revelers enjoy the view from atop the Tower. *Courtesy of Geo. M. Meiser IX from* The Passing Scene *series.*

play weekdays between 2:00 p.m. and 10:30 p.m. (presumably with a few breaks here and there). On Saturdays, the "full Germania Band" would entertain visitors during the same period.

The Tower "was brilliantly illuminated," reported Allentown's *Morning Call* that same July, "with a double row of lights, and from the city it resembled a fairy toy castle, illuminated at Christmas time. The odd and striking mountain top picture could be seen as far as Robesonia, and passengers on all incoming trains viewed the illumination with great wonder and satisfaction."[175]

Weiss, who called the Tower's dance floor "the largest and best in Reading," fondly recalled dancing the one-step and the two-step, as well as the schottische, waltz and even the maxixe to an orchestra of eight or ten pieces led by Harry Fahrbach. The Tower floor was also large enough, unlike many others, to perform the horse trot—a dance that apparently required plenty of open space due to its high speeds. Popular tunes (around 1914) included "Beautiful Ohio," "Alexander's Rag Time Band" and "The Trail of the Lonesome Pine."

Weiss went on to describe the following memories of climbing to the building's apex:

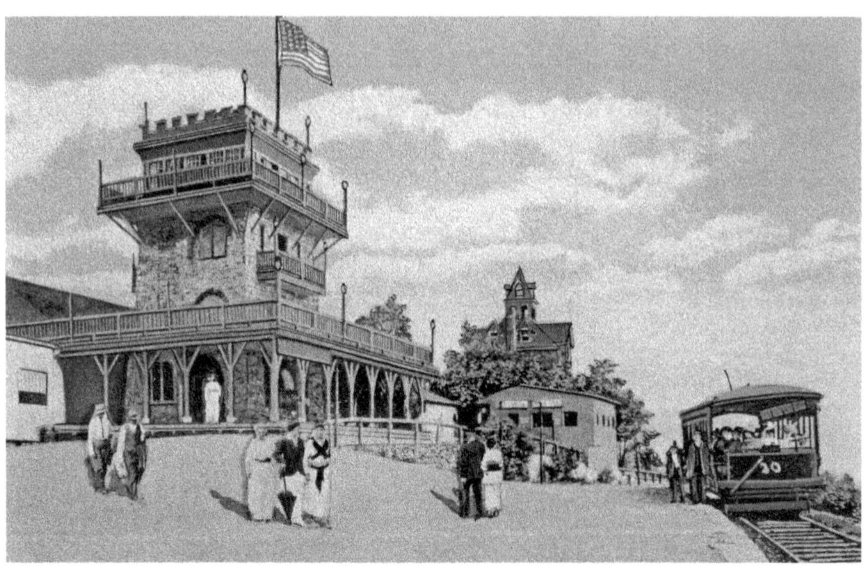

A lovely illustration of the Tower and its railway station, with the Summit House in the background. *W. Chas Lewars.*

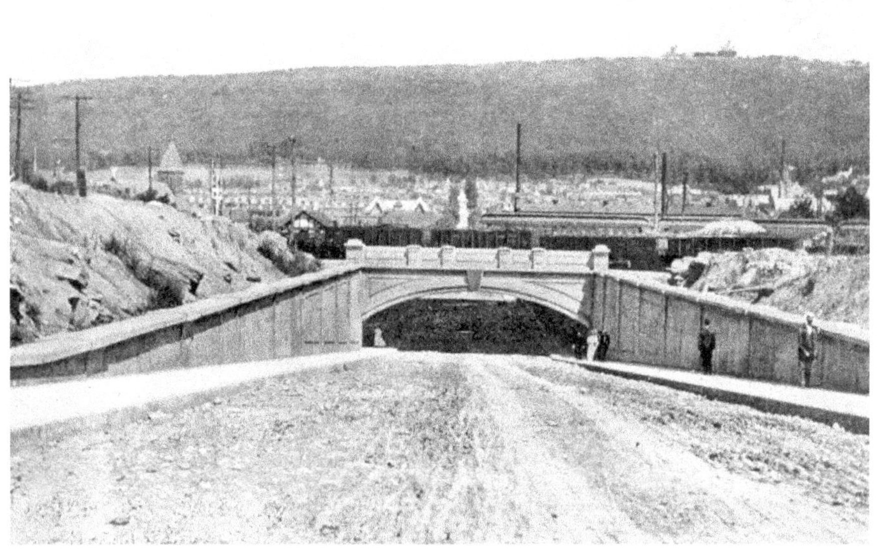

A cool shot from the city of Reading, with the Tower and Summit House visible on Mount Penn. *Charles J. Adams III Collection.*

> At intermission, or perhaps during a dance, you took the young girl up the six or eight flights of stairs to the top of the Tower. This platform was unlighted and open to the stars, and over the parapets you could see the blinking lights of the city....Up there you had the feeling of height and distance and broad vision that your children and grand-children were to have in an airplane. It was a place for romance. Though we have no statistics on the matter, it has been ventured that more romances started on the top of the Tower than in any equal area in Berks County.[176]

In June 1892, William Schwartz's Summit Hotel (with a gala concert by the full Germania band, of course) joined the Tower at the mountain's highest reaches. Known for its vast, two-story veranda—"the coolest spot on the mountain"—as well as an observatory extending twenty-five feet above the main roof, the new hotel could accommodate up to one hundred overnight guests and double that for banquets. In addition, it opened the majority of its grounds for picnicking and amusement, even providing graphophone concerts for children. "To sit there in the cool of the evening and watch the turning on of the electric lights in the city below," the hotel's promotional material once read, was "like seeing a thousand stars born in the sky above."[177] A supper menu from the hotel is available in appendix F.

8

RESORT TOWN

It was not merely the Mount Penn Gravity Railroad that enabled Reading's resort status to reach world-class levels, but rather the confluence of numerous factors. The city's emergence as a manufacturing hub, as well as the growth of the Philadelphia and Reading Railroad during the mid-1800s and the resulting money and influence it brought to the area, obviously contributed considerably. This, combined with a wealth of natural resources so near to the downtown area, offered the perfect match of urban and bucolic.

"Reading as a summer resort has attractions superior to many highly-praised localities by the sea or on the mountains," wrote an optimistic *Reading Times* in 1889, illuminating the seemingly unlimited pleasure-seeking options for both residents and visitors. Among others, "a splendid system of horse and electric railways…the river, with its little steamers plying up and down at all hours…romantic views [and] parks well shaded…vine-clad hills in the neighborhood, which call up the sun-illumined vineyards along the Rhine…gurgling brooks and placid streams where fishing may be indulged in…the delights of music…inspiration from crowded thoroughfares."[178] (And this was before the major attractions were even open.)

Reading's citizens themselves formed another—perhaps unheralded, in the grand scheme of things—crucial element to this story. As has been evidenced by our willful winemakers, Kuechler and his Foosgangers and the businessmen who finally brought the railroad to reality, the people of Reading at this time highly valued the pleasures of life. Many were, of

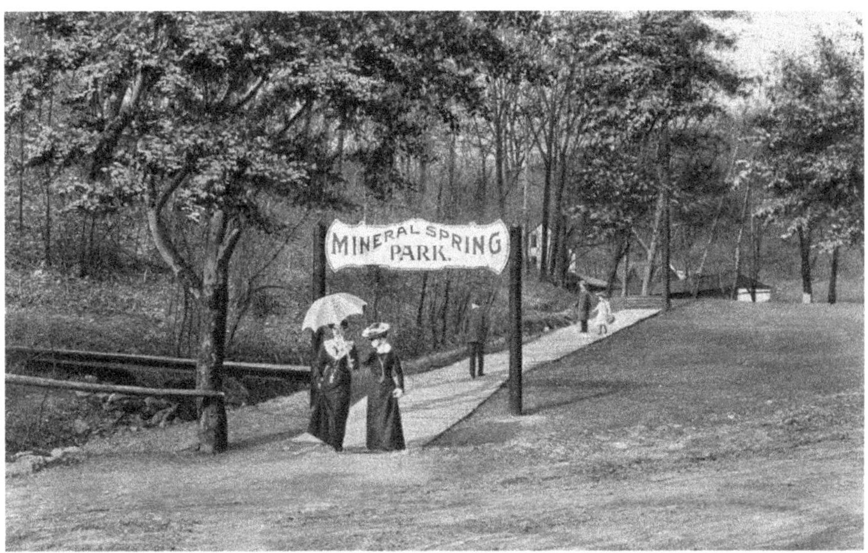

The entrance to Mineral Spring Park. *Joseph A. Webb Collection.*

course, dedicated professionals, but they also took their fun seriously enough to build an industry around it. An 1893 book titled *Reading, Its Representative Business Men, and Its Points of Interest* added the following observations:

> As can be easily seen from the great development of its suburban resorts, the people of Reading, of all sorts and conditions, are very fond of amusement. They delight in them, according to the old frank and free Teutonic style. They are an open-hearted people and see no reason whatever why life should be taken with a grave and melancholy countenance, rather than with hearty and moderate enjoyment. You will always find them sociable, uncensorious and very pleasant people to meet. In the summer, frequent little trips and picnics help to speed the heated months away. In the winter also are frequent balls, carnivals and entertainments. It has been often remarked by travelers that in many larger cities of the country, there is not one half as much pleasant social life and entertainment as marks the constant round of the seasons in Reading.[179]

It might seem baffling today to call Reading "one of the best known cities to visit in the country,"[180] yet this was absolutely a common sentiment during this flourishing period, when the P&R Railroad regularly ran excursions

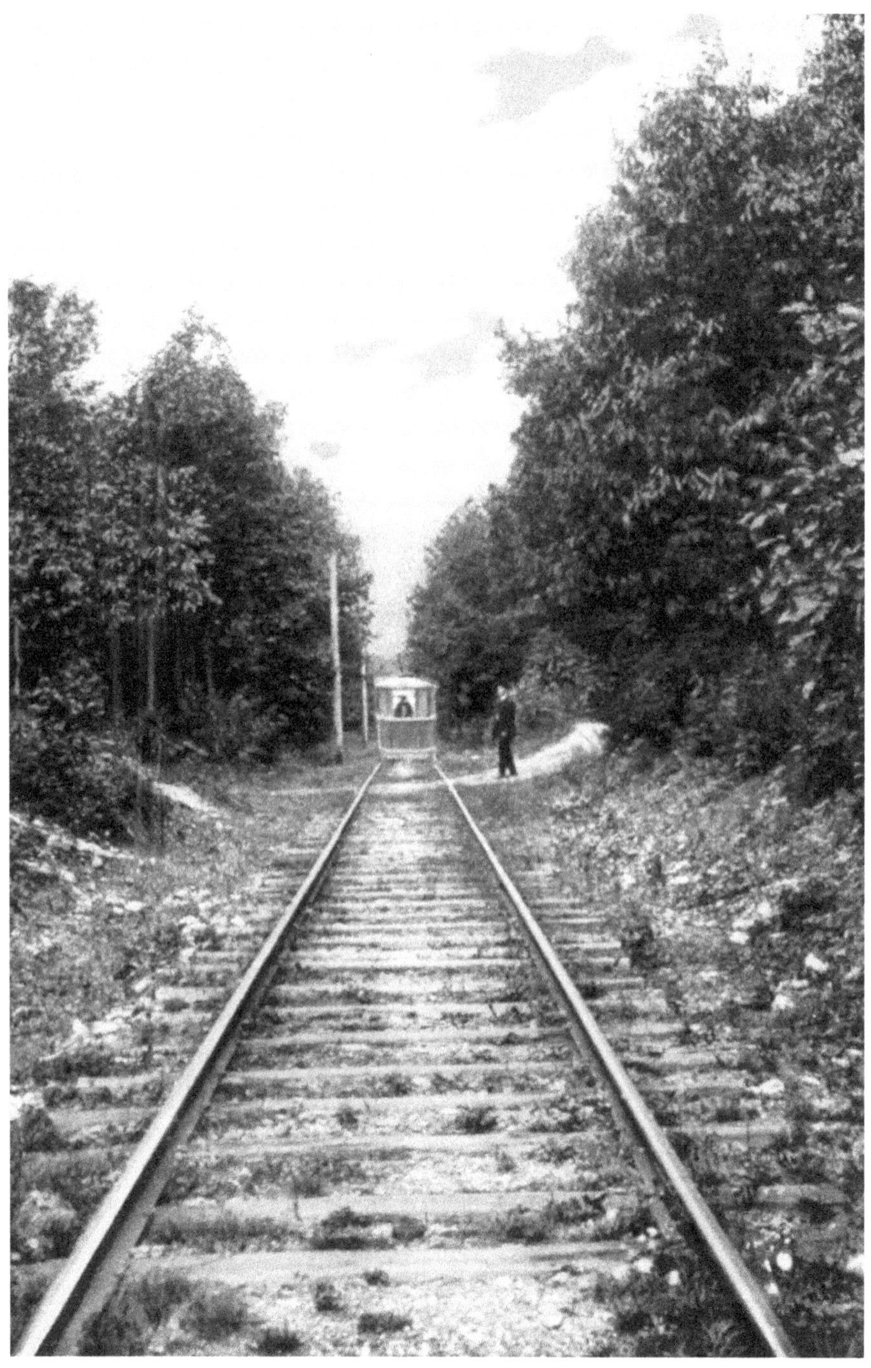

A scene along Neversink Railroad. *Charles J. Adams III Collection.*

from as far as New York State and conventions of various organizations visited from all over the United States.

And so the Gay Nineties took hold, with success begetting success. Not only would the Gravity Railroad spawn many resorts on the mountain to join Kuechler's Roost, but other similar attractions would continue to emerge throughout the greater Reading area for many years to come.

Neversink Mountain Railroad

Though its origins arguably dated back further than the Gravity Railroad, construction for a similar attraction over nearby Neversink Mountain began the very same week as on Mount Penn, and the road itself opened several months later, in August 1890. It would quickly become paramount for any Reading visitor to enjoy both elevated rides before departing the city, and while debate surely occurred on which was superior, it was readily agreed that both offered glimpses of nature and countryside that were as marvelous as any in the state or even country.

Neversink's entertainment history actually began in 1840, with the opening of the White House Hotel, the area's first mountain resort, and closest to Reading's downtown. It was, however, Joseph Ganser's purchase of about eighty acres on the mountain's western peak in the early 1880s, and subsequent building of the Highland House Hotel, that truly kick-started growth on Reading's "other" mountain.

In 1883, Ganser constructed an incline railway (basically a funicular) from the base of Neversink at Thirteenth Street up to his property, with the original intention of moving construction material, but also with an eye on using it for passengers once the hotel was completed. And, even if the Highland House would not open until later in the summer of '84, the incline railroad began regularly taking pleasure riders in the spring of that same year.

Shortly before the railway and resort's opening, the *Reading Times* took an opportunity to sing the praises of "Mount Ganser" in its inimitable way:

> Its towering height, its sweep of city, farm, and field. Its silver thread of river and companion mountain tops and the teaming life below—over a busy municipality throughout the broad expanse of valley, form ever changing, ever beautiful pictures. Citizen, artist and poet have treasure

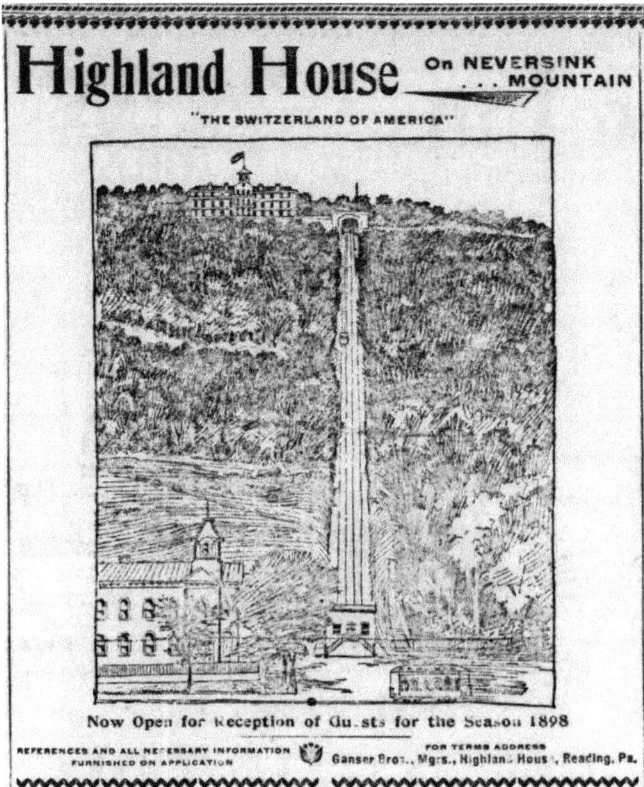

This ad shows Joseph Ganser's "incline plane," leading from Reading up to the Highland House. *Newspapers.com.*

> untold laid bare from familiar Neversink and the wealth of landscape, gorgeous sunset, fruitful valley and perfect view is of that which never grows old. Enchantment enters into the possession of other and broader dominions. It has royal entertainment for delighted subjects. It lays before them kingdoms of dazzling beauty and magnificent reaches of domain in moments of time, and it brings to the doors of Reading an attraction that cannot fail of recognition from all over the country.[181]

Ganser's "incline plane" also held the distinction of being the area's first actual mountain railway, though its more utilitarian design would limit its reputation-building prowess in comparison to eventual competitors. In fact, it was closed permanently in 1907, once it became clear that the Neversink Mountain Railroad was preferred by Highland House visitors. Ganser also built a toboggan ride nicknamed "The Cannonball" in 1889, and while it provided some amusement to his customers, it failed, in the public's eyes, to match the allure of the mountain's namesake railway.

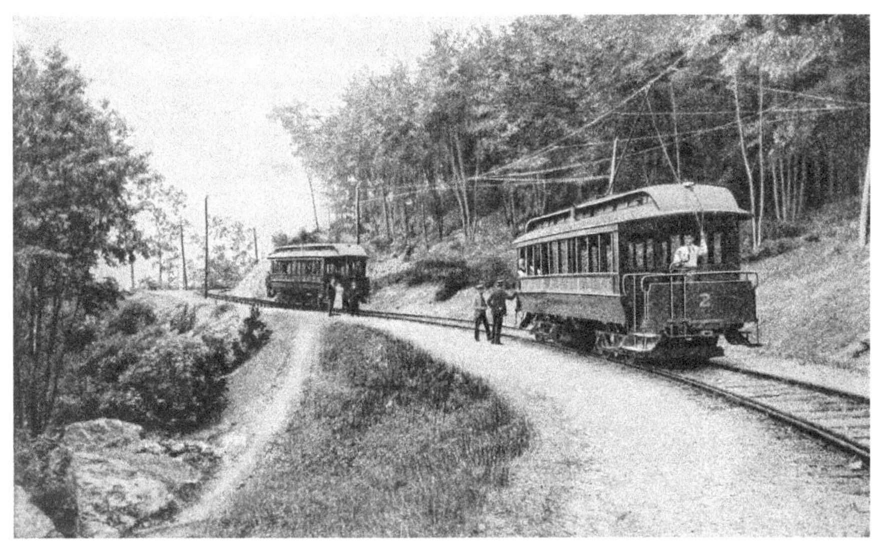

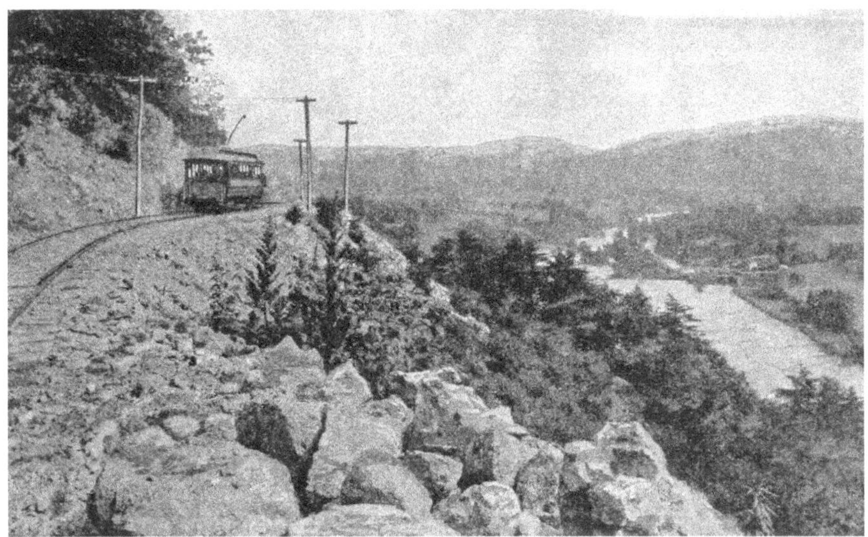

Two views of train cars on Neversink Railroad. *Streetcar Railway Review/Internet Archive.*

When the actual Neversink Mountain Railroad first opened, it was of particular interest as the very first electric railroad to run on hydroelectric power, "one of the most notable triumphs of engineering skill, anywhere in the State or country," noted one writer of the time. Located at the big dam on the Schuylkill River just below Reading, the innovative power plant featured two mammoth (forty-five-inch diameter) "Hercules" turbine waterwheels, each with 250 horsepower.[182] (For more details on the railroad construction, view appendix H.)

Compared to its sibling on the opposite mount, Neversink's railroad had clear accessibility advantages. Its official starting point, for example, was situated at the corner of Ninth and Penn Streets, easily boarded from Reading's downtown. Perhaps even more importantly, Klapperthal Station, at the road's other end, was shared with the Main Line of the P&R Railroad. Thus, the nearby Klapperthal Park and Pavilion—which the *Philadelphia Public Ledger* described as "a most charmingly sylvan retreat, surrounded by lofty forest-covered mountains, down which purling streams of clear spring water wind like silver threads"[183]—offered an enticing prospect to anyone approaching Reading from the east.

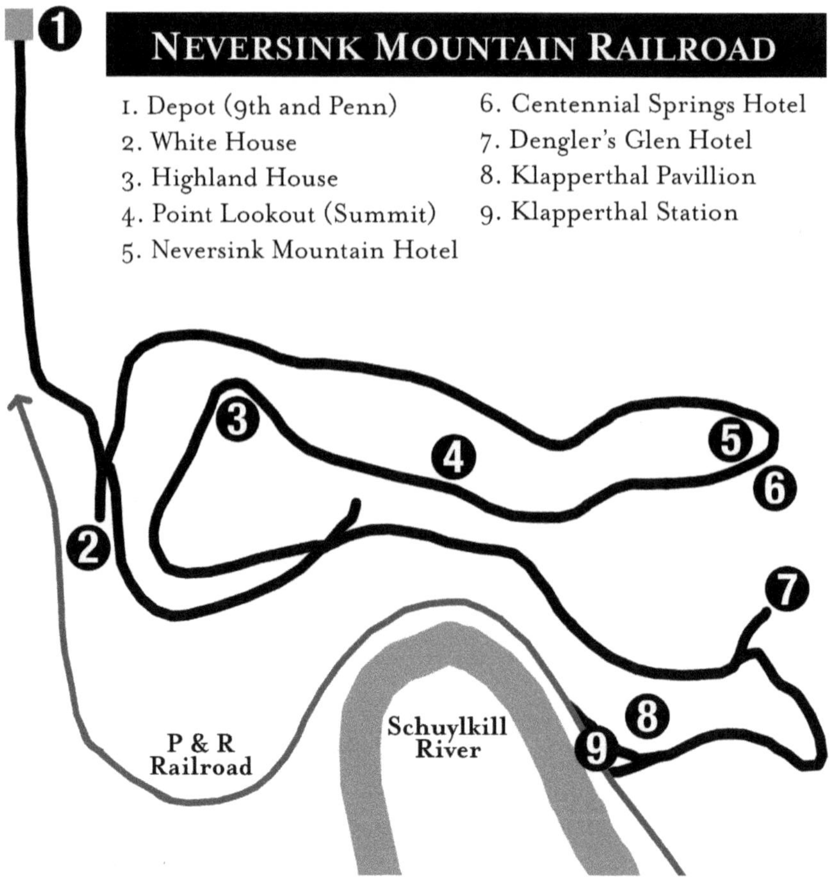

A map of the Neversink railroad route. Based on a 1981 Gottschall drawing. *Drawing by Mike Madaio.*

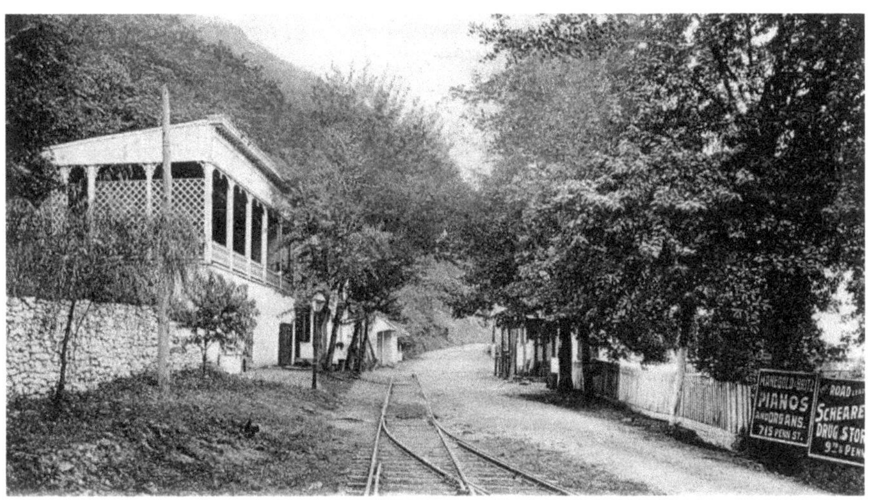

A postcard showing the White House on Neversink. *Joseph A. Webb Collection.*

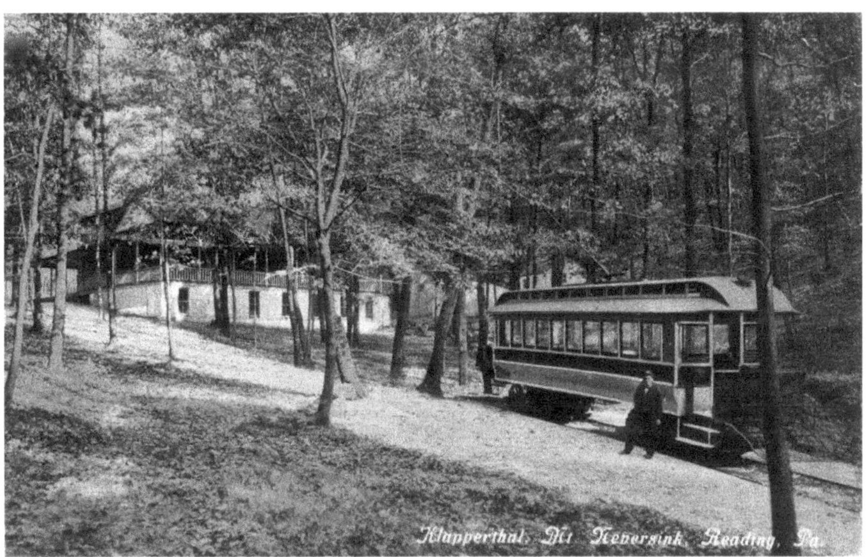

A postcard depicting Klapperthal Park and the depot on Neversink. *Joseph A. Webb Collection.*

In the early 1890s, several new resorts cropped up on Neversink to serve the influx of explorers, including Dengler's Glen Hotel, Centennial Springs Hotel and the Neversink Mountain Hotel. The latter was distinguished—perhaps auspiciously so—by the fact that it catered exclusively to out-of-town guests, advertising only in non-Reading papers and even going so far

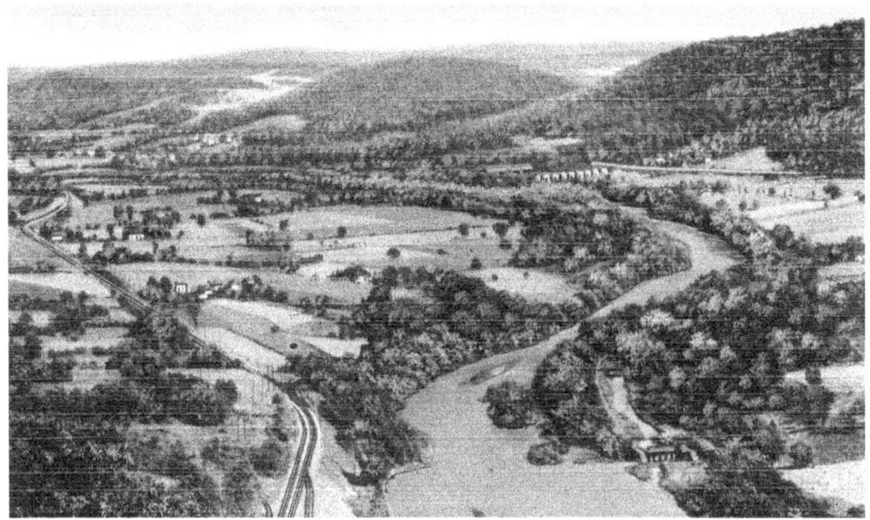

A postcard depicting the view from Point Lookout, on Neversink. *Wikimedia Commons.*

as to make it clear that city residents were unwelcome there. (In the end, it would only be remembered as another high-priced project doomed to failure by its backers' hubris.)

Another popular stop was Point Lookout—Neversink's answer to the Black Spot—which offered such a wonderful view that the aforementioned party of guests from the *Philadelphia Public Ledger*, upon arriving, were said to have broken into spontaneous applause.[184]

A particularly good description of the Neversink experience can be found in a written history of the Reading Railroad company. It reads like so:

> The ride over and around it is a series of delightful surprises. As the train begins the ascent a charming panorama is unrolled before its passengers. Spread out beneath is a brave array of public buildings, skyward-pointing church spires, factories, business houses, dwellings of all degrees. The smoke from the many towering chimneys is swept clear by the mountain breezes, and the bright red of the brick buildings seems empowered in the many shaded greens of the well-wooded parks and umbrageous avenues. An amphitheater of hills bounds the horizon, Mount Penn to the north marshaling the heights and serenely viewing Mounts Washington and Jefferson.
>
> Well may enthusiastic lovers of the beautiful in nature declare that the scenery here visible has no superior in the famed natural show places in

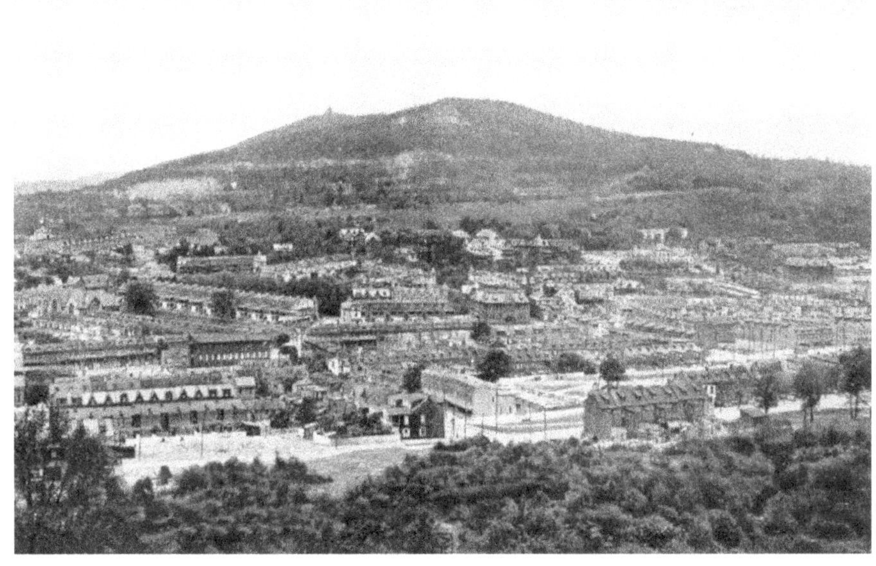

A view of east Reading from Neversink. *Charles J. Adams III Collection.*

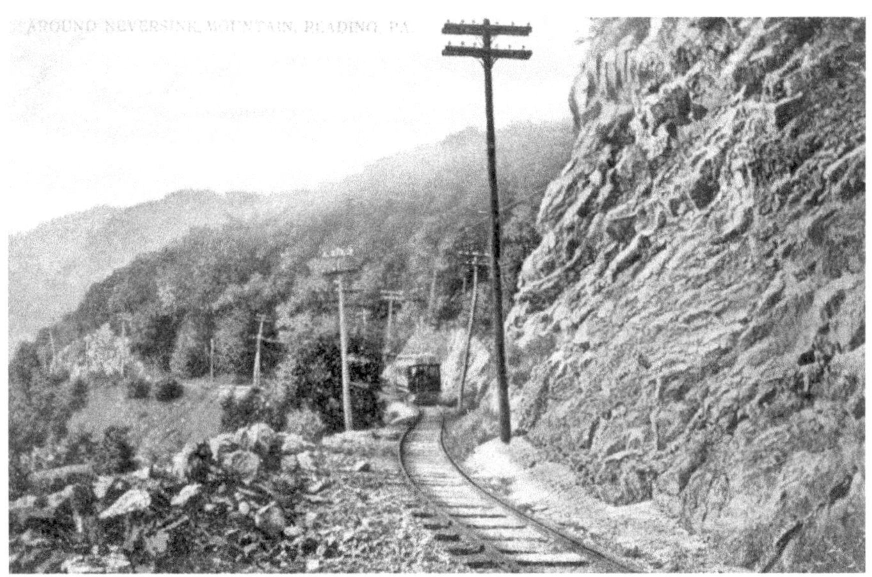

A view along the Neversink Mountain Railroad. *Charles J. Adams III Collection.*

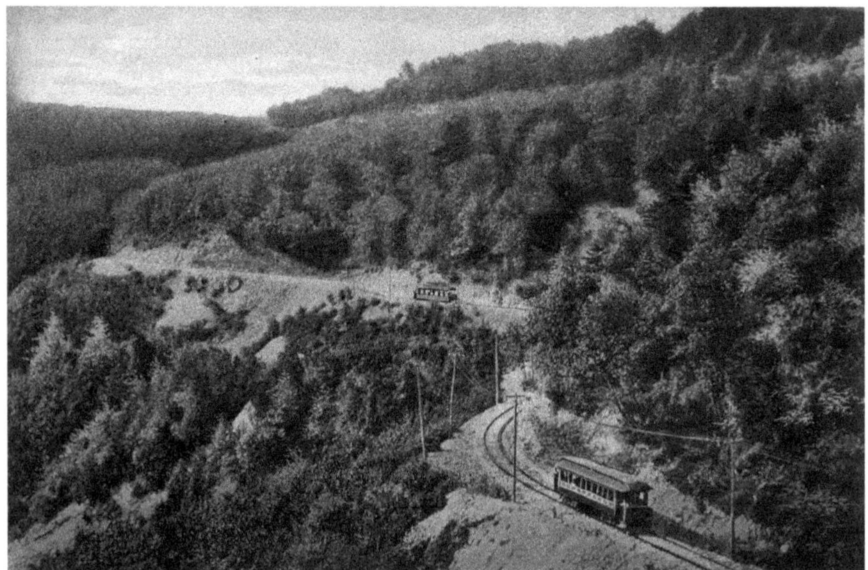

The Neversink railroad from above, circa 1907. *Joseph A. Webb Collection.*

> the Old World. The river, turning and twisting like some mammoth contortionist, glistens like a silver mirror far beneath. Twenty miles away, across a great sea of grain and grass, the eye catches the bold line of the Blue Mountains and follows their undulations to the Gap beyond Harrisburg, fifty-four miles distant. The landscape in every direction is rugged and romantic, and unfolds a series of views of unexcelled beauty and grandeur.[185]

MOUNTAIN WINE HOUSES

Over on Mount Penn, an influx of new resorts created competition for the already-established winemakers covered in previous chapters. Kuechler's response, in 1890, would be to again claim grand plans for a stone hotel, though he actually did little more than apply for a liquor license and occasionally advertise his potato roasts. His patrons were still abundant.

Reiniger, on the other hand, built an improved path from the railroad's closest stop to his vineyard and wine house along the descent and began to serve light fare alongside his popular wines. After the elder George Reiniger passed away in 1892, his two sons (Daniel and John) ran the family business together until John's death in 1901, after which his son George stepped in. In 1911, the family split up, with Daniel purchasing the business outright from his brother's estate and his nephew starting his own winery just down the road. The younger George never grew his own grapes, however, choosing instead to purchase fruit for winemaking.

LAUTERBACH SPRINGS

An interesting character named Fred Kiedeisch (occasionally spelled Kiedaisch) ran the first notable wine house on the way up the mountain—and only one on the ascent—shortly past Egelman Park. Born in Württemberg, Germany, in 1860, Kiedeisch arrived in Reading around 1882, quickly finding work at a stonecutter (the trade he learned as a young man). He purchased a seventeen-acre farm on Mount Penn around 1887 and relocated his large family—they had eight children—from 356 North Eleventh Street shortly thereafter. Dubbed "Lauterbach Springs" in honor of the tributary river in Württemberg, the property featured excellent natural springs that supplied fresh water.

Each season, Kiedeisch produced several thousand gallons of wine from three vineyard sites around his large property. Grapes included Clinton, Concord, Ives Seedling and Niagara. His most popular wine, made with the former two grapes, produced a pale, slightly sweet wine aged in large oak barrels. (More detail about Kiedeisch's winemaking methods can be found in chapter 4.)

He also brewed a sought-after sparkling cider with apples from his own orchard, producing about twenty-five large barrels of the stuff—which was made by adding sugar to regular cider and allowing it to ferment—per year. The quart and gallon bottles were wired shut in attempt to contain the volatile beverage, remembered Fred's son Charles briefly before his death at age ninety-seven, but that didn't stop them from regularly exploding.[186]

To prepare for the influx of visitors who would inquire from the nearby Gravity Railroad stop, Kiedeisch built a third story onto the stone farmhouse, ensuring his family had plenty of room away from the large kitchen and dining rooms on the first floor that would serve guests. The meals prepared by Kiedeisch's wife, Pauline, in fact, became one of the main draws of Lauterbach Springs. Her specialty was a platter of pork, potatoes and sauerkraut, alongside two slices of renowned rye bread. (Originally priced at

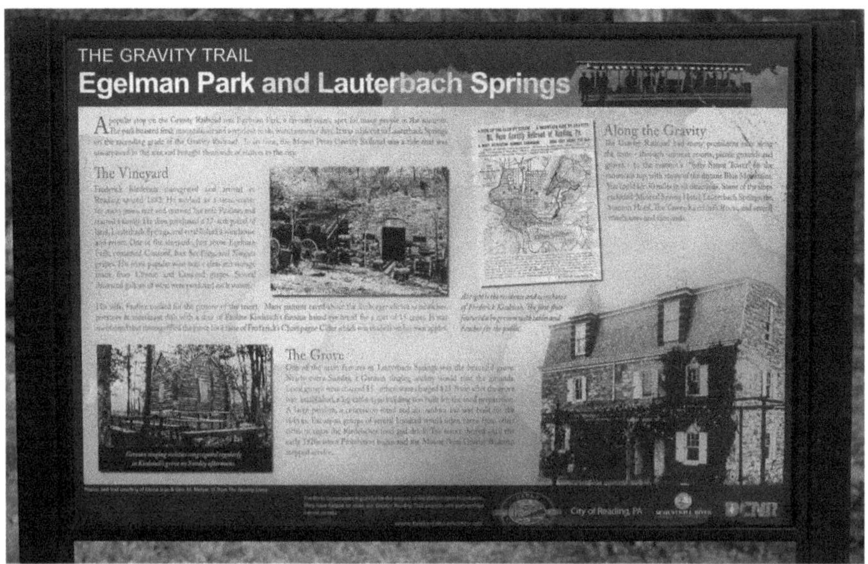

A Gravity Trail sign in modern-day Egelman Park that features Fred Kiedeisch's Lauterbach Springs. *Author photo.*

fifteen cents, the dinner eventually went as high as forty!) The kitchen also churned out a large quantity of ham, cheese and Limburger sandwiches to help wash down the copious glasses of wine and cider.

Fred Jr. operated the Lauterbach Springs Bottling Works in a small frame building behind the wine house, producing soda that was sold both on the premises and around town. "Those who remember his fruit-flavored soft drinks—especially lemon pop," wrote George Meisler IX in *The Passing Scene*, "claim they were really something special."[187]

The other big draw on the property was a large, pretty grove near the Egelman Reservoir. This spot became a destination for excursion groups from all over the region, which could rent it out for five dollars per day if local or twenty-five if not. Because the grove was a reasonable distance from the wine house, a log cabin—along with a large pavilion and small frame concession stand—was erected to prepare food nearby during the warmer seasons.

On Sundays, this grove was the exclusive domain of German singing groups such as the Harmonie-Maennerchor, the Liederkranz or the Cannstatter Volkfest-Verein. (Fred himself was a notable tenor.) As a result of these festivities, the entire family (and often others), would spend considerable time at the grove on Mondays—the designated cleanup day—preparing it for the following week. Fred's granddaughter fondly recalled, to *The Passing Scene*, how she spent many a Monday searching the spot for coins that had dropped to the ground during the previous day's festivities. Usually, she noted, the searchers were quite successful.[188]

Despite the advances of his wine house, Kiedeisch remained active as a stonecutter, most notably helping to construct stone pillars and walls in Reading City Park, including a curious heart-shaped stone that became a prominent feature in a sandstone wall near the old Penn Street entrance. Unfortunately, Kiedeisch's talents would inadvertently contribute to an early demise; he passed away, according to his sister, from "stonecutter's consumption"—the side effects of inhaling a lifetime of stone dust—in 1907, at the age of forty-seven. In his stead, his wife and children continued Lauterbach Springs—once referred to as "Mecca"[189] to Philadelphia-based Germans—successfully for many years.

Though beer was not sold on site, the Kiedeisch family was willing to procure it for interested parties—typically from local brewer Barbey's—for a mere one dollar per barrel service fee. In time, these "beer parties" at the Lauterbach Springs grove developed quite a reputation. When the City of Reading annexed part of Lower Alsace Township in 1917, for example, officials set these parties directly in their sights, claiming that their trash was polluting the Egelman Reservoir, which at the time provided water for fifteen

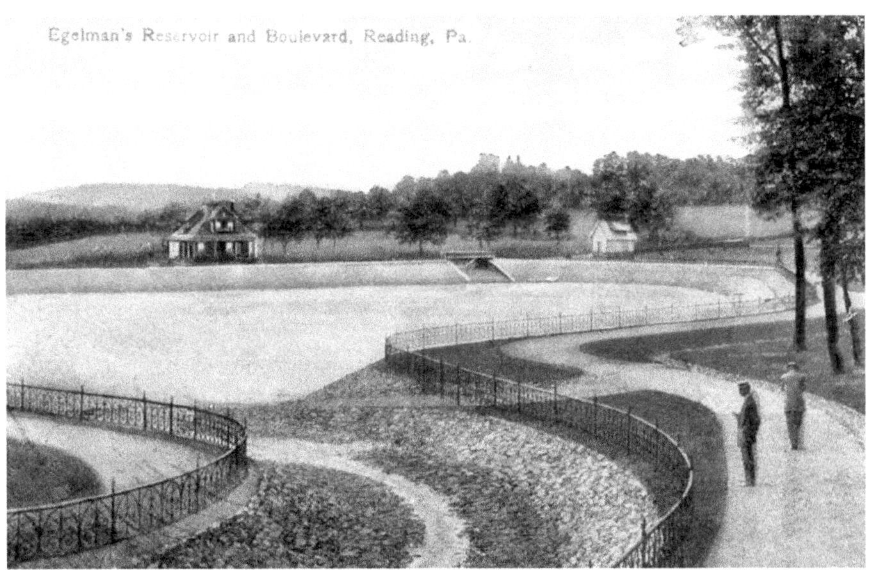

An Egelman's Reservoir postcard. *Charles J. Adams III Collection.*

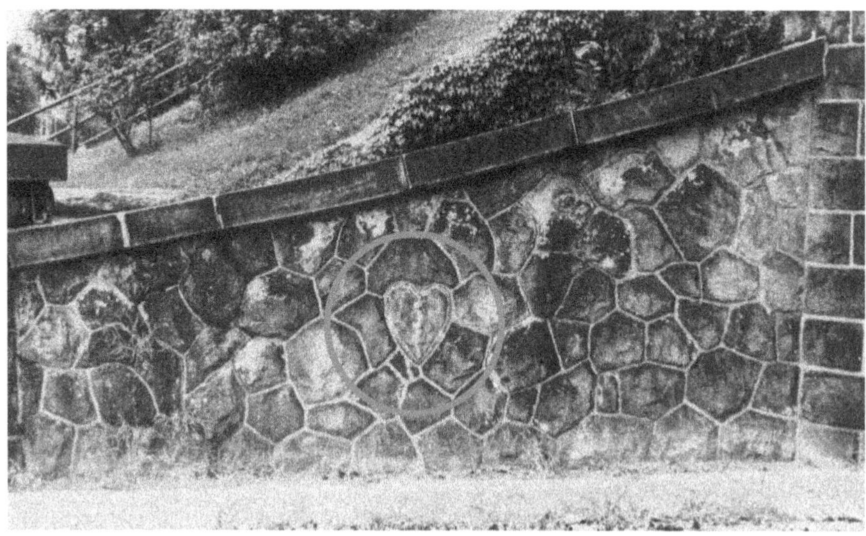

Fred Kiedeich's "heart stone," shown in the wall at the entrance to City Park. *Joseph A. Webb Collection.*

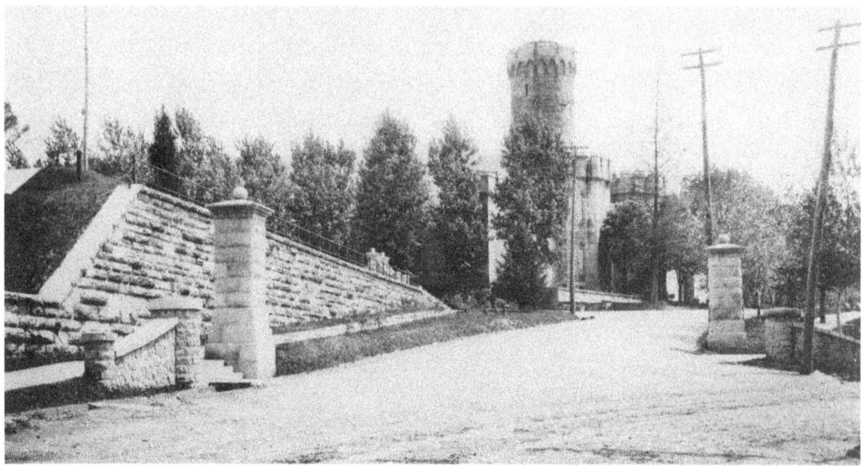

The City Park wall that featured Kiedeisch's "heart stone." *Joseph A. Webb Collection.*

thousand citizens. A councilman named Frank Tyson called out the sanitary condition of Lauterbach Springs specifically and noted, "The mayor will see that there are no more beer picnics in the woods." It is unclear whether these threats were ever carried out.

This was not the only time the law bumped up against life at Lauterbach Springs. In 1911, both Pauline Kiedeisch and her son George pleaded guilty to selling liquor (wine and cider) on a Sunday without a license. George was sentenced to three months in jail—a seemingly excessive punishment from this modern viewpoint—and the family was fined $500.

To share one final, amusing anecdote about the Kiedeisch farm, in 1899 an elephant that was part of a visiting circus escaped in Reading, enjoying a brief rampage that would eventually end at Lauterbach Springs. The *Philadelphia Inquirer* provided the following account:

> With trunk high in air and trumpeting loudly the elephant started through the City Park, crushing choice shrubbery and plants under his ponderous feet and overturning urns and fountains, until he reached the lake, where he plunged into the water and enjoyed a bath.
>
> He then proceeded out Mineral Spring Avenue, keeping in front of a trolley car and followed by several hundred men and boys. The elephant disappeared finally in the thickets of Mount Penn, and was at large several hours. Passengers on the Mount Penn Gravity Railroad occasionally caught a glimpse of his bulky frame.[190]

The beast's keeper eventually tracked it down, without incident, on the Kiedeisch estate. The man appeared in the nick of time, it seems, as his arrival found a number of farmers (presumably the Kiedeisch family included) surrounding the animal with pitchforks. Later, Kiedeisch would sue the elephant's owners, claiming it uprooted his gardens, tore down fences and injured apple trees. The amount sought was twenty-five dollars.

Steigerwald's

Once the Gravity rail car had passed the summit and begun its descent, it turned off the Skyline Drive ridge to run along the current Line Road, past Kuechler's Roost and Wildwood Park, before angling back toward the depot. Near this point was a stop where many alighted to visit both the Reiniger and Steigerwald wine houses, the latter run by an affable gentleman named Thomas Steigerwald.

Born in 1831 in Bavaria, at the age of eighteen "Der Steigerwald" came to Reading, where some other family members had already settled. He immediately went to work as a baker's apprentice and, in 1854, started his own bakery business, which he would continue—mostly in Reading, with a short stint in Danville during the Civil War—for more than twenty years. In 1875, while attending the funeral of William Miller and his wife on the farm where they'd most recently lived, Steigerwald met William Heister, the owner of the same seventy-six-acre farm. Shortly thereafter, he purchased the property.

Prior to the Gravity Railroad's opening, the baker-turned-farmer established himself as one of the leading agriculturists and wine growers in Berks County. He even raised cranberries in a piece of swampy land on the property. Though only a portion of the farm was devoted to viticulture, in good years, he was known to produce several thousand gallons of wine.

Once the railroad began transporting a steady stream of visitors, Steigerwald devoted more of his time to the wine house—he took much enjoyment in hosting guests—and less to farming. He would, however, continue producing wines well into his eighties, earning him the title of oldest winemaker on the mountain.

As with other stops along the road, Steigerwald's food and wine were well regarded. In 1899, one particularly satisfied diner described the hotel's chicken and waffle dinner as a "a culinary poem with many accompaniments in blank verse."[191]

The *Reading Eagle*, commenting on an 1895 visit to Steigerwald's, noted "good wine, Sweitzer cheese, rye bread and a romantic view from the ridge of Mt. Penn, overlooking the valley below." If visitors came on baking day, the paper continued, and were "fortunate to get for lunch some of Mrs. Steigerwald's matchless rye bread with caraway seed, and crust that is tender and delicate as the best of pie crust, with more excellent butter churned on the premises in the old fashioned way, then they will agree that life is worth living."[192] All that and a "fine old bottle" of Alsace red would run said happy guest forty cents.

In the mid-1880s, a group of boys exploring the woods on Steigerwald's property came upon an old hut that contained an ancient bake oven. An inscription on the stove featured a picture of the goddess of fortune alongside a mysterious poem:

> Du falsches Glueck [Thou false Fortune]
> Du gibst und nimmst aus [Thou givest and takest from out]
> Deine Gaben, was wir [Thy gifts, that which we]
> Ein Glaubens, Kind [Children of faith]
> Dir zu schaffen haben [Create for Thee][193]

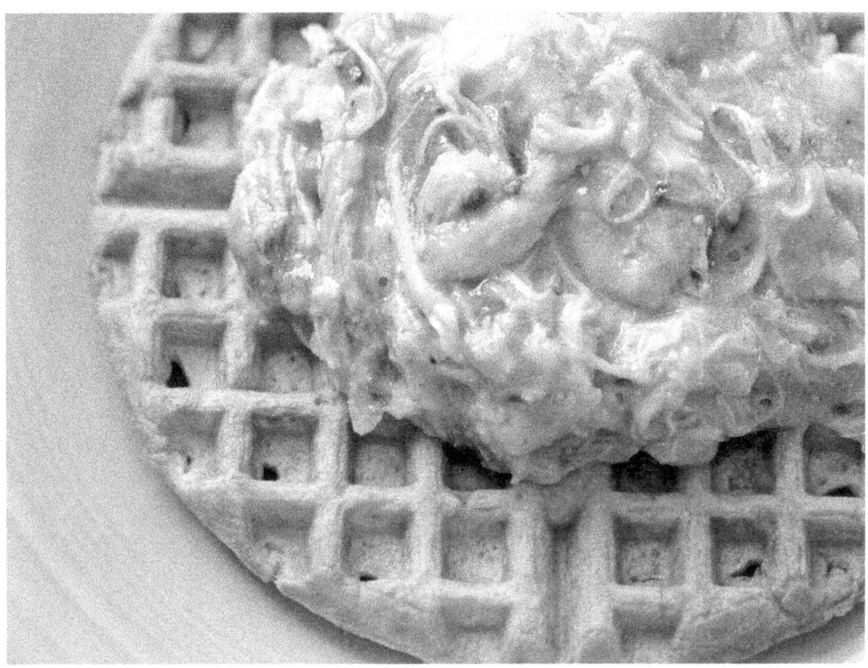

Berks-style chicken and waffles features stewed, not fried, chicken and gravy. It tastes better than it looks (definitely). Recipe in appendix G. *Author photo.*

This discovery was the object of much curiosity at the time. Originally assumed to be the work of Baron W.J. Stiegel—who was thought to have built the very first iron stove in Pennsylvania—this item bore the date 1726, twenty-four years before the baron arrived in America..

Spuhler's

Perhaps the most popular resort on Mount Penn during the Gravity era was Spuhler's Hotel, located along the descent, back toward Kiedeisch's place and Egelman Park. In its best year, the winery produced over twenty-five thousand gallons of grape, elderberry, blackberry and other wines and served as many as two thousand visitors on a given weekend.

The resort's founder, John Spuhler, was a Lower Alsace native born in 1847. After learning carpentry at an early age, Spuhler helped his father build houses in and around Reading before going into similar business on his own. In 1884, he purchased twenty-six acres on Mount Penn, which, in addition to grapes, would feature apple, pear and chestnut trees, berries and pumpkins. Shortly after the railroad's opening, Spuhler began constructing a substantial stone structure, featuring a mansard roof and wide porches on two sides, as well as a back building containing nineteen rooms, all by his own hand. Seats for guests were, according to the *Reading Times*, "liberally distributed throughout the grounds," and the property was "flanked on three sides by beautiful woods."[194]

Spuhler imported grapes from New York for his first vintages while waiting for his own vineyard—which featured mostly Clinton and Concord grapes—to mature. Later, as business boomed, he purchased and cultivated two other tracts on the mountain, one fourteen acres and the other nine. In addition, he managed a two-hundred-ton icehouse that helped supply other resorts such as Kuechler's Roost.

"Of the wine houses on the slopes of Mount Penn served by the railroad," recalled David Rowland in the *Historical Review of Berks County*, "Spuhler's was probably the most widely known." The hotel, he continued, "became famous throughout the East for its wines and food. Spuhler's pig roasts were renowned, with as many as 800 persons being served from noon until midnight."

The specialty of the house, *spankerfel* (roast little pig), was simply brined, then basted in butter to crisp the skin as it slowly cooked. It was dressed with gravy from its drippings as well as sauerkraut, stuffing and mashed potatoes. Like many other resorts of the time, Spuhler's also served its fair share of baked clams and chicken and waffle suppers.

PLEASANT VIEW HOTEL

Unlike some of these resorts, the Pleasant View Hotel story began much earlier than the Gravity Railroad's first ride. Original owner and winemaker Richard Moll first purchased farmland on the mountain in the 1870s, which he kept while also running a brewery and saloon at Ninth and Franklin Streets. Having arrived from Baden, Germany, in 1864, he developed a reputation in town for his taxidermy, with a large collection of native birds adorning the walls of his saloon.

In 1885, Moll purchased eight acres along Friedensburg Road on the eastern side of Mount Penn, with the intent to "retire" to the mountain

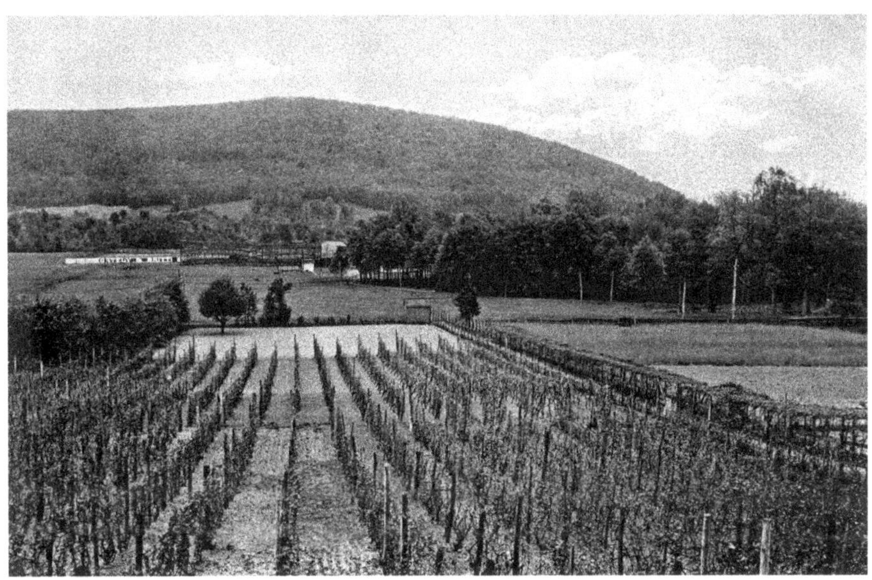

Clam Bake

Pleasant View Hotel

Above Carsonia Park

EVERY FRIDAY EVENING

Pleasant View Hotel

Twenty minutes from Fifth and Penn streets, Reading's most up-to-date suburban Hotel. Large, spacious Dining Room and Parlor. Banquets and Suppers at short notice. Stony Creek and Boyertown cars, one fare, direct to place.

CHAS. F. SMITH, Prop.

Consolidated 'phone.

Above: This lovely postcard shows the vineyards and view from the Pleasant View Hotel. *J. George Hintz.*

Left: Ads for the Pleasant View Hotel, 1911. *Newspapers.com.*

and start a summer resort. He subsequently built a three-story rustic Swiss pavilion on the hill immediately opposite the original farmhouse and residence. Though it was somewhat removed from the eventual Gravity Road, the property featured a stairway leading up to the popular mountain paths of the time. The farm would eventually produce somewhere upward of three thousand gallons of wine per year, as well as other fruits.

After Moll passed away in 1894, Albert Smith purchased the farm and made considerable improvements, including a large veranda on the south side of the hotel facing Carsonia Park. Under Smith's direction, the resort would become one of the most popular in the area, known for its Friday evening clambakes and, of course, chicken and waffle suppers. (Several banquet menus are available in appendix D.)

The resort's view, wrote the *Reading Times* in 1899, was "one of the most charming in the county of Berks, comprehending, as it does, finely-cultivated vineyards and truck-gardens, woods and meadows, orchards, Carsonia Park and several ranges of mountains in the distance."[195]

When Smith died in 1903 of dropsy, the local paper noted that, although he was "a plain, unpretending, quiet citizen," he "endeared himself to the many patrons and guests of his wayside inn by a native goodness of heart and strict attention to business."[196] Both Mrs. Smith and their son Charles would go on to run the hotel—which remained popular through the 1930s—successfully.

Theo Benz

As noted previously, baker-turned-barman Theodore Benz acquired John Fehr's original "Mineral Spring Vineyard" in 1885; it so happened to sit just north of the future Gravity Railroad depot. Like many of the other characters in this story, Benz was a multitalented German immigrant who was active in many local organizations and thus was a popular fellow about

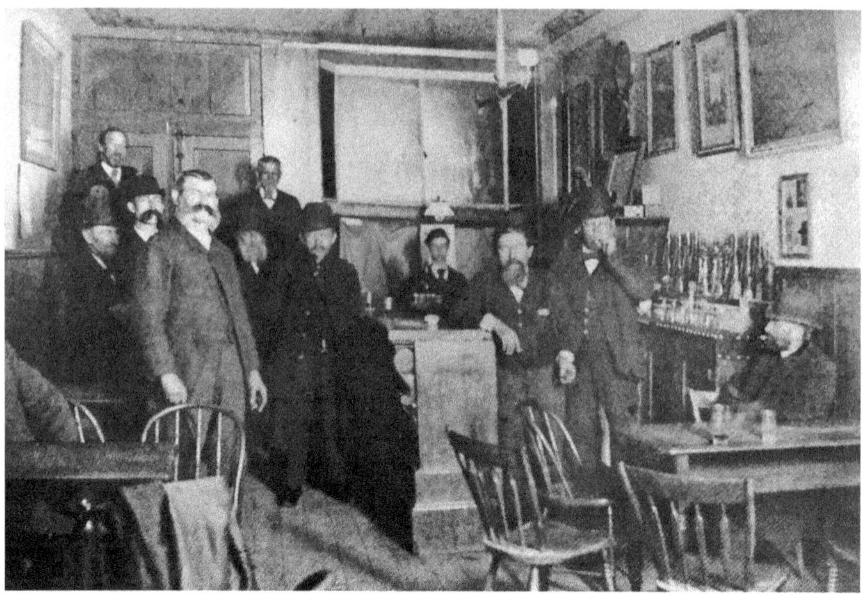

A rare interior photo from a Reading wine house, in this case that of Theo Benz, who is standing behind the bar. *Courtesy of Geo. M. Meiser, IX from* The Passing Scene *series.*

town. After arriving in 1856 as a baker, he engaged in the oyster business for several years before enlisting and fighting in the Civil War in the mid-1860s.

Once he returned from combat, he resumed baking for almost a decade before opening a popular saloon at 928 Penn Street, which he ran until 1892. After the Benz family had moved permanently to his vineyard property (also around 1892), he operated a wine house there for several years, no doubt helped by its convenient access, via a long flight of steps, from Mineral Spring Park

CENTENNIAL SPRINGS HOTEL

Over on Neversink—in contrast to the grape lovers of Mount Penn—beer was often the beverage of choice. Only Moses Graeff, proprietor of the Centennial Springs Hotel, made wine with any seriousness. On about ten acres of a total twenty-eight that made up the property, he cultivated approximately ten thousand grapevines, including Clinton, Catawba, Niagara, Ives Seedling and more. This produced several hundred barrels of wine each season, which was stored and aged in "one of the most complete and substantial"[197] wine vaults of its kind, built into the mountainside on the property.

Born in 1829 on a farm in Maidencreek township (ten to fifteen miles north of Reading), Graeff was exposed to both agriculture and hotel management while growing up. He came to Reading in 1857, initially finding work as a builder, then entering the malt business in 1863. He even briefly served on the board of the city's popular Lauer Brewing Company.

Graeff's resort—which was named after a group of springs that became public in the centennial year (and provided water to the hotel)—opened in the spring of 1891 on the mountain's southern side. Among other natural benefits, it boasted easy access from both the Neversink Mountain Railroad as well as the Klapperthal Station on the P&R line. "The view from the wide porches of the hotel is one of the most picturesque in the county of Berks,"[198] noted the *Reading Times* in 1898, one of many similar sentiments expressed by writers of the time.

Despite being the "perfect paradise for the seekers of health and recreation,"[199] the hotel was never a particularly profitable business, and Graeff began to look for prospective buyers in the early aughts. In 1907, Reverend Monsignor George Bornemann, pastor of Reading's St. Paul's

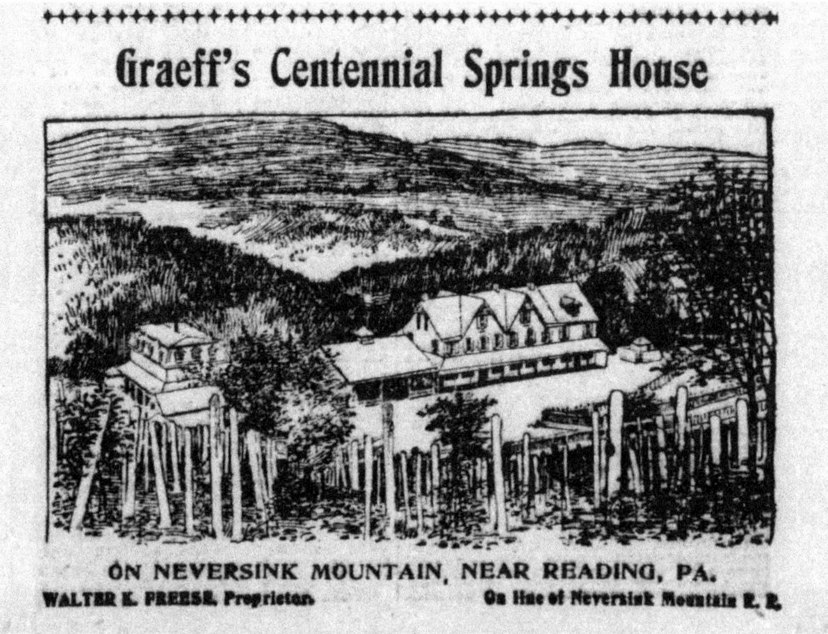

An ad for Moses Graeff's Centennial Springs resort, 1897. *Newspapers.com.*

Catholic Church, purchased and then donated the property to the Berks County Tuberculosis Association for use as a sanitarium. (TB was a particularly serious problem at the time, and this voluntary quarantining was common.)

Interestingly, the sanitarium's patients were charged with maintaining the vineyards during their stay (as much as they were able), and sales of the resulting crop—as many as ten thousand pounds of grapes per year—were essential in keeping the nonprofit center in operation. The fruit was harvested and vinified by none other than George Reiniger.

When there was no longer a need to quarantine TB patients so aggressively, around 1930, the project was abandoned. And since no subsequent buyer could be found for the property, it was destroyed. The entrance to the old wine vault, however, can still be seen from the Upper Glen/Klapperthal hiking trail on Neversink (though forest growth makes it rather difficult to reach).

Boulevard & Pagoda

Construction of Mount Penn Boulevard—a road for carriages and pedestrians that led from City Park up to the White Spot (the second-highest peak)—began in 1893 and was completed in 1897. The *Philadelphia Times* heralded its opening with the following passage:

> It is only a few years since the Mount Penn Gravity Railroad of Reading became famous as a marvel of fine engineering, being without a parallel. It was decidedly the wonder of those days that are scarcely past. We are now presented with even a greater feat of ingenuity and execution in the form of a drive through the same mountain, constructed on the same principle of gradual ascent and descent, winding around and around the mountain, disclosing superb views that are varied with each turn and the whole having the charm of extending otherwise limited and contracted park territory that numbered only acres and was not adapted to driving purposes....Electric roads over the mountains have long delighted not alone the people of Reading who have by these means been lifted to their heights and surprised with the beauty of the scenery,

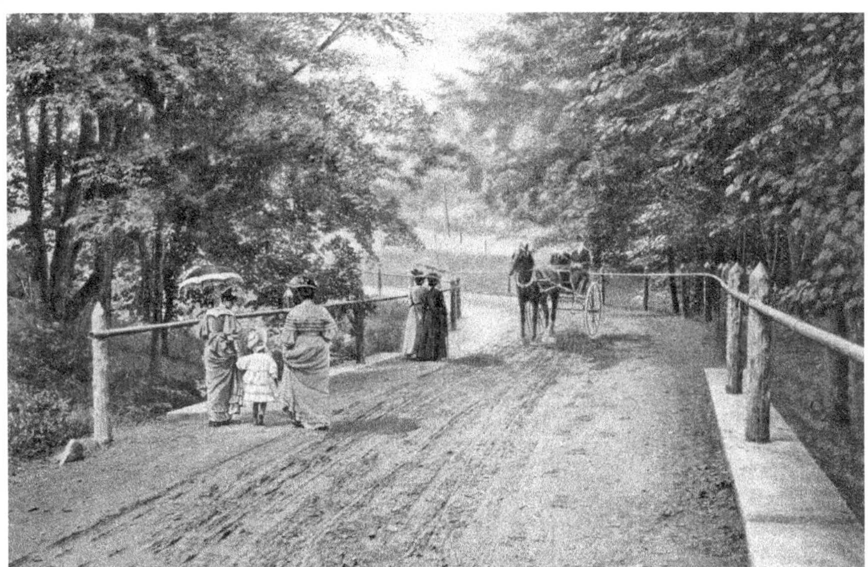

Pedestrians out for a stroll along the Mount Penn Boulevard, 1909. *The Hugh C. Leighton Company.*

> but strangers as well have journeyed here for these views, which compare with the finest. These electric roads are now supplemented by the drive, which is unequaled in any city in the country, and whose fame is already noised abroad before its entire completion.[200]

Around the turn of the century, a man named William Abbott Witman purchased ten acres of land near the Boulevard and White Spot, intending to quarry the rock. Once he embarked on this business, however, many in Reading resented the way his quarry defaced the city side of the mountain, and considerable pressure was put on Witman to abandon the operation. As he was contemplating a run for mayor (he'd eventually lose the 1908 democratic primary), in 1906 Witman ceded, changing course to build a luxury resort that would salvage the location.

This led to construction of the Pagoda—a strangely incongruous Asiatic structure that sits atop Mount Penn looking over modern-day Reading—which has become an enduring, beloved symbol of the city. Witman abandoned his project after losing an oddly heated battle over obtaining a liquor license (likely due to semirelated political battles), and it only opened years later as part of the city park system. Ironically, this failed attempt to capitalize on the period's resort culture is the only intact remnant of the Gravity Railroad era today.

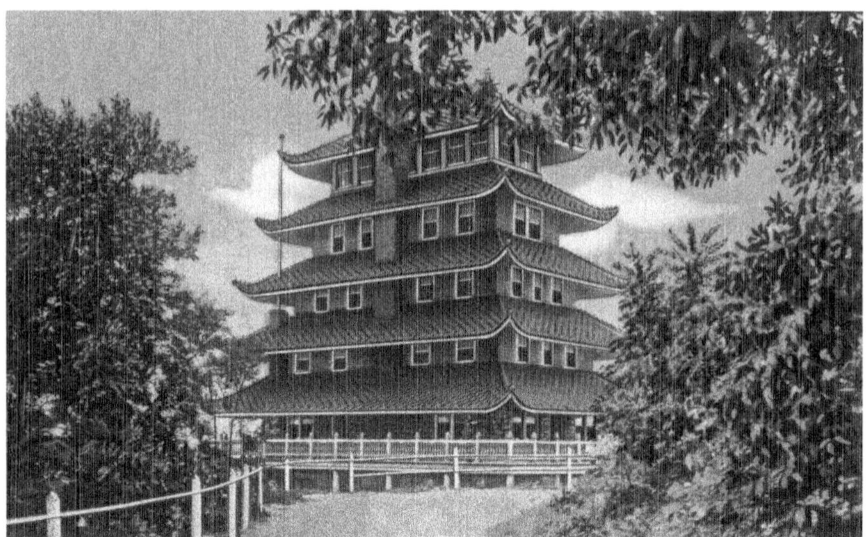

Above: The Pagoda, as shown on a postcard. *Wikimedia Commons.*

Opposite: The Pagoda on Mount Penn, with the Highland House on Neversink in the background. *Charles J. Adams III Collection.*

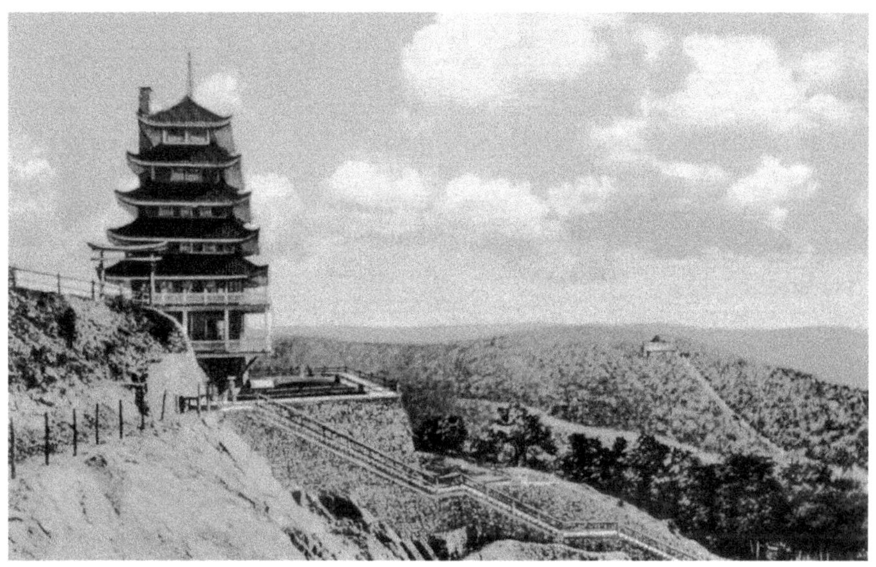

A BONA FIDE DESTINATION

Aside from the aforementioned attractions, there were, in fact, many other resorts and amusements that emerged during this time in Reading, as one would expect with any top leisure destination. It truly is both staggering and sobering to understand just how much there was to do and how many people were entertained. And while it would be tedious, at this point, to list out every single saloon, hotel and resort available to the public during this era, it's certainly worth considering the overall scene.

Legendary entertainers from across the country frequently visited, performing concerts in City Park and the many other parks and pleasure grounds that dotted the area, as well as theaters in town. Operas, dramas, minstrelsy and circus-like acrobatic performances were common. Vaudeville shows were also popular, along with the nickelodeon movie houses. Excursion boats ran on the Schuylkill regularly, most notably the moonlight cruises that always featured live music.

Though the idea of Pennsylvania Dutch cuisine has today been denigrated to roadside smorgasbords and mass-produced shoofly pies, back then it was common to find widely renowned cuisine all over town. Beyond the previously discussed local wines, a number of highly regarded

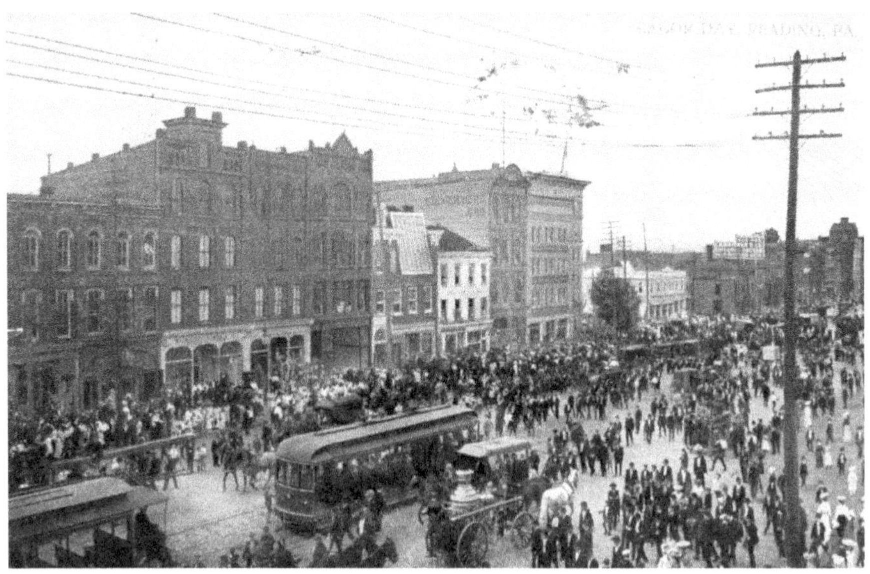

Revelers celebrate Labor Day on Penn Street in Reading, circa 1908. *Charles J. Adams III Collection.*

breweries produced quality beer, no doubt influenced by the traditions of the Fatherland.

The Gravity Railroad era also saw the emergence of Coney Island–style amusement in both Pendora and Carsonia Parks, which would compete for attention with the Tower yet also supply endless streams of visitors for the many hotels and resorts in both the mountains and city. A never-ending plethora of organizations, clubs and other groups held regular banquets, parties and special events all over Reading, some coming from great distances to experience the city's charms. When perusing the newspapers of the period, each day seemed to list more of these than the last.

In August 1915—to illustrate further one particularly good example—the Southern Philatelic Association (stamp collectors) convention took place in Reading. As part of their recap, *Mekeel's Weekly Stamp News* described the event as "unexpectedly large" and "unusually representative," no doubt—at least in part—due to the city's broad appeal as a summer destination.

A variety of blurbs, detailing both the technical details of the conference as well as some of the fun times had, covered three full pages of the text-heavy newsletter. "Six, sixty, or six hundred breweries in Reading!" read one amusing account. "It makes no difference, enough liquid refreshment has never been brewed to satisfy the thirsts of *some* stamp collectors."

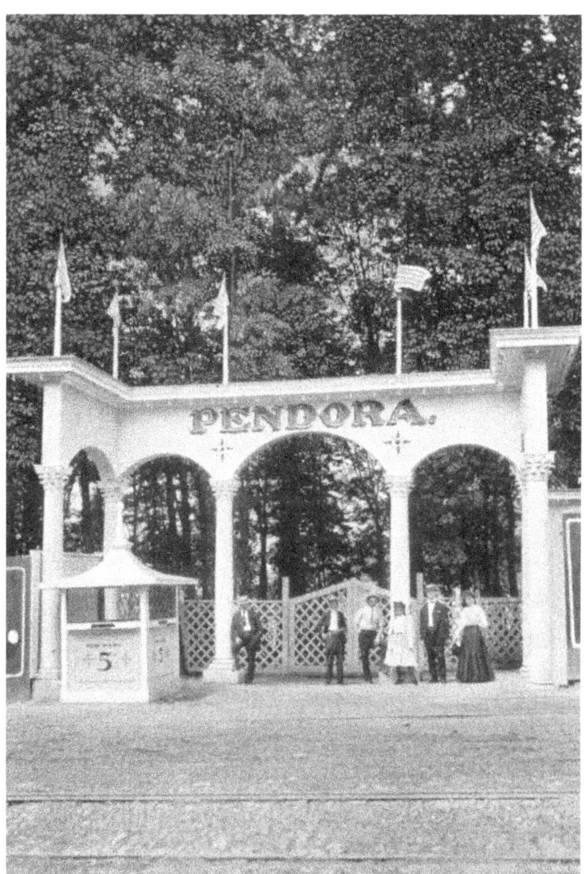

Right: A view of Pendora Park's entrance. *Charles J. Adams III Collection.*

Below: A group of railroad executives known as "The Syndicate" pose with the Ringgold Band during an outing in Reading. *Wikimedia Commons.*

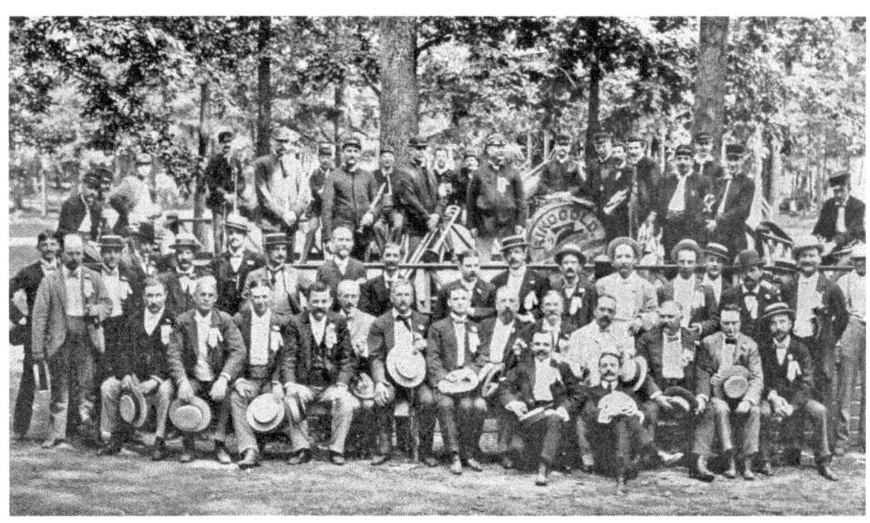

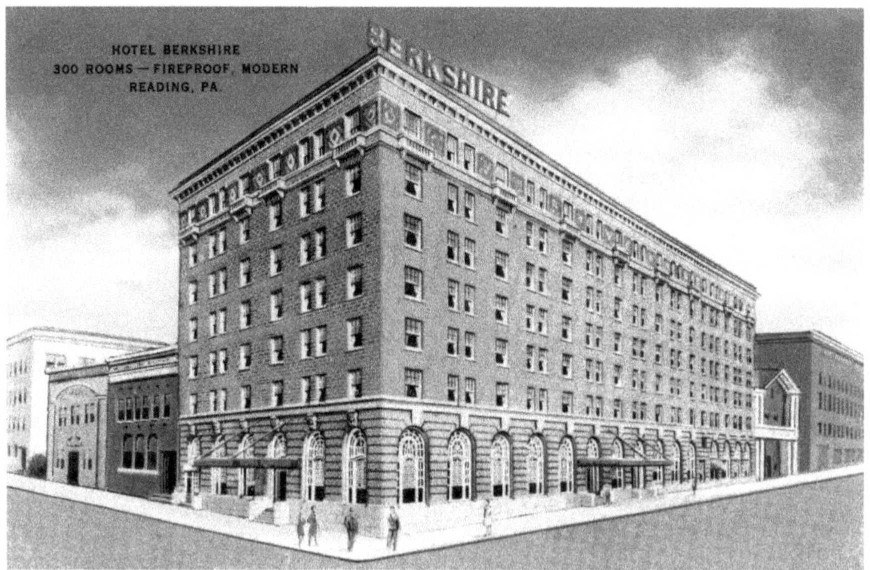

The Berkshire Hotel, home base for Miss Gushie Gurgle and the stamp collecting convention. *Joseph A. Webb Collection.*

The crown jewel of this recap was a column titled "Such a Lovely Time," credited to a Miss Gushie Gurgle. "I know you are all just dying to hear all about the fun we had at Reading," she began. "Have you ever been there? I hope you have, for if you have not, you just can't understand how perfectly lovely it all was. You know the people are so hospitable they just entertained us every minute—met us at the train and told us that the town was ours."

Among a packed agenda of speeches, "jolly" receptions and banquets, all replete with food and refreshments, the author took specific time to describe trips up both Neversink and Mount Penn. "Friday," she recalled, "we stopped at the tower and danced; Cliffie Kissinger, Brody and Percy Mann all danced beautifully. Percy is so much like Vernon Castle. We didn't want to leave there, but the car was ready and we went on to Kuechler's Roost. I wish I had time to tell you all about the Roost; it was started by a funny old hermit who lived up there all alone. Now it is a popular resort. We sat around the round table, drank lemonade, ate pretzels and had such a good time."[201] (The entire article, which is well worth reading in its entirety, is included in appendix I.)

Looking back, it seems both absurd and perfectly reasonable to say that Reading was, during this period, as exciting of a place to be as just about any other. It doesn't feel like exaggeration to add that, especially during the summer, there was something interesting to do, see or hear every single night. Lastly, it's hard not to be overwhelmed with both awe at the amount of entertainment choices available to residents and visitors and envy toward those lucky enough to have had the opportunity to experience them in all their glory.

9
PASSING THE TORCH

While the railroad was still growing into its explosive popularity at the turn of the century, the Roost—which was gradually improved over time, but had never become the magnificent stone hotel the hermit originally envisioned—entrenched itself as one of the most popular resorts on the mountain. A visit in 1898 was described as such:

> After greeting "Mine Host" Kuechler the party sat under the grape vines and enjoyed a good look at Dame Nature who put on one of her prettiest smiles. Games and other recreation was [sic] indulged in and [at] 5 o'clock the party sat down under the spreading trees and enjoyed one of the most delicious suppers that could have been produced anywhere on earth. Pure mountain air is a splendid appetizer and hunger is a splendid chef and there were no dyspeptics round that table judging from the hearty laughter that greeted every bon mot, repartee or jolly good story, which, like good wine, improves with age....After feasting and enjoying the scenery and incidentally several good cigars, the party returned home shortly after 7 o'clock delighted with the trip to "the loveliest spot which mortal man has ever laid his eyes upon."

Around the turn of the century, however, Kuechler—who was approaching seventy—began to show signs of slowing down. He suffered from nagging health issues that often required long periods of convalescence and were likely helped by neither his insistence on staying at his rustic home during the coldest months nor his near-constant pipe smoking.

SANTA CLAUS VERY ILL
IN HIS LONELY HOME

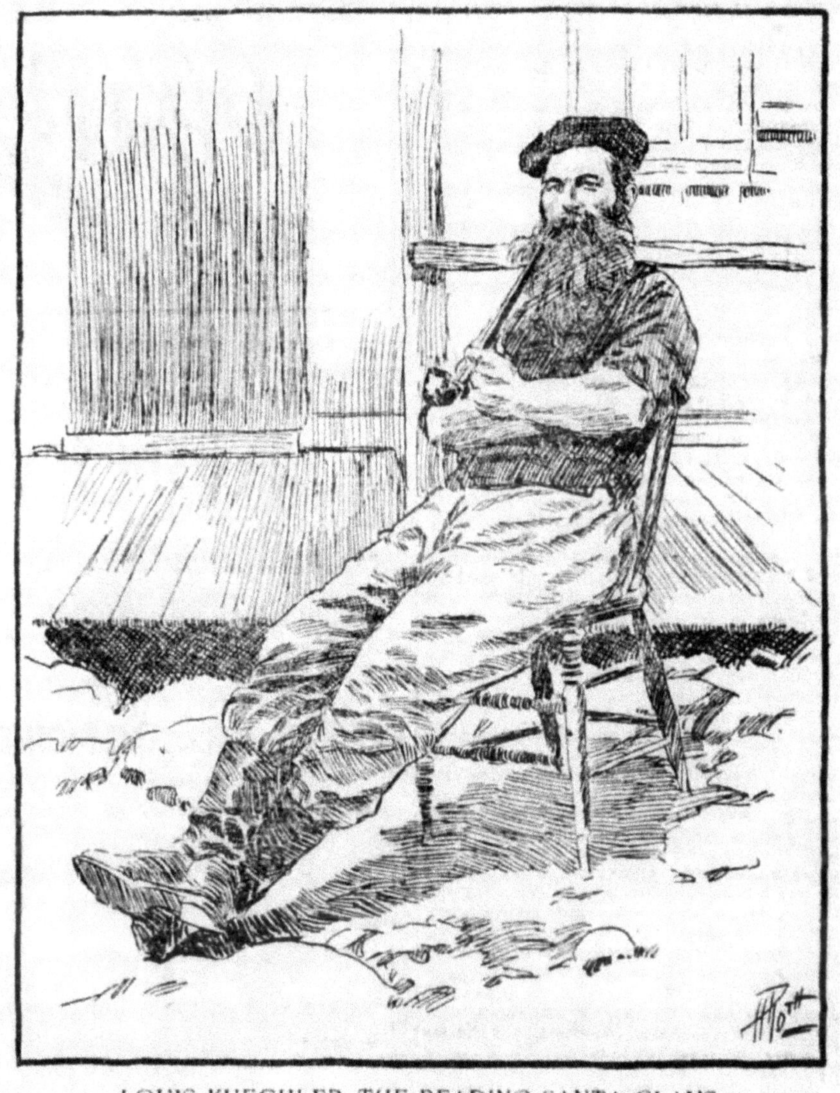

LOUIS KUECHLER, THE READING SANTA CLAUS

A *Philadelphia Times* illustration to accompany the story about Kuechler's health, 1900. *Newspapers.com.*

Pulitzer Prize–winning poet Wallace Stevens, son of Foosganger Garrett, described the seventy-two-year-old hermit in 1902: "I visited Kuechler on his hill-top and found him still and pale—his beautiful beard spread over his bosom, the gleam of an invisible sword darting about him."[202]

In January 1904, suffering from complications of asthma and dropsy (edema), Kuechler passed away after a brief stay in St. Joseph's Hospital (which, ironically, sat at the former spot of Vollmer's winery). Such was Kuechler's notoriety and influence that his death was headline news not only in Reading but also in Philadelphia, Allentown, Wilmington and as far away as Chicago.

In a somber yet uplifting obituary, his friend Tom Zimmerman wrote:

> To say that Mr. Kuechler was a typical host, is but to echo a long existing truism which found frequent expression upon the lips of thousands who partook of his hospitality. Frequenters of this mountain hostlerie will not soon forget how his handsome face would be aglow with pleasurable welcome to all his guests as they entered the modest, one-storied hut on the crest of the mountain, about four miles from Reading, where warm-hearted hospitality had been dispensed with lavish hand for nearly a quarter of a century.
>
> Mr. Kuechler was a well-bred German, a man of artistic tastes and capabilities, a lover of classical German poetic literature, and a model landlord. In personal appearance he was a stalwart, rosy-cheeked fellow, who, when his eyes were atwinkle with merriment, didn't look unlike the familiar picture of Santa Claus. He had a head which would have adorned the shoulders of a king: there was about it the lofty spirit of majesty in its almost leonine massiveness, and yet not without a quiet dignity that bespoke the innate gentility of soul that illumined the expression of his beaming blue eyes. It may with truth be said of him, that he had good-will in his face, sunshine in his heart, and hospitality in his hand.[203]

Another moving eulogy came from the *Lancaster New Era*, which added the following about Kuechler and his Roost:

> Its surroundings were the "forest primeval" below, and the ozone and stars above, not to mention the Gravity railroad, which approached the vine-clad retreat near enough to make the short walk thither desirable rather than otherwise, but not the return. There, in that spot, sacred to

> all good fellows, Mine Host Kuechler dispensed for a consideration those fluids and other hospitalities that will no doubt secure him a marble statue or a brass tablet in the near future. What that hospitality meant we know from personal experience, for we have enjoyed it in the shade of the giant trees that girdle the hallowed spot.[204]

In the years following Kuechler's death, Garrett Stevens launched his prolific secret career, sharing—in addition to "A Foosganger's Evening"—the following two tributary poems anonymously via the *Reading Times* (the first in 1906 and the second in 1908), with his authorship only to be revealed after his own passing.

THE HERMIT'S BURIAL
By Garrett Stevens

Cross-legged
And clad in sombre suit—anxious and
expectant
On every leaf and naked limb sit elf
and fairy.
Fay and nymph; while 'round each
mossy rock
And gnarled root flit sentinels of
sprite and
Goblin rare! Sadness everywhere and
wonder, too,
For at this hour for years and years,
in calm
Or storm, it was the wont of Kuechler,
living there.
To don his cap and stroke his beard,
and saunter down
The stony path and talk with them.

The humble cot in which he dwelt is
silent now
And none can guess the reason for
this strange neglect
And seeming rare disdain. For barking
squirrel

And chattering hack have frisked
about from tree to tree
And vainly sought by every trick familiar
To draw the loved hermit forth. The
whip-poor-will
Has thrice and thrice again his plain-
tive note resounded
And sits with cocked ear attent upon
the
Sweet imitative answer which cometh
not.

Cricket and chipmunk and north wind.
As messengers sent, have rapped
and rapped again
At paintless door and cracked window
pane
And returning sadly say that only
the stars
May know what is amiss, but whisper
this:
"This very eve when the sun went
down."
The shadow of the 'Schwartze Geist
Crept up the vale and hovered at the
door
Of the hermit in his mountain home!

Hark!
Up over fern and rock and straggling
bush
Comes Ulalla's call! See on the east-
ern hill
Luna flashes signals bright. Each
senseless
Stone, each shapeless root, turns to a
Moving thing. Alive, alert, are now
each

Elf and sprite and nymph and fairy
god,
For peering through the silent wood
they see
At Kuechler's gate the Schwartze
Geist,
O'er death triumphant, beating back
the demon phantom.
And with robes apart they see him
bear in fond embrace
The spirit they have known and loved
so well.

Adown the path his patient feet have
worn
Glides the uncanny bearer, fearless,
and to the host
Fast gathering there, he beckons, and
from each frosted leaf,
And naked limb and fern-hid rock and
root,
Flitting shadows rise and move, and
soon
In endless line they form a misty
troupe;
And quick o'er pathless wood and feck-
less field
And busy mart they make their way
Like flimsy cloud to a place of sepulture.
Where strong men stand about and
weeping women,
And crape and mourning equipage
abound.

There, 'round a place where upturned
earth is thrown
A surpliced priest is chanting of the
mortal

Who has put on immortality, and in
voice
That has no triumph, drones how
Death
Is swallowed up in Victory! "Dust to
dust,"
Saith the book, and a moan comes
from the throng;
"Earth to earth," saith the priest, his
form strict following,
And all that is earthly is soon en-
tombed.

But the black ghost unseen still is
kneeling,
And from his burden seems to sadly
separate;
And then the spirit smiling, to his bearer
clinging.
And to his loved mountain wistfully
turning.
Is swiftly borne aloft, like flash of rad-
ium light.
Is whisked away and only Hepler,
standing there,
'Neath his raised cap reverently peering.
As upon the dull coffin he drops his
symbol clods.
Has seen the fleeting troupe o'er the
crest
Of Penn departing, dissolve in familiar haunts.

And even now.
And until the eastern hills are again
alight.
This spirit still abides on mountain
side.

And with each elfin friend holds con-
verse fond.
And all that Nature's God has vital-
ized is loved;
And all who hallow and not desecrate
this sanctuary
Can there in peace repose. But woe
betide
The luckless lout or heated dame.
Who will on pleasure bent these sa-
cred hills profane.
For demons and imps, real devils, too.
Are spirits in his train—to work dire
ill
To those who will their host disdain.[205]

***

IN MEMORY OF KUECHLER'S ROOST

By Garrett Stevens

For the Judge and Tom, Doc and I.

"In the open gates
Of Ivory tower
On Zion's crest
His spirit waits."

On this fair mount
Removed from city's noise and man's selfish quest,
The passing years of time he counts
As the pleasing hours of an evening rest.
What to him the moans and groans and crunching bones
Where human hopes lie wrecked, or the wild huzzas that crown some victor great in royal test—or the honeyed tones of wooing lovers clasped breast to breast! These pass o'er his Aeolian chords, bringing no smiles or tears or empty words.

His spirit waits
And greets each morning sun of promise new, and patient sees at night the light of other worlds bedeck the heaven above and only

> the trees, the rocks and voiceless things can tell vain man his purpose here. With these he holds sweet converse in Nature's tongue and waits God's own good time—and round him grow the works of busy man disturbing this sweet sanctuary.[206]

Honoring a Legend

In 1909—just about five years after his death—a special tribute, held at his former home, celebrated the life of Jacob Louis Kuechler and featured the unveiling of a new portrait by E.E. Hafer, a local artist and friend of the hermit. The painting, which measures thirty by forty-two inches, shows Kuechler with trademark pipe alongside a grape arbor on the west side of his old shack. On a table stands a bottle of wine, of his own vintage, and a glass. As of the writing of this book, the piece hangs proudly in the Berks History Center museum.

Michler played toastmaster for the evening, while Zimmerman—who else?—gave the keynote address, alongside a banquet featuring Kuechler favorite chicken and waffles, plus native and German wines.

Several of Kuechler's friends gave brief speeches during the course of the evening, recapping the impact the hermit had on their lives. One particularly good example came from Richmond Jones:

> I am happy to be in this little company, assembled to recall pleasing memories of the old hermit of the mountain, with whom, on this lovely spot we whiled away so many happy hours. How often in the blinding snow or pelting rain we climbed these hills to seek the shelter and the warmth and welcome of his little cabin, which seemed more charming within as the weather was rugged and boisterous without. The contrast exalted the comfort of his snug little quarters, the glowing cannon stove defied the howling winds and the aeolian harp, perched upon the low roof, mocked and made music of the storm, Bacchus brewed the punch, Minerva kept the log book, and between the two, provided, a measure of scintillating wit for every comer. It was Olympus.[207]

During Zimmerman's speech, he read a prepared statement from Wallace Stevens, who was living in New York at the time and thus unable to attend himself. Though this was well before Stevens's first book (1923's *Harmonium*)

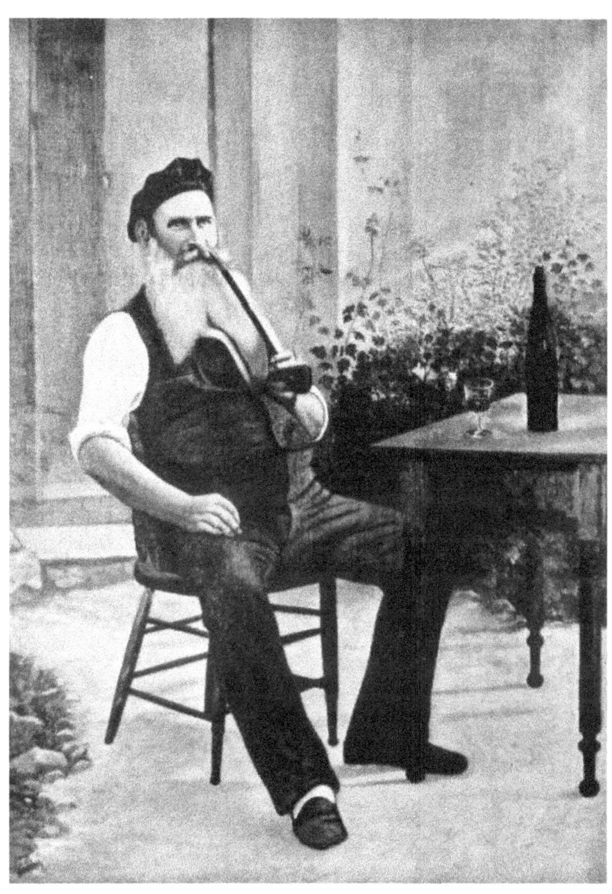

Left: The portrait of Jacob Louis Kuechler, by E.E. Hafer. *Lincoln Financial Foundation Collection/Internet Archive.*

Below: A menu from Kuechler tribute held at the Roost on February 10, 1909. *Newspapers.com.*

Consomme

Celery Olives Pickles

Chicken and Waffles

Sweet Potatoes Canned Corn

Chicken Salad Mayonnaise Dressing

Cheese

Vanilla Ice Cream Assorted Cakes

Coffee

Native Wine German Rhine Wine

Imported and Reading Cigars

would be published, it gave a glimpse of the soon-to-be famous poet's potential for lovely wordplay.

> And so the genius of the mountain woods has flown! He was such good company, and has gone to join such good company that one catches himself wishing, wishing he might be there, too. There must be an end, of names and of dignities and whatsoever there is of the earth. Where is Mowbray? Where is Mortimer? Nay! What is more, where is Plantagenet? They are entombed in the urns and sepulchres of mortality.
>
> Mr. Kuechler's death leaves the loved hill as a desert to me now. Reminiscences (older than his wines) have through years of absence, refreshed me; the airs of his Aeolian Harp! The new blossoms from his mountain garden; His dim lamp lighting up the "Roost"! His kingly face rimmed with royal beard! I even recall the tones of his guarded voice, tuned low and sweet, as he recited from Schiller some loved line. Ah! he was charming; and his "Geiste" was real to him. The sprites and fairies and goblins were his familiars, and no worldly fellow should have invaded his sanctuary thinking this king loved to serve for aught but for good company's sake.
>
> He will meet the Fooszgaenger in Paradise, in the Ivory Tower—with Michael and Peter and Gabriel—and it is not for the busy and vain to say he was foolish. For under the stars that hung so close to his humble home, he seemed to be communing with spirits; the mere pleasure-seeking idler could not understand.[208]

Though most of Zimmerman's comments were pulled from previous works already quoted here, he concluded with the following coda:

> But the good old host of the "Roost" is gone forever! His spirit soared to far greater, heights than the eyrie whereon, with the instinct of the eagle, he spread his wings many years ago. Who knows but that, through the coming years, the spirit of this kind, genial soul will continue to hover about the "Roost" and its surroundings like an angel of sweet companionship, which the passing periods of generations of those about Reading will not wholly efface, for the glory of the "Roost" has been embalmed, not only in the hearts of thousands of the living here and elsewhere, but in the unfading literature of the historic page.[209]

10

THE NEW ROOST

After Kuechler's death, his family briefly leased the Roost to an Albert Barto, who secured a liquor license for the establishment. No records, however, indicate that Barto was able to launch any business there before Carl A. Schaich bought the property outright in January 1905. Another native German (born 1863, in Nurtingen), Schaich had worked as a tanner at the leather manufacturing firm of Winter & Goetz for several years after he had arrived in Reading around 1901.

Not coincidentally—it can be assumed—one of Schaich's bosses was Ferdinand Goetz, son-in-law of Louis Kuechler and the executor to his will. Curiously, however, Goetz passed away (from a stroke) in October 1904, before Schaich completed his purchase.

On Thanksgiving Day, November 30, 1905, Schaich married Catherine Seabold of Philadelphia, the daughter of German immigrants, with an ensuing celebration held at the Roost. Like Kuechler, the two were said to be innately talented hosts, Schaich's friendly and welcoming demeanor perfectly complementing his wife's renowned skills in the kitchen. The couple also welcomed one child, Carl Jr., in September 1906—the only baby to ever grace the property.

As summer visitors rapidly grew with the popularity of the railroad, it became obvious that Kuechler's weather-beaten hut would need to be upgraded. As such, in 1907, Schaich took on a major renovation, replacing the original building with a Swiss-style inn made of local stone. The result would become the "most picturesque resort in Berks county."

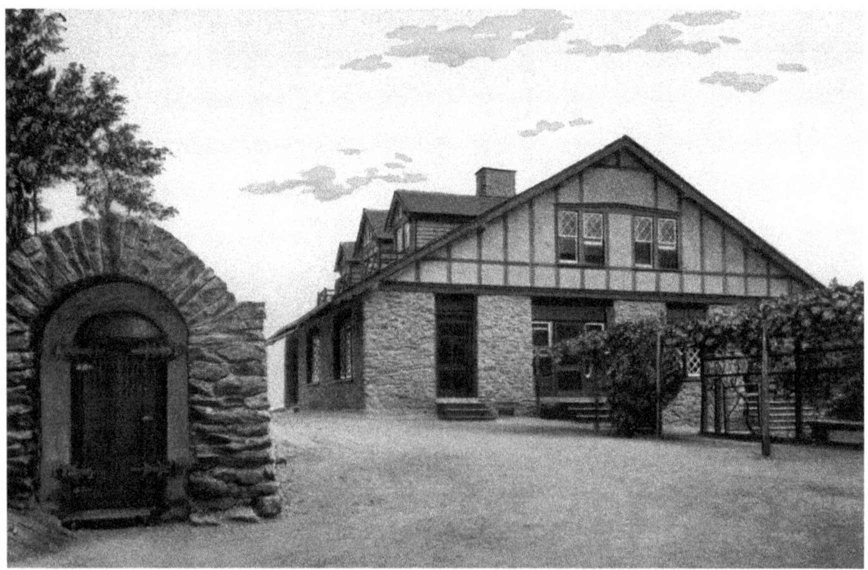

A postcard showing the new Kuechler's Roost and the wine cellar. *J. George Hintz.*

Upon the opening in August 1907, the *Reading Times* described the property as "a splendid bungalow of stone, similar to pretty inns found everywhere in Germany." One highlight was the huge open fireplace in the living room. Schaich spared no expense to illustrate the transformation from rustic to luxurious, as, when visitors reached the Roost station, they found the path leading to the resort decorated with blazing Chinese lanterns and the new building trimmed with German and American flags intertwined with still more lanterns. A dinner of barbecue spring chicken welcomed the guests, who gathered in three large rooms decorated with the foliage of sassafras, chestnut and oak.[210]

A few years later, the *Times* again provided the following descriptive commentary:

> If Herr Kuechler could come back to earth and see the handsome structure that supplanted his primitive hut, in which he loved to offer his friends good cheer, and in which he so long led a hermit life, he would be truly astonished. Low and squat, one and three-quarter stories high and built of stone quarried in the neighborhood, it is at once pleasing to the eye and comfortable as an abode. Its interior is finished in hardwood mission type, and the furniture and furnishings are in complete harmony.

KUECHLER'S ROOST

A Cool and Delightful Spot on Mount Penn. Famous for good meals, liquors, wines and beer. Under new management. Give me a call.

KARL SCHAICH, Prop'r

An early ad for Schiach's Roost. *Newspapers.com.*

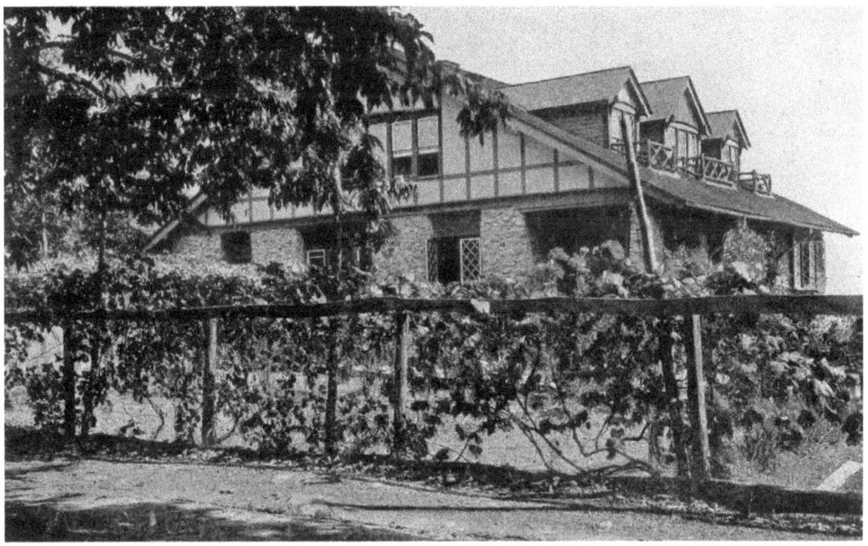

Another view of the new Kuechler's Roost. *Lincoln Financial Foundation Collection/Internet Archive.*

> A broad verandah juts from the south side of the building and affords a splendid resting place for those in search of repose at the fag-end of a day of rush and business.[211]

Over time, the new owners would continue to upgrade the property; this included importing top-quality mahogany furniture from Germany and installing electric and phone service, as well as a massive refrigeration chamber in the basement. Two new bowling alleys, constructed in a one-story outbuilding, provided club members with a popular Saturday night activity. Guest rooms offered refuge for overnight revelers. High demand for space on the veranda resulted in the erection, in 1910, of a rustic pavilion directly east of the Roost building. Yet another new pavilion was added in 1915. The *Reading Times* described the former as such:

> This structure, like the chalet, is of stone of native quarrying while the roof is constructed of shingles supported on hewn logs. The floor is of hardwood. In this pavilion, on the verandah and in the Roost proper, on summer days, are constantly many groups of guests.
>
> The pavilion is an especially delightful place to spend a summer evening, for no matter how hot it may be in the city a pleasant and cool breeze stirs about the Roost. The views of the sunset from the pavilion and verandah are superb. As the great orb of day slips down beyond the western hills the last rays filter like gold through the tree tops, making the beholder, of clear conscience, at peace with himself and all the world.[212]

Tafelrunde

The wealthy and influential German community that made up the Foosgangers remained interested and involved in this new Roost, in all probability helping to pay for the renovations. As part of the new design, a special clubroom in the corner of the resort became the group's exclusive domain, complete with a twenty-by-thirty-foot pavilion lined with elaborate flower boxes for their private use during pleasant weather.

The club dubbed itself "Tafelrunde auf Kuechler's Roost," after the centerpiece of the club room, a round, hand-carved *stamtisch* (the word for "regulars' table" in German), designed by founding member Robert Carl Rahm. This unique table featured a sixty-inch quarter-sawed oak top, on which the names of the group's earliest members are engraved, as well as vine and wine imagery, and was supported by a mission pedestal. Though Rahm—along with Ferdinand Thun, Henry Janssen and Gustav Oberlaender—is most often credited as founder of the Tafelrunde, it's hard not to also notice the name "T. Zimmerman" looming large toward the edge of the table.

Twelve mission-style armchairs—produced by Louis Heilbron's furniture factory located at 940 Penn Street—matched the table, each featuring its own intricate carving pattern. In addition, a cabinet in the clubroom held

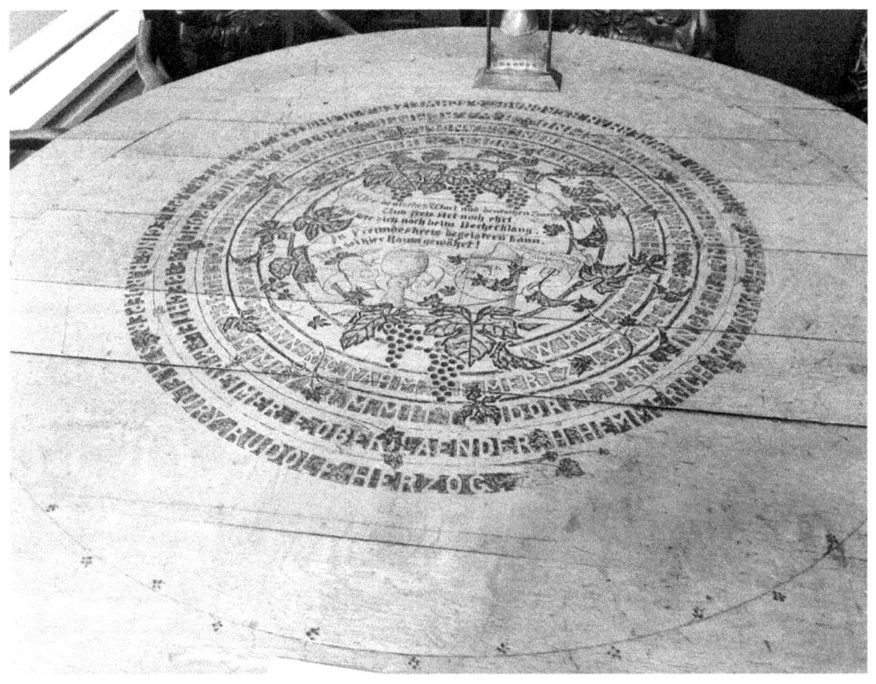

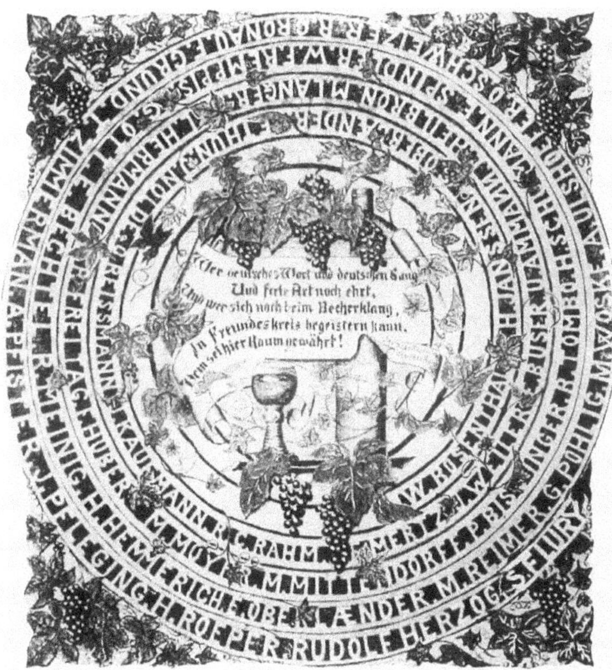

Above: The Tafelrunde, in the Berks History Center. *Author photo.*

Left: An illustration of the Tafelrunde carving. *Lincoln Financial Foundation Collection/Internet Archive.*

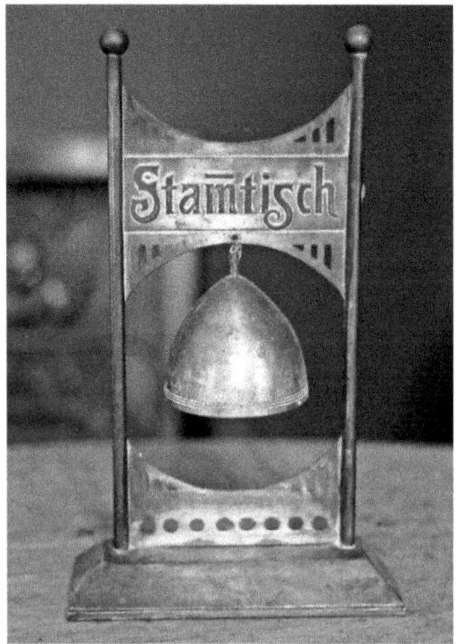

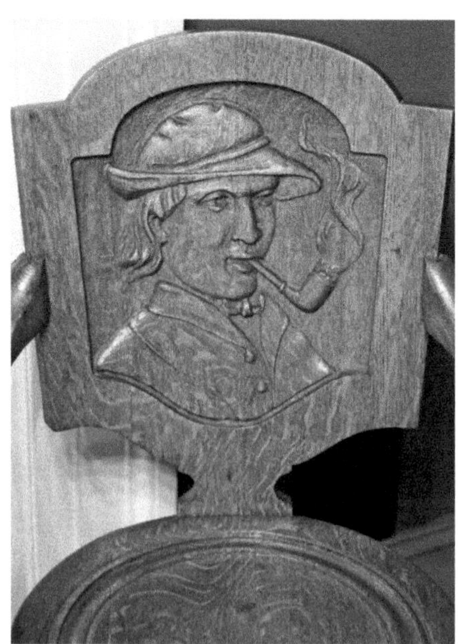

Left: The Stamtisch sign that sits atop the table, now at the Berks History Center. *Author photo.*

Right: One of the hand-carved chairs that matched the Roost Stamtisch. At the Berks History Center. *Author photo.*

imported crystal-clear drinking glasses for every member, all sporting a pewter lid and personal monogram. Further decorations imported from Germany created the semblance of a tavern in Schaich's native Württemberg.

As were the Foosgangers, the Tafelrunde was an august and erudite group, known certainly for drinking around their table, but also for thinking. Each of their regular Saturday afternoon meetings thus began with a literary session, followed by supper, sociability and, finally, after many glasses had been clinked, singing.

BEYOND THE ROUND TABLE

Like the original Roost—in fact more so—it was quite common for Schaich to host large parties and banquets. Perusing the newspapers of the time, one would often discover notices such as the following, titled "Delightful Outing":

> A party of 50 of the most prominent German-Americans of this city and Wyomissing enjoyed a delightful outing and dinner at Kuechler's Roost, last evening. The affair was entirely informal and comfort and good fellowship alone were the aims of the party.
>
> The dinner centered around chickens and waffles. The table adornments were very pretty and attracted considerable attention. There was only one speech made. This was by Ferdinand Thun, and it was of a felicitous character. There was no toastmaster. There was singing and a general good time until 11 o'clock when the party boarded a special car on the Gravity road and returned to the city.[213]

Though the Tafelrunde was markedly German in nature, and certainly the regular German American clients did frequently host private dinners there, the Roost's appeal—helped of course by its proximity to a railroad stop—was not limited to a particular nationality. In fact, the resort's halls just as commonly hosted class or family reunions and meetings of other private clubs or professional organizations.

"Readingites generally showed much partiality to 'Kuechler's' when they desired to spend a day on the mountains," reported the *Reading Times*. "Among politicians 'The Roost' had a quota of adherents and in years gone by many important 'slates' were devised within its quiet walls."[214]

Fryer backed up the assertion that thinking of the Roost as only German was incorrect. "It was cosmopolitan," he wrote. "There was an annual Swiss day, and every day was an American day, with frequent parties, banquets and balls, and dining and dancing in the moonlight."[215]

Food served in Schaich's time did draw mostly from German and Pennsylvania Dutch traditions; chicken (stewed or grilled) and waffles was the specialty, and the highest priced item at one dollar, including dessert and coffee. Though German-style meats and cheeses made up the vast majority of the regular menu (a version of which is available in full in appendix E), local and international influences occasionally made themselves known through items like corn, olives and caviar.

In 1910, the *Reading Times* described a Roost banquet staff members had recently attended, highlighting several of the above items in further detail:

> Then came the epicurean treat of the evening when a comely young woman decked a table with snowy cloth and brought on a substantial and delicately prepared rural feast....There was the soup, followed by barbecued chicken and the accessories and potatoes French fried to a

KUECHLER'S

ROOST

Mt. Penn's delightful resort. Chicken and waffle suppers, quick lunches, choice wines. Take Mt. Penn Gravity cars. Bell 'phone.

CARL SCHAICH, Prop.

A 1910 ad for Kuechler's Roost, emphasizing chicken and waffles. *Newspapers.com.*

> golden brown; young green corn on the cob and a plentiful supply of delicious ham, a choice of whole wheat and pure rye bread, waffles that were at once crisp and dainty, the whole coming to a close with ice cream and coffee of superb flavor.
>
> While the feast was going merrily on, to the southeast arose the moon blood red, as though perspiring from the heat of the day. Now and then a cloud sailed across its face and hid it from view or, when then cloud was slender, only partly obscured it. At such times an affect [sic] was produced such as artists love to paint. With joke and quip, good fellowship adding zest, the feast came to a close and an added hour was spent.[216]

Pennsylvania Dutch and Their Cookery contains several recipes associated with Kuechler's Roost, though it does not specify which era—other than a stewed chestnut dish attributed to Schaich. Also included are Hasenkucha, a casserole of rabbit with Dutch potato stuffing; Baked Ham with Spiced Oranges; Corn Meal Mush and Lamb Kidneys; and Tomato Cakes.

Schaich did continue raising vines and making wines from the Roost vineyard, if with far less priority than Kuechler. He also served Reiniger's local product alongside a broad variety of German choices, primarily white but some red. The most expensive item was a bottle of Mumm Champagne—

which would run about $50 in 2019—at $4.50. Beer also became a popular choice. A full wine list from this era is available in appendix E.

During Reading Fair week, in September 1916, Schaich passed away suddenly. Part of his obituary read:

> Carl Augustus Schaich, a leading figure among the German-American population in this vicinity, and proprietor of the famous "Kuechler's Roost" on Mt. Penn, died at 7:30 last evening from pneumonia at the "Roost," where he has acted as the genial host to thousands of pleasure seekers from every part of the United States. Ill not quite three days, his death was a shock to many friends. Especially among the Germans throughout the city was there general lamentation.[217]

Catherine Schaich persevered as proprietor, remaining successful as patrons continued to flock to Reading's mountains each summer.

11

END OF THE LINE

More broadly, the Gravity Railroad's popularity grew quickly and steadily through the 1890s and early 1900s, with estimates surpassing 70,000 riders for the first time in 1893 and 100,000 in 1896. Though events and weather did cause these numbers to fluctuate, estimates suggest that at least 50,000 passengers enjoyed the attraction each year between 1893 and 1919, with an average around 80,000.

In January 1919, the Eighteenth Amendment was ratified, meaning Prohibition was imminent, bringing with it a threat to every business on the mountain. This same year, however, the line boasted a record total of 140,205 riders, who perhaps sensed the looming end of their good times at this hallowed spot and made sure to get in on them before they disappeared.

It is easy to fault Prohibition alone—and the so-called noble experiment certainly deserves a fair share of the blame—but the reality is that a number of factors combined to kick-start the beloved attraction's demise as the decade ended. Like so many similar stories, it mostly came down to the bottom line: cash money.

Despite the railroad's continued and expanding popularity, the company had consistent difficulty turning a profit. It had particular trouble covering expenses during the early years, when construction took place and the locomotives ran on steam. At the outset of the project, $100,000 in bonds were sold, yet an additional $60,000 was needed in 1891. Originally promised by April 1902, the bonds' deadline was later extended to 1919, then 1922 and finally 1923. In 1894, prospects were so dim that a committee

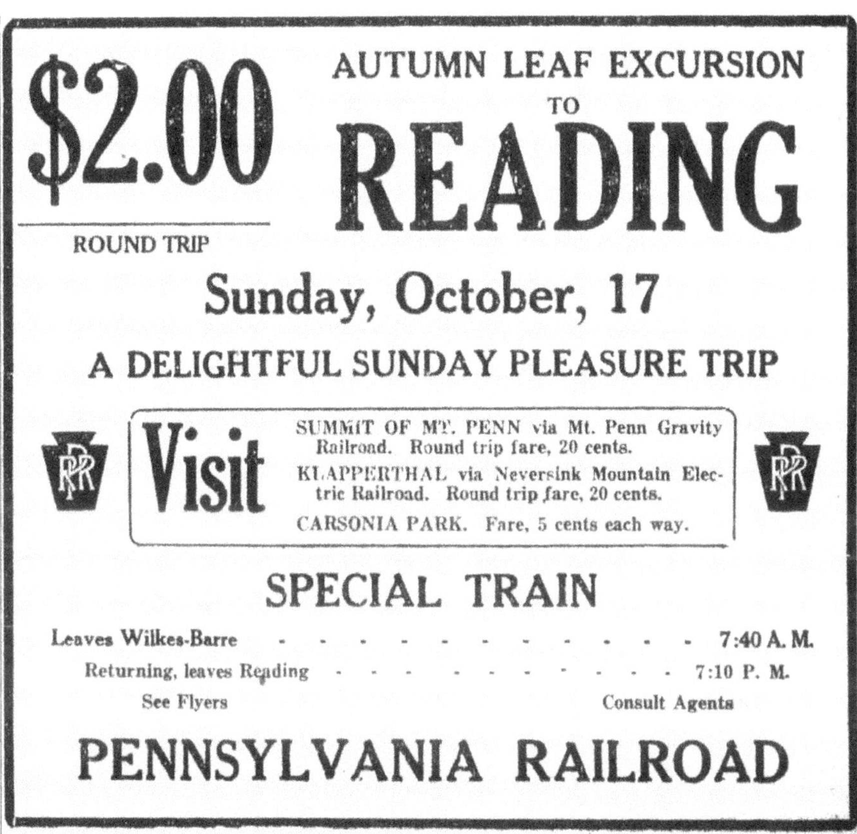

An ad for an autumn Gravity Railroad Excursion, 1915. *Newspapers.com.*

on railroad reorganization recommended to stockholders that the road be sold at judicial sale. While this did not occur, the company took out a second mortgage the following year and, typically, went into debt after paying these mortgages. In 1898, electric cars replaced the old steam engines, providing significant savings and allowing the line to become (mildly) profitable for the first time. Starting in 1907, dividends of 2–3 percent were paid to stockholders annually until around 1919.

According to J. Bennett Nolan, a former director of the Gravity Railroad, the company consistently flourished on Decoration Day (Memorial Day), the Fourth of July and Labor Day, but other days it just got by. Another former director named Arthur Rick noted that some younger members of the board attempted to raise fares, but more established members prevented this from ever occurring. (Ticket prices did increase from twenty cents to thirty-five over the twenty-year period, but apparently this was not enough.)

TRAGEDIES AND THEIR AFTERMATH

Some of the company's financial troubles relate to fatal accidents that occurred during the first two seasons. On Friday, August 22, 1890, the brakes on a Gravity car failed near the summit, causing it to careen wildly down the mountain—estimates had its top speed at eighty miles per hour—and jump the track on the coincidentally named Cemetery Curve (because it was near Aulenbach's Cemetery). Five people perished (and later a sixth, due to injuries in the rescue effort), and about twenty suffered injuries. The following year, on November 5, 1891, a car's brakes again failed—this time due to wet leaves—and the car smashed into a cut above Mineral Spring Park, killing both the driver and brakeman and injuring four passengers. Though train accidents were not exactly uncommon at the time, both incidents made headlines around the country.

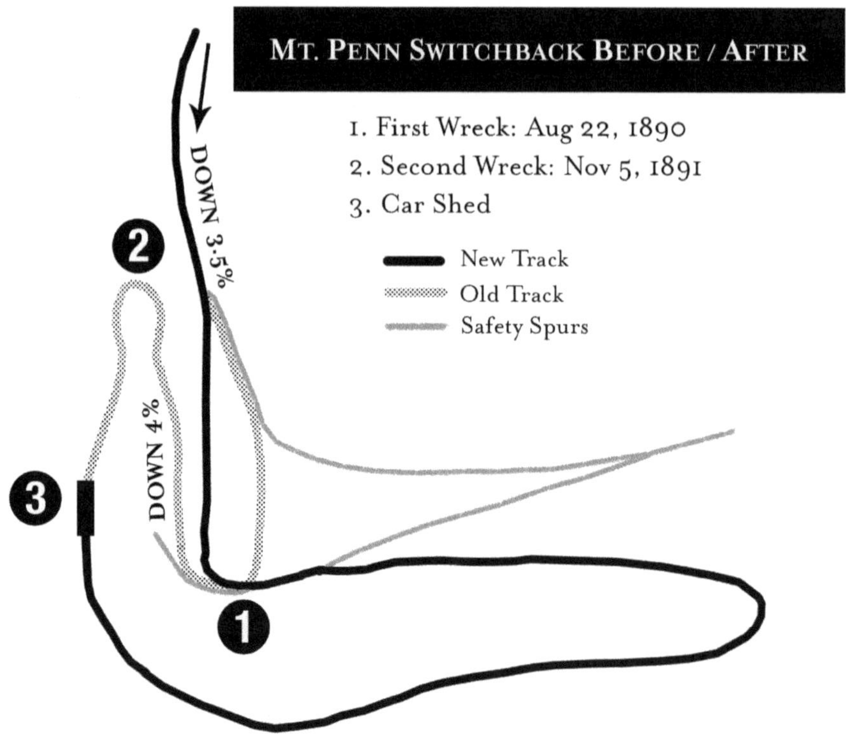

A map depicting the safety adjustments made in 1891–92 after fatal wrecks.

Because each of these derailments occurred at approximately the same spot on the descent, near a particularly vicious curve, the winter of 1891 saw a number of safety improvements. In addition to a switchback to replace the dangerous curve, a new runaway track was added. No further accidents occurred, and the switchback was removed in 1902 once the entire line had been electrified.

These tragedies had little bearing on the ride's receipts. Traffic was heavier than normal the weekend following the first and biggest wreck, for example, including 1,500 excursionists from Philadelphia. After a jury found the Gravity Railroad company responsible, however, long-term settlements with the families of the injured and deceased would bleed off profits for the entire life of the project.

UP IN FLAMES

Fires were a constant threat during this period, especially in areas where civilization encroached on natural lands. (City buildings were also quite vulnerable.) Perusing newspapers of the time, stories about these incidents on Mount Penn and Neversink are easy to come across, and firemen were often featured prominently in news coverage. At some point or another, fires wreaked havoc at Kuechler's, Spuhler's, Reiniger's and Lauterbach Springs. It was, then, not particularly surprising that fire damage also played a key role in the Gravity Railroad's downfall.

On July 4, 1919, patriotic revelers at Kuechler's Roost took their festivities too far, and the resort burned to the ground, ending a thirty-seven-year reign atop the mountain. "Authorities believe that careless

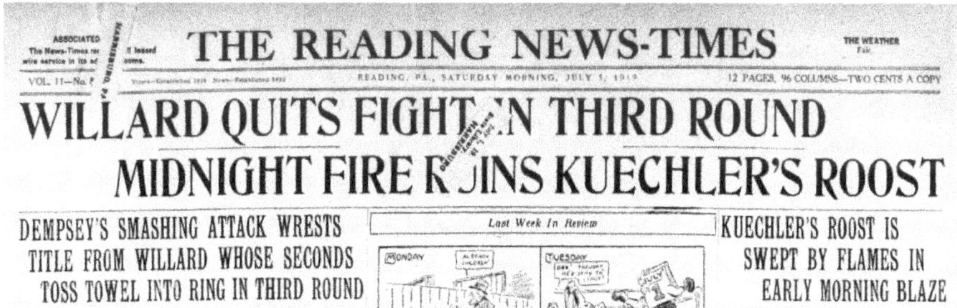

THE READING NEWS-TIMES

VOL. 11—No.

READING, PA., SATURDAY MORNING, JULY 5, 1919

12 PAGES, 96 COLUMNS—TWO CENTS A COPY

WILLARD QUITS FIGHT IN THIRD ROUND

MIDNIGHT FIRE RUINS KUECHLER'S ROOST

DEMPSEY'S SMASHING ATTACK WRESTS TITLE FROM WILLARD WHOSE SECONDS TOSS TOWEL INTO RING IN THIRD ROUND

Last Week In Review

KUECHLER'S ROOST IS SWEPT BY FLAMES IN EARLY MORNING BLAZE

The *Reading Times* front page, the day after Kuechler's Roost burned to the ground, July 5, 1919. *Newspapers.com.*

Fourth of July celebrants left burning remnants of fire crackers lying beneath the pavilion,"[218] reported a downtrodden *Reading Times* the following day, adding that fourteen unlucky hotel guests were forced to flee in their nightclothes, forgoing their valuables. The fire, which started in a 190-foot square pavilion just southeast of the main hotel, spread so quickly that within ten minutes, it was said, spectators knew the entire property was doomed. And, in fact, by the time firefighters from Reading reached the scene, the building was practically destroyed. (They were, thankfully, able to contain the blaze to a single property.)

The paper went on to describe the scene at what it dubbed "the best known resort in the county" like so:

> The fire threw a great circle of red across the top of Mount Penn and hundreds of Reading citizens saw the glow in the eastern sky. The flames swept through the hotel with terrific speed, eating their way from room to room with incredible swiftness....Forty-five minutes after the outbreak...the building was a mass of flames. At 1 o'clock the roof collapsed, sending showers of sparks high into the sky....The four stone walls alone remained standing early this morning, although firemen constantly played streams on the smouldering debris.[219]

As part of an estimated $30,000 in losses, the Mountain Log Book perished in the fire, lost forever to history—save the tidbits collected and published by Zimmerman. Thankfully, however, the handmade stamtisch and chairs, along with Kuechler's portrait, were saved and today stand together in the Berks History Center.

In the days that followed, much criticism was leveled at the Roost, for it was believed by the Reading fire chief and his fellow firefighters that the place could have been saved with the simple preparation of having had a fire extinguisher on hand.

Post-fire coverage remained optimistic about the future. "It is likely that the hotel will be rebuilt," wrote the *Reading Times*. "It is the most famous mountain resort hereabouts and has been visited by many celebrities."[220] And while Catherine Schaich did make a half-hearted but ultimately doomed attempt to continue the business in the remaining bowling alley, the rest of the Roost was never resurrected. Schiach summed up her situation with the following bleak words: "I came to the Roost a happy bride, and left it a sorrowing widow. Death took my husband, fire destroyed my home, and Prohibition ruined my business."[221]

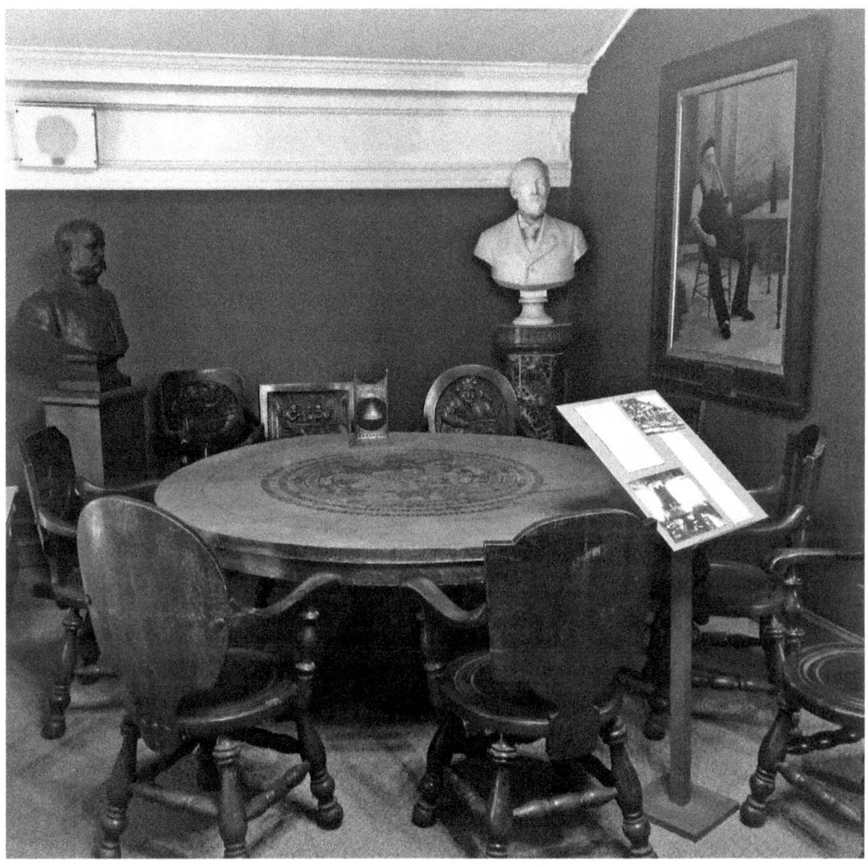

Kuechler's portrait watches over the Roost Stamtisch, at the Berks History Center. *Author photo.*

Although the loss of the mountain's flagship resort was a devastating blow, especially as it coincided with the onset of Prohibition, the railroad pressed on. Ticket sales decreased quickly—to less than half the 1919 numbers—yet in early 1923, the company expressed optimism for the oncoming season, noting an increase of ten thousand passengers from 1921 to 1922, as well as a number of equipment and roadbed improvements made that winter.[222] On April 20, 1923, directors of the company performed their final inspection before the season, declaring everything in excellent shape to open on May 8.

Just several days later, around 6:45 p.m. on April 23, 1923, city residents began to notice flames at the northwest corner of the Tower's dance pavilion. The fire—described by the *Reading Eagle* as "the most spectacular ever witnessed anywhere in the county"[223] spread quickly, helped by a strong

Kuechler's Roost
MOUNT PENN, READING, PA.
Open again for business, serving dinners, etc., as usual.
Mrs. CATHARINE SCHAICK,
Proprietress.

Above: Catharine Schiach put this ad in Philadelphia's *Evening Public Ledger* after the Roost fire in August 1919. *Library of Congress.*

Right: The *Reading Times* front page after the Tower fire, April 24, 1923. *Newspapers.com.*

TOWER BURNS

Old Mountain Landmark Destroyed—Fire Origin Mystery

THOUSANDS WATCH FLAMES

Hotel Is Saved—All Other Buildings Wiped Out

northwest wind, and everything on site was decimated: the Tower, the bowling alley, refreshment stands and all of the outbuildings. It is particularly upsetting to consider the destruction of carvings—initials, addresses and dates inscribed by visitors from all parts of the country, serving as a guestbook of sorts—that blanketed the interior of the Tower. Yet only the bare stone walls remained, severely cracked by the intense heat, rendering them useless. The nearby Summit Hotel was—thanks to the efforts of fire wardens and volunteer Boy Scouts—spared any damage.

"Thousands of people in the city stood in the streets, on housetops and in the city park to watch the flames lay in ashes the city's oldest mountain landmark," recapped the *Reading Times* the following day. "The structure was known to every visitor that came to this city," the article continued, "and was the mecca for thousands during the summer months. Picnics attracted many and it is a rarity to find even a resident of the city who has not visited the building. Picturesque, it was the object of every official delegation and one of the expectations of everyone who intended to be in the city. Its fame was spread country-wide, for it is doubtful if any other city could boast of a duplicate."[224]

Save the Tower?

On April 25, the company's board of directors declared that they would not invest in a new resort at the same spot. Furthermore, they added, unless someone else stepped up to reinstate a social destination atop the mountain, the railroad would shutter permanently. "It is squarely up to the people of Reading whether they want the Mt. Penn Gravity Railroad to keep going or not," remarked board president James Rick Jr. "We have conducted it for 32 years without getting anything out of it and we are not willing to spend any more money on the proposition."[225] (Yikes.)

Just five days later, however, Rick was leading a splinter group made of younger members from the Gravity board, one of two recently activated plans to save the railroad. "In a very short time," Rick stated, "we hope to be able to present concrete figures to the public, regarding our plans, and will then go before them and seek their co-operation in organizing a company to promote them." These plans never seemed to materialize or, if they did, failed to make an impact.

At the same time, members of the city council were investigating the possibility of purchasing the land for a municipal park. Though optimism ran rampant at the start of this conversation, it was quickly decided that the city could not afford the minimum $100,000 asking price. Additional ideas were considered that year (such as a toll road for cars), but none ever came to fruition.

The railroad did operate during the 1923 season, starting around Memorial Day. Having been closed since 1919, the Summit Hotel reopened and held dances each Wednesday and Saturday evening. In early 1924, however, the railroad company defaulted on interest for bonds held on its first mortgage, and a Berks court ordered it to be put up for sale. On March 8 of that same year, prominent Reading banker and businessman George D. Horst purchased the company's full holdings at auction for just $12,650 (which, for those keeping score, is more than $87,000 below the original asking price). Shortly thereafter, Horst dismantled the railroad and sold the equipment for scrap.

The property's new owner did little with it over the next ten years, but he became an early supporter of the Skyline Drive project and consistently stated he would donate his land to the city if this ever became reality. He finally followed through on this promise in 1933, but sadly passed away, in 1934, before the long-planned drive opened the following year.

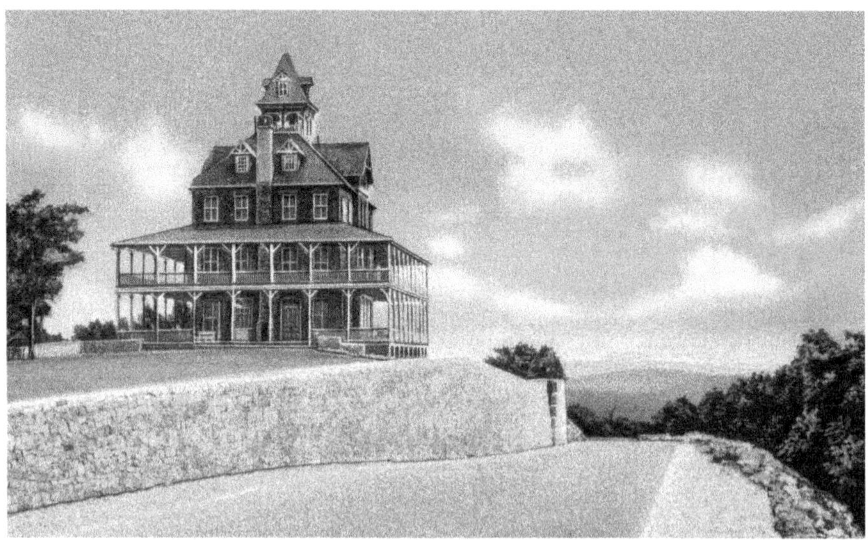

The Summit House, alone atop the mountain, once Skyline Drive had opened. *Wikimedia Commons.*

It is particularly interesting how initial reactions to both the Roost and Tower fires assumed that the resorts would be saved and continued. These institutions had, after all, become part of the fabric of life in Reading. This viewpoint, was, of course, naive in that it failed to fully understand the financial limitations at play. Looking back, it's quite difficult to imagine a situation where investing in a railroad that had never made a lot of money would have been fiscally prudent, especially considering the rise of the automobile and the realities of Prohibition.

The True Impact of Prohibition

The Volstead Act, in actuality, did little to reduce alcohol consumption in Reading; in fact, it probably had the opposite effect. Those who wanted a drink could find one, and without much trouble. But its impact on the region's culture went much deeper and still reverberates today.

The initial development of winemaking in this area was a direct result of immigrants bringing a part of their countries' culture to their new home. The European tradition of wine lived on as part of a healthy lifestyle, to be enjoyed as food, with food, with family and friends. Sure, it made you feel good. But it was not drunk to get drunk.

"To a secluded—suggestive for misbehavior—spot on Mt. Penn, for many years, men, women and children came and enjoyed themselves in a rational manner," recalled John Michler of Kuechler's original hideaway. "There is no record, there has never been mention made of an instance where a disturbance occurred at 'Kuechler's Roost.' He showed that a mountain resort can be conducted decently and in order, and without intoxication."

"Those not feeling it, did not fit," added Benjamin Fryer. "People of that sort merely want a place to drink, gulp it down, and order another round. John Barleycorn was not at home here. John becomes noisy and is out of place where friends gather for sociability. The juice of the grape invites song and cements friendship, while distilled grain produces argument."

Prohibition enabled this so-called John Barleycorn. He was forced underground, where liquor that did its job quickly and brutally became the norm. With the constant risk of raids—despite Reading maintaining 75 percent of its saloons, not counting speakeasies—getting drunk quickly became normalized, as did losing control. In 1923, for example, the Reading police charged three times as many people with drunkenness as they did in 1920.[226]

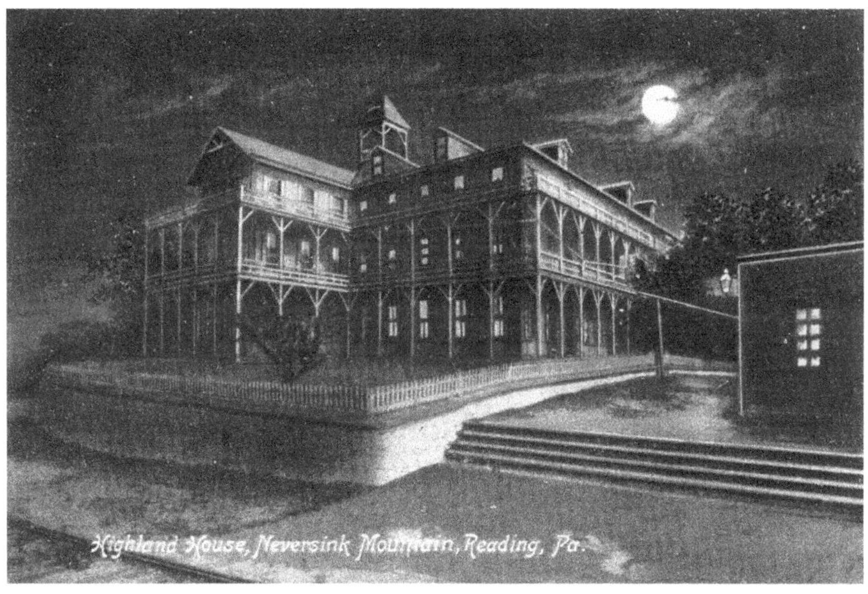

The Highland House lit up at night—said to be a common view during Prohibition, despite the resort's official closure in 1917. *Joseph A. Webb Collection.*

Once the merciful end to this not-so-noble experiment finally arrived, many of the mountain vineyards—some of which had thrived for more than eighty years—had already been abandoned or replaced. Ed Spuhler, who tended bar at his father's eponymous resort for many years, summed it up simply: "Repeal," he remarked, "will not bring back those leisurely days at the turn of the century." The idea of wine as a vital part of life, in the grand European tradition, had quickly disappeared.

When initially researching this period, it seemed that the Gravity Railroad was the key catalyst for this explosion of culture in Reading. Digging further, however, helped illustrate how the railroad was instead the logical extension of a culture that already existed. It's even worth venturing to say that without the original winemakers who remained so dedicated to establishing the industry in those early years, the later resort era may have never materialized. This is, of course, not to say that there weren't other economic and societal factors, yet it serves to reiterate how important the wine industry's growth was to the area. And how much Prohibition hurt that.

A few of the old places—Spuhler's, Pleasant View, the Summit Hotel—resurrected after repeal, but local wine was no longer a focus. Daniel J. Reiniger did reestablish his family winery, but he used imported grapes from New York State rather than local ones. In 1954, he sold the business, and with it the last connection to winemaking on the mountain. (The new owner relocated the company to Jermyn, Pennsylvania, north of Scranton, until the late 1960s, when it eventually went defunct.).

Let's be clear, however; it's not as if grape-growing came to an abrupt halt on January 17, 1920. Federal agents did not swarm Mount Penn to tear up every vine. It's actually quite easy to find mention of Berks vineyards in the 1930s, although in these cases the reference is more likely to a small plot on private land. The problem, as it so often is—and has already been discussed with regards to the railroad—was money. Without a commercial industry to drive forward research and innovation, motivation dissipated. A farmer could no longer expect to earn a living growing grapes, so his attentions became, by necessity, focused elsewhere.

In Pennsylvania specifically, establishment of the Pennsylvania Liquor Control Board (PLCB) after repeal had a particularly destructive effect. It wasn't until the passage of the Limited Winery Act in 1968 that individual wineries could sell their products directly to the public. Before that, sales could only be made through state liquor stores, which at that time were most definitely not in the business of promoting or helping any wineries, let alone local ones. Grape growers could sell their

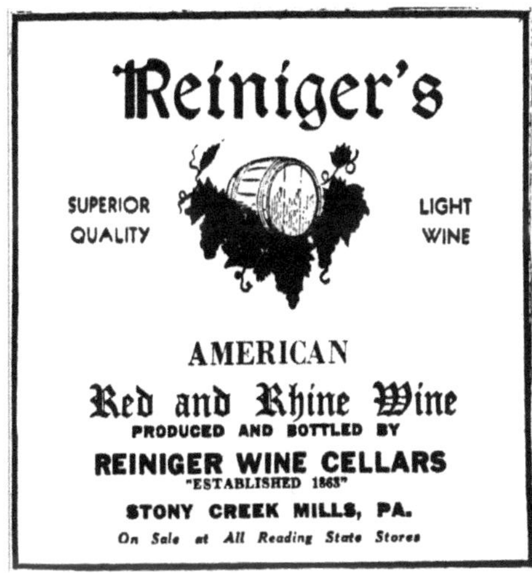

Left: A Reiniger Cellars ad, 1936. *Newspapers.com.*

Below: A post-Prohibition ad for Spuhler's Hotel, 1933. *Newspapers.com.*

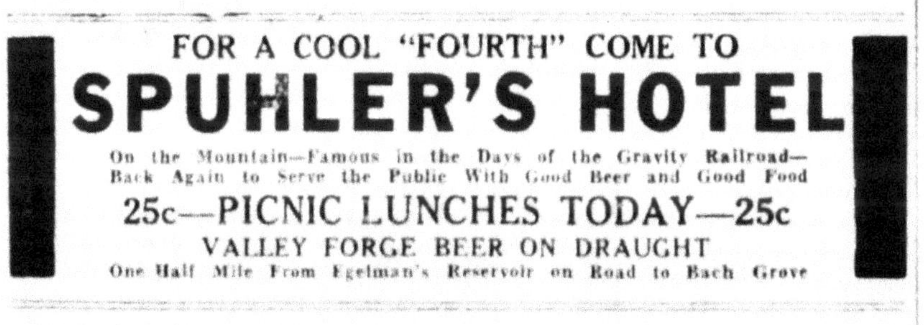

fruit to out-of-state winemakers (in New York, for example), but this was not lucrative.

In 1941, the PLCB issued just eleven winery licenses—including to Reiniger Wine Cellars—most of which were to importers or distillers who likely bottled cheap wine that was grown and made elsewhere. As nine of the eleven listed addresses were in Philadelphia or Pittsburgh, it seems unlikely any were "wineries" in the sense we'd think of today.

It wasn't, therefore, until Dutch Country Winery opened in Lenhartsville on April 17, 1976, that commercially viable, locally focused winemaking returned to Berks. As such, when thinking of Prohibition's impact on the area, it is not enough to solely consider the period from 1920 to 1933. The reality is that the local wine industry lost *fifty-five years* of research, experimentation and progress. At a minimum. Furthermore, the Berks County Wine Trail—a modern sign of the industry's importance—wasn't established until 2004.

Speaking with some of the current winemakers in the area, it's clear that there was not much in terms of local knowledge to pull from when they started. Tom

"State Has Wineries"

This simple headline, featured in Pennsylvania newspaper the *Evening Standard* during April 1977, says it all. It would be funny if it wasn't sad.

Calvaresi, for example—whose eponymous winery (founded 1981) is the oldest currently in operation in Berks, though he is no longer involved—described visiting some of the plots that were vineyards in the old days. They were long past usefulness; his interest was mere curiosity. Otherwise, most new entrants look to advances in the Erie area, or even the West Coast, for inspiration. This is fine of course, and probably would be done even if the Reading industry had persisted. But with wine, there's also the French concept of terroir to consider; the idea that every parcel of land has a unique combination of weather, soil, pests and so forth that affects winemaking differently. Without farmers focused on learning about which areas generate which characteristics, which grapes work on which plots and more, there's little hope to improve a region's wine quality over time.

An illustrative example came from William Smith, the winemaker at Ridgewood Winery in Birdsboro (established 2013). He spoke of a plot of land he'd identified in Boyertown that he felt was ideally situated to grow *Vitis vinifera* grapes. Fifty years from now, assuming he continues with the plan to experiment there, we'll know whether his hypothesis is true. And probably which grapes thrive there. Yet because the industry was stagnant for so long, today we can't be certain.

Compare all of this to the brewing industry, which even the most casual observer can understand is far more prolific and influential in the Pennsylvania of today. Breweries did not stop production during Prohibition. Yes, they were supposed to brew only "near beer" of less than 0.5 percent alcohol by volume (ABV), but the reality is that most continued to churn out plenty of regular beer as well. In fact, these brews became more potent, often jumping to more than 4 percent ABV, versus an average of around 2.75 percent in the years prior to Prohibition.[227] (A particularly interesting statistic when considering 4 percent is the lowest level that most beers today contain.) Post-repeal, the PLCB rules that stifled winery growth spared brewers, enabling beer to become a much more accessible and lucrative beverage in the commonwealth, not to mention world class in quality.

As a lover of wine—not only the beverage, but the culture it creates—for me, it is devastating to think of what could have been, had winemaking on Mount Penn continued to thrive during the twentieth century. Nothing would have been guaranteed, obviously; Reading has certainly been through its fair share of troubles in the years since. Still, to think that wineries in the area are just now, forty years since they were reestablished, starting to produce quality wine on a consistent basis, it's impossible to wonder where we might be today with that extra half century of development. And with a society that still believes in wine as life, the way it once did.

12

LINGERING GHOSTS

It is not insightful to suggest that Reading has changed drastically since 1920. The area was particularly hard hit by the demise of industry (especially the Reading Railroad) after World War II, and by 2010, it had earned the unenviable distinction of the U.S. city with the highest poverty rate.[228] That said, there are some remnants of the winery and resort era to be found—for those who know where to look—and the region's natural resources remain extremely accessible.

As a whole, the Pennsylvania wine industry continues to grow and improve, Berks being no exception—while not as prominent within the statewide wine industry as it was in 1900. And while nobody is growing grapes commercially on Mount Penn or Neversink, if it once was a great place to produce wine, it doesn't seem a stretch to suggest it could be again.

Berks County now boasts more than fifteen wineries, with events and tastings held throughout the year. Of this group, Pinnacle Ridge, Sutter Ridge and Manatawny Creek have had particular success with *vinifera* and continue to expand their influence throughout the region. Pinnacle Ridge, for example, is now available in Wegmans, ACME and Giant stores, and several bars in Philly serve its keg wine.

As described by William Woys Weaver and discussed in the introduction, the cuisine popular at Reading wine houses has all but died out from a commercial perspective, replicated in touristy, lackluster diners or replaced by more modern fare. (Berks-style chicken and waffles can, occasionally, be found on special at area restaurants and at the Reading Terminal Market in

Philadelphia.) On the positive side, the Ringgold Band—which merged with the Germania Orchestra in 1901—still exists and plays dates in and around Reading regularly.

The Berks History Center museum, as mentioned previously, has a small but important collection of artifacts from the time, including Kuechler's portrait and the stamtisch table and chairs from the new Kuechler's Roost. Over in the BHC Jaansen Library, George Meisler IX's *The Passing Scene* series showcases an astonishing collection of photographs, even more than could be featured in this book.

Some ruins of the Gravity Railroad also exist, according to the Pagoda-Skyline historical organization. An old gravity railcar stands beside a residence at Hill Road & Glenn Road, and another sits to the side of the Lower Alsace Township building on Carsonia Avenue. A cement slab to the south of the Lindbergh Viaduct and stone pillars on the north side indicate where the Gravity station once stood. Portions of graded rail beds are evident around Mineral Spring Park, and some of the railroad's paths now cross portions of Hill Road, Haag Road, Spook Lane and Angora Road.

Mount Penn, of course, is far more accessible now than it was back then, with the William Penn Memorial Fire Tower—built on the foundation of the original Tower—easily accessible by car via Duryea and Skyline Drives. For

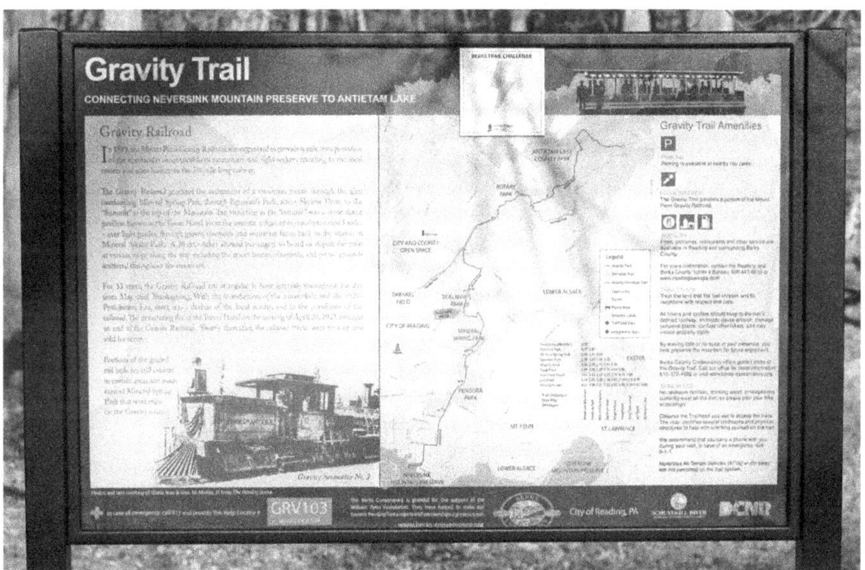

A sign along the Gravity hiking and biking trail in modern-day Reading. *Author photo.*

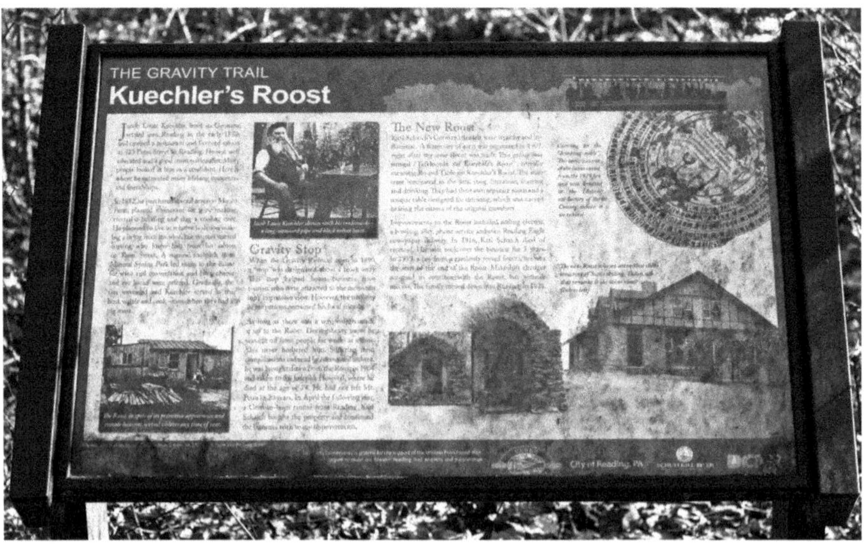

A sign near the former site of Kuechler's Roost, along the Gravity Trail. *Author photo.*

those with energy and enthusiasm, however, it may be preferable to do it the Foosganger way, hiking the "Gravity Trail" from Pendora, Mineral Spring or Egelman Park, up the mountain to Kuechler's Roost and Antietam Lake Park, which has incorporated the former Wildwood Park. (Cheaters can drive to Rotary Park and join the trail near the back of the fields, just below the Roost property.) Similar paths can be found to the Pagoda as well as on Neversink. Expect to see plenty of mountain bikers, who have reclaimed many of these trails as their own.

Not too long ago, I hiked up to the Roost alone. My experience was not that different from young Kuechler's: though I did encounter a pack or two of bikers early on in my trek, when I reached the hallowed spot, it seemed I was the only soul on the mountain. Aside from the remnants of Schiach's wine cellar—which is in surprisingly good condition—and foundations of the lodge, plus maybe a few once cultivated, now wild grapevines, there was no evidence of modern life anywhere in sight, and all I could hear was birds chirping. As I breathed in the mountain air, relished my solitude and felt my own workaday cares melting away, I couldn't help but think that Kuechler himself would've wanted it this way.

Appendix A

CHRISTOPHER SHEARER ON HOW WINE IS MADE

Mr. Shearer Tells How High Grade Wines Are Made.

The Famous Winemaker Describes the Process by Which He Obtains Such Excellent Results—How Quality is Maintained.

C.H. Shearer, the well-known vineyardist, who has spent the greater part of his life in the production of high grade domestic wines at Tuckerton, this county, was in this city the other day, and in the course of a conversation with a *Times* representative, spoke entertainingly on what constitutes good wine and how it is obtained.

"Good wine," said Mr. Shearer, "should contain these qualities: The color of red wine should be a deep madder. The scintillating lights playing in the wine glass must appear light and dark crimson, sometimes verging to the purples and deep, rich reds. The sheen ever [sic] the wine should not be umber or brown, but of a silver hue, with here and there tiny flashes of rare ultramarine. A poor colored wine is yellow, red or umber. The flavor must be agreeable and very grapy. The more pronounced the grape flavor, the better the wine.

"The effect on the tongue should continue for some time and be without any foregone taste. Above all it should leave a clear head. It should be invigorating and strengthening. It should not cause heat, headache nor thirst. When being poured into a glass a whizzing sound, such as the running of silvers and produces, should be heard, and the wine must leap up into a multitude of pearls. There must, in addition to the wine ether, be an aroma. It should not be over much intoxicating and it must be extra dry. When being served, an excellent wine will fill the room with the odor of grapes. Such are the qualities I am endeavoring to obtain in the wines I make.

"But how do you make wines in which all the qualities you have named are preserved?" asked the *Times* representative.

"First of all," replied Mr. Shearer, "I endeavor to have the grapes as ripe as possible. When they are not so I have them spread out on the barn floor and also on sieves, where they are left until the stems are perfectly dry. Next the grapes are carefully picked from the stems, all the rotten and imperfect berries being thrown away. By doing this I not only increase the saccharine matter, but also refine the combination of acids, the coloring properties, the flavor, and, in fact, all the fruit and gummy parts. The latter is always injurious to wine, and especially so where green berries and stems are permitted to remain. It not only destroys the grape flavor, which is so desirable in wine, but imparts a disagreeable and musty taste. The same may also be said of the gelatine acids.

"To get an idea of the dross, examine the bunches of grapes as they grow in the vineyard. You will find numberless half grown and green grapes, some dry, rattling and mouldy grapes, particles of dead leafage, spider webs and vermin and a network of stems, all of which are elements destructive to the production of good wine. All these obnoxious parts must be kept out of the wine casks.

"I agree with the Count de Odart, a rich vineyard proprietor of France, who says in his 'Observations sur le moment des Vendages,' that in order to produce good wine the berries must not only be carefully picked, but must be exposed to the air, spread out on hurdles. The Count, since 1833, has confined himself to this process and now makes a wine that markets at from three to four francs a bottle. Before the observance of this method the same vineyard produced wine which netted only from three to four sous [a five-centime coin] a bottle."

"Is there not considerable deception practiced by wine producers in order to make the business profitable?" asked the *Times* man.

"Yes," said Mr. Shearer, "there is. I am sorry to say. But my endeavor has always been to produce the best wine possible and I think I am succeeding. My chief aim always has been to strive for quality and not quantity. I am now producing three grades of wine from the same grapes, which I am satisfied will meet the requirements of even the most fastidious."

"What is your process for making three grades of wine from the same grape? Is it a secret?" was asked of Mr. Shearer.

"No, it is no secret. I'll tell you how I do it," said Mr. Shearer. "After the grapes have been thoroughly cleansed in the manner I told you, I run them through a roller mill where they are mashed. The crushed grapes are then placed in fermenting barrels, and the open ends of the casks carefully covered with cloths to prevent dust, dirt and other foreign matter from getting into the mash and also to prevent the grape flavor escaping. When the grape shells rise to the surface, the mash is stirred to keep the juice and shells mixed. The first turbulent ferment about half over, the shells are permitted to rise to the surface and a rubber hose is passed through the floating shells and the liquid drawn off from the bottom. The liquid thus drawn off is placed into large casks in the cellar, where it undergoes low fermentation. This first run I style 'C. H. Shearer's X Pure Grape Juice.'"

"The remaining juice and shells in the barrels are stirred twice and three times a day, until the turbulent fermentation is over. This juice retains the best of the fruit parts in the shells. The whole mass is next placed into a press and the remaining juice extracted. This is known as 'C. H. Shearer's XX Pure Grape Juice.' The pomace is then returned to the fermenting barrels, where it is mixed with sugar and water, after which a new ferment sets in. When the ferment is over the liquid is pressed from the pomace and labeled C. H. Shearer s Light Table Wine.' The chemical composition of the last wine is about the same as that recommended by Dr. L. Gall, whose system is practiced throughout the entire civilized world, which is in consistency a little more than one-third grape juice, a trifle less than two-thirds water and about two pounds of sugar to the gallon. No utensils used in wine making should be rinsed with water, but should be cleansed with good brandy, as is done in the Bordeaux regions."[229]

Appendix B

GERMAN AND PENNSYLVANIA GERMAN POEMS FROM MOUNTAIN LOG BOOK

(via *Reading Times*)

Many entries were scribbled in German or Pennsylvania German, which I've done my best to reproduce here. (If any mistakes are noticed, please note that I don't speak German or Pennsylvania Dutch, and the scans of these old newspapers are not always crystal clear.)

First, this poem from Samuel A. Baer, published on December 14, 1897:

Heut ist's feucht, heut ist's kuehl,
Doch sin mir lustig, un ziemlich flehl.
Am Kuechler's Roost da ist's gut sein,
Der Platz ist schoen, un die Luft ist rein;
Un der Kuechler selbst mit schoenem betragen
Weis was zu thun un immer was zu sagen.
Fuer Kaelt un Zahnweh 'giebt er Wein-punch,
Fuer Hunger un Durst an Elsaxer Lunch
Gesundeheit, Kuechler!—mit seliger Lust
Leb' lang un froehlich in deiner Roost

(rough translation)
Today it's wet, today it's cool,
But I'm funny, and a lot of trouble
At Kuechler's Roost it's gonna be good

The place is beautiful, and the air is pure;
Even Kuechler himself is beautiful
What to do and what to say.
For cold and toothache he gives wine-punch,
For hunger and thirst, Alsace Lunch
To health, Kuechler!— with blissful desire
Long may you live in your roost

***

"Kuechler's Ruuscht," one H.L. Fisher's most singular poems—according to Woys Weaver—was originally part of a holiday letter to friends.

Kuechler's Ruuscht

(Der Ehrvoller Alsace Fuszganger Klubb Gewitmet)

Hail, mine own hill—ye bright'ning hilltops, hail!
Hail, sun that gild'st them with thy looks of love;
Sweet fields! ye lindens, murmuring to the gale
And ye, gay choristers, the boughs above:
And thou, the blue immeasurable Calm,
O'er mount and forest, motionless and bright—
Thine airs breath through me their reviving balm,
And the heart strengthens as it drinks thy light!
Thou gracious Heaven! man's prison-home I flee—
Loosed from the babbling world, my soul leaps up to thee!

—Schiller, Hempel's translation.

"Drei Meil hinnig Red'n," do isch 'en Weiberg
Un der Weeg nuf isch ziemlich geh;
Dort leewe die Herre so luschtig wie Lerch
Un freue sich, dort, in der Heh!

Im Frihling, so wan die Fegel z'ruck kumme
Un singe un peife so sche;
Im summer—die Luft, wohlreichend mit Blumme—
Wie lieblig isch's dort in der Heh!

Im Herbscht, wan der Wald isch brau, geel un roth,
Un de Fegel, die, singe, "Adee,"—
Wan die Felder im Dhaal sin gree mit der Soot
Wie herlich isch's dort uf der Heh!

Im Winter, wan Bam un Felder sin bloosz,
Un's Blimli schlooft unner 'm Schnee
Wan alles isch schtumm un weisz wie der Doot,
Doch heemelt's em a' uf der Heh.

Der Weeg nuf isch uwerecks, eng, un krumm,
Un laaft uwer Felse un Schtee;
Was gewwe die luschtige Fuszganger d'rum,
Mil Wei un Gesang uf der Heh?

Im Morge, so wan die Sun sich erhelt,
Un Aurora gukt wie der Roth See—
Am Owet so wan die Sun unnergeht,
Wie 'r getzlich isch's dort uf der Heh.

Der Schnee maag so dief sei—bis an die Knie,
Doch traue mer als zu de Bee;
Mer saddle juscht uf un laafe dort hi',
Un schtelle dort uf—uf der Heh.

En jede, der, traagt sei eegne Lascht nuf—
Ja, des muss er dhu—all allee;
Wie 'n Dampfgaul, doch macht er als, "huff! huff! huff!"
Un der Dampf schteigt hooch in die Heh!

Ich hab schun geleese fun Himmel uf Erd,
In Lender weit uwer de See—
Was ware sie all zumm'e Fuszganger weerd,
Im Hausel, do, hooch uf der Heh!

Ich hab, a'h schun g'heert fum e' "Hausel am Rheln,"—
En Hausel, "net grosz un net klee;"
Doch, geb mer die Freiheit, Ferknege, un Wein,
Im Hausel, do, hooch uf der Heh.

'S isch net in Geld, un het mer die Welt,
So wet mer doch immer noch meh;
Hier sin mer so luschtig un frey wie die Held'
Un die Adler, do, hooch in der Heh.

So liftig un heftig wie'm Adler sei Nescht,
Uf de Alpen—weit uwer 'm See—
So schtandhaft wie'm Kaiser sei Schloss un sei Fescht,
Schteht's Hausel, do, hooch uf der Heh.

Im Winter bloost Boreas grimmig un scharf,
Un die Luft isch lewendig mit Schnee;
Dan schpielt alt Eolus sei bescht's uf der Harf,
Uf 'm Hausel, do, hooch uf der Heh,

Es Wasser, die Luft, un alles isch rein—
Do gebt's ke' Malari, O! nee;
Ke' Hausel am Neckar, ke' Palascht am Rhein,
Wie's Hausel, do, hooch uf der Heh!

Es kummt a'h, net bal, en Ketzer do heer—
Ke' Kranket, ke' Krampet, ke' Weh;
Un es gans Johr-rum wert's Fessli net lehr,
Am Weiberg, do, hooch uf der Heh,

Es Leewe isch flichtig un kurz bey uns' all,
Un der Wandel isch krimig un geh:
Doch heemelt em a' der Hall un der Schall,
Am Weiberg, do, hooch uf der Heh,

Eudlich, "Aschen zu Aschen un Schtaab zu Schtaab,"
Un en Felse zum Denkmal-Schtee!
O, dan schenk uns hier, en friedliches Kraab,
Un Seeligkeit, dort, in der Heh![230]

***

This poem, attributed only to "Fussgaanger & Co.," was published without further comment in the *Reading Times* on January 17, 1907:

Kuechler's Roost

Im Sonnenschein, von Reading her,
Geh uebern' Berg ich kreuz und quer
Und wenn es regnet oder pust'
Eil ich grad-weg's nach "Kuechler's Roost."

Jedoch vom Roost herab ins Thal,
Das ist ue' Sach', oft sehr fatal,
Nachdem ich mich gelabt benn Wein,
Und wacklich bin auf beide Bein!

Und trank ich Reading's Flaschenbier,
Dann ist's wohrhoftig kein Placrier(?)
Weil sein Volumen "H (2) O"
Stark reagirt, wie immer so.

Drum de Moral davon nun sei—
"Eil' schnell an jeder Kirch" vorbei
Hin auf den Berg! In die Natur!"
Denn Sonntag's giebt's hier Kaffe nur.

Nicht fest gebauut, an Reading's grosses Leiden—
"Das Kirchengehen"—sei der brave Mann;
Er soll dasselbe ganz und gar vermeiden,
Wo die Natur hier Berg und Thalersaun.

Die in der Pracht der Reading Jungfrau gleichen.
Die hoch entsueckt die Pfade mit ihm fusst.
Und gluecklich ist, wenn unter hohen Eichen,
Das traute Heim sie gruesst auf "Kuechler's Roost."

Appendix C

GERMAN POETRY PENNED BY KUECHLER

EINGEFANDT

Ueber'm Berg lag Nebel den ganzen Tag.
Mit der Nacht kam Sturm und Regen
Der "Bachofen" hinter'm Berg that einen Krach,
Und: Bums! Da war er gelegen
Und aus den Trümmern flog der Storch empor,
Der klapperte mit dem Sturm im Chor

Und als man die Geschichte näher befah,
Lag neben der Mutter ein Junge Da.
Der liesz sich dann hören durch's ganze Haus
Und schrie so laut er nur konnte heraus,
Und der kleine Walie rief ängstlich aus
Papa! Jag' doch die Katz hinaus !!!

Under Elsass, Jan 1894[231]

***

Appendix C

The Lawyer and the Farmer, or, Lard and Oleomargarine

Es wohnt ein Bauer in Elsaszland,
Sein Name ist gar wohlbekannt.
Auch hat er einen guten Klang,
Denn Guthart heist der bied're Mann.

Allwöchentlich zum Markt er fährt
Mit Sachen, die der Mensch begehrt,
Als Kraut und Rüben, Käs und Butter
Und sonst beliebtem Menschenfutter

Auch bringt er jeden Morgen früh
Die süsze Milch von Schweizerküa
Nach Grof's berühmten Restaurant,
Das Jedermann ist wohlbekannt.

Herr Guthart ist ein smarter Mann,
Der such Küchenabfall brauchen kann,
D'rum nimmt er auch, so zu und ab,
Des Oeftern heim von Grof's "die Schlapp."

Es wohnt auch in Reading ein Gentleman,
Ein Rechtsgelehrter und Ex-Congressman,
Der zur Erholung in frischer Luft
Gern die Berge von Elsasz Taunschip besucht.

Die Wege sind ihm wohlbekannt
Durch's ganze liebe Elsaszland,—
Do kam er jüngst, so kreuz und quer,
Auch durch Guthart's Baurel daher.

Begrüszt Herrn Guthart mit Wort und Hand,
Fragt nebenbei auch nach dem Viehstand.—
Da bemerkt er zwei Ständer in der Yard
Deren Inhalt gar sonderbar duften that.

"Was haben Sie denn in den Fässern hier?
"Machen Sie daraus wohl Wein oder Bier?"—
Herr Guthart aber platxt grad' heraus :
"Da mach' ich das feinste Schmalz daraus!"

Da sprach unser Lahjer aus treuem Herzen :
"Herr Guthart, Sie belieden wohl zu scherzen?
"Sie haben vielleicht so'n verflixte Maschin
"Und machen daraus wohl Oleomargarin?"

Da lachte Herr Guthart ganz fürchterlich
Und sprach, indem er den Schnurbart strich—
"Ihr Herr'n vun der Lah versteht's freilich net:
"Do mach ich jo mei Säu mit fett!"[232]

Appendix D

MENUS FROM PLEASANT VIEW HOTEL

Annual Supper of the Bohemian Club, Pleasant View Hotel

Oyster cocktail
Cream of tomato soup
Celery—Olives—Pickles
Stewed chicken
Cranberry sauce
Apple sauce
Stewed onions
Sweet potatoes
Lancaster dried corn
Waffles
Baked filling
Neapolitan ice cream
Pudding cake
Wine
Coffee
Cigars, cigarettes, etc.[233]

Press Club Dinner

"Excellently prepared and daintily served menu"

Chickens and waffles
Green peas and green beans
Mashed potatoes
New beets
Creamed potatoes
Tomato sauce
Sliced tomatoes
Apple sauce
Lettuce
Cheese
Banquet wafers
Pies, custards, ice cream
Cigars[234]

Kline, Eppihimer & Company Annual Banquet

Oyster cocktail
Cream of tomatoes
Celery—Pickles—Olives
Stewed chicken
Baked filling
Waffles
Stewed onions
Dried corn
Cranberry sauce
Apple sauce
Cold slaw [*sic*]
Shellbark ice cream
Cakes
Demi tasse[235]

Appendix E

"NEW" ROOST MENU AND WINE LIST

A menu from the early to mid-1910s, found at the Berks History Center Library, reads like so:

Regular Dinners, Including Dessert and Coffee

Spring Chicken and Waffles	$1.00
Stewed Chicken and Waffles	90¢
Tenderloin Steak	85¢
Sirloin Steak	75¢
Ham and Eggs	60¢
Roast Beef, Veal or Lamb	60¢
Cold Cuts	50¢ and 75¢

Cold Meals Served on Short Notice

Westphalia Ham	35¢
Ham, Boiled	25¢
Tongue, Smoked	25¢
Potato Salad	15¢
Lettuce Salad	15¢
Olives	15¢

Sardines, per box	35¢
Russian Caviar	60¢
Cervelat Wurst	20¢
Cervelat Wurst, Imported	25¢
Swiss Cheese (Emmenthaler)	25¢
Limburger Cheese	20¢
Kräuter Käse with Butter	20¢
Sandwiches, to order	10¢
Coffee, Tea, Chocolate or Milk	5¢

Wine List

Domestic Wines

	Quart	Pint
Home made Red Wine	.40	.20
California White or Red Wine	.50	.25

Rhine Wines

Vintage WHITE—

1911—St. Martiner	.90
1911—Budenheimer	1.00
1908—Niersteiner	1.20
1911—Niersteiner Burgweg	1.35
1906—Rudesheimer	1.60
1907—Liebfraumilch	1.85
1906—Schloss Johannisberger .... Seal Furst v. Metternich	2.75
1908—Marcobrunner .... Seal Schloss Reinhartshausen	3.00

RED—

1909—Oberingelheimer	1.25
1905—Assmanshauser	1.75

Steinwein-Boxbeutel

1911—Wurzburger Stein Riesling	2.00

Imported and Domestic Cigars and Cigarettes

Moselle Wines

Vintage	Quart	Pint
1910—Trabener	.90	
1910—Piesporter	1.25	
1911—Mulheimer	1.25	
1906—Erdener Treppchen	1.60	
1911—Eitelsbacher Karthäuser Hofberger	2.00	
1911—Graacher Himmelreich	2.50	

Bordeaux Wines

	Quart	Pint
Medoc	1.10	
St. Julien	1.60	

Champagne and Sparkling Wines

Imported	Quart	Pint
Burgeff Extra Cuvee, Extra Dry	3.50	
G.H. Mumm & Co. Extra Dry	4.50	2.25
Duc de Montebello, Brut	4.50	2.25

American Sparkling Wines	Quart	Pint
Gold Seal	2.00	1.00
White Top	2.00	

Pilsner beer on draught . . . . per glass 10¢ and 20¢

Mineral water, various Liqueurs and Cordials

Imported and Domestic Cigars and Cigarettes

Appendix F

MOUNT PENN SUMMIT HOTEL, SUPPER MENU

Broiled

Beefsteak, plain, with Onions or Tomato Sauce
Lamb Chops
Ham
Liver and Bacon

Fish

Eggs

Fried
Boiled
Scrambled
Omelette, Plain
Ham Omelette
Parsley Omelette
Poached on Toast

Cold Meats

Roast Beef
Ham
Tongue

Potatoes

Fried
Saute
Saratoga Chips

Bread and Toast

Plain Bread
Rye Bread
Griddle Cakes
Dry
Buttered
Milk Toast

Coffee
Chocolate
Tea[236]

Appendix G

RECIPES

Berks-style Chicken and Waffles

½ cup butter
½ cup all-purpose flour
2–3 cups chicken stock, warmed
Frozen peas, optional
Cooked, shredded chicken thighs, or supermarket rotisserie chicken, shredded

Make a roux: melt butter over medium heat and mix in flour until a smooth paste is formed. Cook, stirring regularly, until roux is golden brown. Do not use if burned. Whisk in chicken stock slowly, until desired gravy consistency is achieved. Add chicken and peas and simmer until warmed. Serve over hot waffles.

HASENPFEFFER

Adapted from Tom Zimmerman's recipe, as published in *Pennsylvania Dutch and Their Cookery.*

1 rabbit
Apple cider vinegar
Salt and pepper
1 teaspoon ground ginger
All-purpose flour
½ cup mirepoix (minced onion, carrot, celery)
¾ cup heavy cream
¼ cup currant or grape jelly

Soak a disjointed rabbit in enough vinegar to cover, for 6 hours. Drain, dry with a clean towel and rub with salt, pepper and ginger. Then dip the rabbit pieces into flour to coat. Cook in a frying pan, until well browned. Then sauté the mirepoix until lightly browned. Add the browned rabbit; then add sufficient water almost to cover. Simmer 2–2.5 hours. Take the rabbit pieces out. Add the cream and jelly and stir well until combined. Pour sauce over the rabbit and, as Zimmerman notes, "serve very hot."[237]

Appendix H

THE MOUNTAIN RAILROADS OF READING, PENNSYLVANIA

Read at the Engineers' Club of Philadelphia, May 3, 1890, by William H. Dechant, Active Member of the Club.

The city of Reading has a population of about 65,000 inhabitants, and is situated in Berks County, on the Schuylkill River. The average altitude of its streets is about 270 feet above mid-tide. It has a number of natural advantages, among which are these: The rich farming districts surrounding it; its water supply is taken mostly from mountain streams and springs by gravity; building materials, excepting timber, are abundant within the city limits; commercially, it is important in manufactures, and has excellent railway facilities furnished by the Philadelphia and Reading and Pennsylvania Railroads. The natural advantage to which this paper is especially intended to refer is its picturesque mountain surroundings.

The long crest of Mount Penn flanks the city on the east, running almost directly north and south. The Neversink Mountain bounds the city on the southeast; its crest line is divided into a number of ridges and summits, having a general east and west direction.

The highest part of Mount Penn has an altitude of about 1,120 feet above mid-tide, and the highest part of Neversink Mountain an altitude of about 875 feet. Taking 270 feet as the altitude of the average streets, the crest of Mount Penn would be 850 feet above the city, and the highest part of Neversink Mountain 605 feet. The city limits extend up the foot slopes of these mountains, and the tide of advancement has sent its streets up their sides, until they reach a grade of nearly 20 per cent, in some places.

The mountains are covered by a growth of chestnut, oak, laurel and patches of pine and cedar, with points where no growth exists on account of barren rocks. These mountains are the attractive feature in the landscape of this section; heretofore their summits, commanding magnificent views of the surrounding country for twenty, thirty and more miles in extent, have been accessible only to persons able to endure tiresome climbing, with the exception of a portion of Neversink Mountain which has had a drive constructed by the Klapperthal Company, owning a large part of the mountain, to the highest point, and to an observatory erected at that point, and also by an inclined plane running to a summer resort called the Highland House, located at a point on the mountain in line with Thirteenth Street, and being at an altitude of about 500 feet above the average city streets. The use of the drive was, however, beyond the masses of the people, on account of the expensive feature of horses and carriages, and the inclined plane is not constructed or equipped to be capable of handling crowds, or to attract people in any degree timid.

The matter of a gravity railroad on Mount Penn was thought of five years ago and brought to the attention of a number of the business men of the city, until, one year ago, the enterprise assumed definite shape and work was begun. The preliminary surveys on Mount Penn were not completed before the company of gentlemen owning a large part of the Neversink Mountain incorporated the Neversink Mountain Railroad and began work on that mountain also, so that within the short space of a year the city of Reading will have acquired, in the shape of two railroads, each more than seven miles long, facilities that will throw open the attractions of its mountain surroundings.

The original plan for the Mount Penn Gravity Railroad was to ascend the mountain to its highest point by an inclined plane, and from this summit to descend by gravity along the route, to the foot of the plane near the head of Penn Street; but owing to obstructions placed in the way by property owners near the city, the terminus of the road has been placed in the Mineral Spring Park, near Nineteenth and Perkiomen Avenue, at the terminus of the Perkiomen Avenue street car line, and near the terminus of the city passenger railway. At this starting point, where it has an elevation of about 200 feet above the average city streets, it ascends the mountain 658 feet higher by a heavy grade road, 2 $^{42}/_{100}$ miles long; the uniform average grade would be 5 $^{15}/_{100}$ per cent, but it was found necessary to increase this in a number of places, and in one place, for a distance of 700 feet, a maximum of 6 $^{5}/_{100}$ per cent, is used. The alignment in the ascent is also of necessity severe, having two short curves, about 100 feet long, of 146 $^{19}/_{100}$ feet radius, or 40 degrees, and these on 6 per cent, grades. There is a 49-degree curve (radius 120 $^{57}/_{100}$ feet) on the ascent where the road passes to the front of the crest near the summit; but the grade at this point is only 1 $^{6}/_{10}$ per cent. The most severe curve to operate on the ascent is a 20-degree curve (radius 287 $^{94}/_{100}$ feet) on a 6 per cent grade and 750 feet long. The summit of the road is at the highest point on the crest of Mount Penn, called the "Black Spot." From this point the gravity part of the road begins, descending by 1 to 1 $^{6}/_{10}$ per cent, grades, except around sharp curves, where the grades are increased to compensate for the curvature.

There are two points in the descent where curves of 75 feet radius are used to make turns on the side of the mountain, and two points where curves of 100 feet radius are put in to turn on the crest of ridges. The length of the descent is 5 $^{6}/_{100}$ miles, making a total of 7 $^{48}/_{100}$ miles in length for the whole road. The route of the road in the ascent is through the Mineral Spring ravine and up back of the mountain, until, within about 1,000 feet from the summit, it passes around the crest, to the front of the mountain, where the Lebanon Valley and the city of Reading burst into view. From this point to the summit, and for 4,500 feet north of the summit, the road runs along the front of the crest line, then turns to the east side of the crest and traverses the undulating table-land back of the mountain, circling around prominent points commanding extended views of the valleys toward the east, and passing through more cultivated districts, to the starting point.

The road is in operation. The motive power at present is a Baldwin locomotive weighing about 22 tons. This locomotive is capable of drawing two cars, carrying together 150 people from the starting point to the summit at the rate of twelve miles per hour. From the summit the cars run on by gravity, and the engine returns to the starting point. The speed of the cars on the gravity portion is kept to twelve miles per hour, so that the round trip occupies about 40 minutes. The company has contracted for two more locomotives of the Shay pattern, which are now on the way. These locomotives weigh 28 tons, and are geared engines, especially adapted for running sharp curves and steep grades. They are expected to draw three loaded cars to the summit. With this capacity, and making the trips 15 minutes apart, they expect to be able to handle 1,000 passengers per hour. The traffic on the Mount Penn Gravity has been good. On several occasions, with their present facilities, they were unable to accommodate all the people.

The intention of the persons in charge and interested in the road is to establish hotels and pavilions on its route to make attractive summer resorts for excursionists and others.

The Neversink Mountain Railroad has its terminus at Ninth and Penn Streets, near the heart of the city. From this point, runs southward out Ninth Street and the White House road, about one mile within the city limits. At Ninth and Penn Streets it has an altitude of 282 feet above mid-tide and only 12 feet above the average city streets. About 2,000 feet from the starting point it reaches its lowest altitude on the city side, 230 feet above mid-tide or forty feet below the average streets, and from this point it ascends by grades between 1 and 6 $^{4}/_{10}$ per cent, to the White House, 1 $^{1}/_{8}$ miles from the starting point—the 6 $^{4}/_{10}$ percent, grade being 900 feet long. At the White House the road which has been running in a southerly direction terminates in a switch, and from there runs in a northeastwardly direction to keep on the northern side of the mountain in view of the city. The altitude at the White House is 406 feet above mid-tide, or 136 feet above the average city streets. From this point up the mountain a uniform grade of 3 $^{94}/_{100}$ per cent, is maintained for a distance of 1 $^{8}/_{10}$ miles, to a point where the road turns through a gap around a point of the mountain; at this point the altitude is 770 feet above mid-tide and 500 feet above the average city streets. From this point the road descends by 1 and 1 $^{6}/_{10}$ per cent, grades for 2,000 feet, crossing over a depression in the mountain to reach another summit, which it ascends for 1,500 feet by a 4 per cent, grade, reaching the *summit of the road* at an altitude of 806 feet above mid-tide, 536 feet above the average city streets, and 576 feet above the lowest part of Ninth Street. After passing the summit the road descends by from 2 $^{4}/_{10}$ to 3 $^{64}/_{100}$ per cent, grades to its southern terminus, where it makes direct connection with the Philadelphia and Reading Railroad.

The alignment from the city to the White House has a number of short curves of 75 feet radius through turnouts and around a street corner. Beyond that, the most severe curves are 40 degrees (146 $^{19}/_{100}$ feet radius), and four in number (with others less severe), along the precipitous side of the mountain, and on a 3 $^{64}/_{100}$ per cent, grade. These curves are short, however, the longest one being 195 feet.

The length of the road from Penn Street to the summit is 3 $^{62}/_{100}$ miles, and from the summit to the southern terminus is 3 $^{33}/_{100}$ miles, making together nearly seven miles.

The route of the road has been carefully planned to take advantage of the prominent points of outlook, and also with a view of giving access to the greatest amount of property on the mountain, much of which is very well adapted by the character of its surface for the location of private residences, hotels and summer resorts. From the White House the line passes along the north side of the mountain in an easterly direction, in full view of the city, until it passes around and back of Observatory Point, through what is called Goods Gap. From this point it undulates over the top of the mountain, passing in front of the Highland House and around the western end of the mountain, running thence southeastwardly to its southern terminus, and passing over the famous Klapperthal ravine by a trestle 35 feet high.

The beauty of the scenery along the western and southern sides of the mountain is very much enhanced by the windings of the Schuylkill River and its valleys, of which there is an almost uninterrupted bird's-eye view. Its direct connection with the Philadelphia and Reading Railroad will make it possible to receive and handle large excursion parties promptly.

It is expected that the construction of the Neversink Mountain Railroad will be completed in June next and that the road will be in operation in that month.

The motive power is to be electricity, generated by a waterpower plant located at the big dam on the Schuylkill River below Reading, close to the southern terminus of the road, to which I desire to call your attention later on, after it is in successful operation.

The electrical equipment is being furnished by the Sprague Company; the two motors on each car are to have a combined capacity of 30 horse-power. The overhead system is to be used. This road does not make a circuit as does the Mount Penn Gravity road, but the cars run in both directions over the same route, passing each other at passing sidings located at proper intervals.

Both roads are constructed to the standard gauge of 4 feet 8½ inches, with steel rails weighing fifty to fifty-six pounds per yard, the Neversink Mountain using tram rails within the city limits. Both roads use double-truck cars and will be equipped throughout in a thoroughly substantial manner.[238]

Appendix I

SUCH A FUN TIME

by Miss Gushie Gurgle

Originally published in Mekeel's Weekly Stamp News, *Volume 29, 1915.*

I know you are all just dying to hear all about the fun we had at Reading. Have you ever been there? I hope you have, for if you have not, you just can't understand how perfectly lovely it all was. You know the people are so hospitable they just entertained us every minute,—met us at the train and told us that the town was ours. Wednesday evening, Mr. and Mrs. Kissinger gave a reception; not a stiff one, where everybody just smiles and says sweet things to everybody else, but just a real jolly one, where everybody had a good time. We had lots of good things to eat and the grandest punch,—say, but you should have seen Henry Ades help serve; and he didn't leave until everybody else had gone; he stayed to get an extra dish of ice cream, I guess.

Thursday morning, the convention opened and philatelists were coming on every train. Wasn't it a shame that poor Brody missed the last car out of Kutztown and had to stay there all night.

We had such a grand trip, right up to the top of Neversink Mountain, where refreshments were served, just ginger ale and things. We got back to the hotel just in time to dress for the banquet that Clifford Kissinger gave at the Berkshire Hotel. It was lovely; such a good dinner and so many speeches; they were all good. The last speaker was Mr. McDermott; he told us how hard it was for him to give us that talk as he had written all the speeches given by the other men and didn't have much left. I wonder if he really did.

Friday, we went to Kuechler's roost [*sic*] by trolley on Mt. Penn; we stopped at the tower and danced; Cliffie Kissinger, Brody and Percy Mann all danced beautifully. Percy is so much like Vernon Castle. We didn't want to leave there, but the car was ready and we went on to Kuechler's Roost. I wish I had time to tell you all about the Roost; it was started by a funny old hermit who lived up there all alone. Now it is a popular resort. We sat around the round table, drank lemonade, ate pretzels and had such a good time; and wasn't it lovely of Harry Kantner, Fred Fox and Clifford Kissinger to serve us such a nice Dutch lunch. We enjoyed it so much after our mountain ride. After lunch, Mr. Fowler had a sale; it was such fun to bid and so exciting,—every time I was ready to bid, the auctioneer said "gone" and it was all over.

We had a picture taken and it was fine of everybody except me; I am always so disappointed in my own picture.

Saturday morning we all felt so sad that the convention was almost over. Early in the afternoon we went on an auto ride to the Pagoda on Mt. Penn. When we got back to the hotel, everybody was packing and getting ready to go. The Wallis' and Ponds left by auto for Atlantic City and other eastern points. Mr. and Mrs. Parker motored to their home in Bethlehem. Mr. and Mrs. Eilers and their little girl returned to St. Louis. Mrs. Lycett seemed so sorry to go as she had such a good time. We all feel so very grateful to Mrs. Kissinger who did so much to entertain the women at the convention.

Now we are all looking forward to Washington next year and to meeting Mrs. Mason. We just can't wait.

Appendix J

LIST OF NAMES ON THE ROOST STAMTISCH TABLE

Names on table starting at inner circle

W. Rosenthal
H Janssen
G. Oberlaender
F. Thun
J. Nolde
O. Reissmann
J. Kaufmann
R.C. Rahm
F. Mertz
J. Weiler
E. Buser
U. Ammann
L. Heilbron
M. Langer
L. Herman
P. Freitag
F. Huber
M. Moyer
M. Mittendorf
P. Bissinger
R. Tombo
H. Schumann
E. Spindler
W.F. Remppis
G. Ott
R. Meinig
G. Pohlig
E. Bechtel
M. Reimer
E. Oberlaender
H. Hemmerich
M. Woske
H. Fry
F. Grund
T. Zimmerman
R. Cronan
O. Schweizer
A. Ulshoefer
A. Pfister
J. Pfleging
H. Roper
S.H. Flury
Rudolf Herzog

NOTES

Introduction

1. Benjamin A. Fryer, "Kuechler's Roost," *Historical Review of Berks County* 1, no. 1 (October 1935): 15–18.

Chapter 1

2. Hudson Cattell and Linda Jones McKee, *Pennsylvania Wine: A History* (Charleston, SC: The History Press, 2012), 8.
3. U.P. Hedrick, *The Grapes of New York* (Project Gutenberg, 2014), 160–63, www.gutenberg.org/ebooks/45978.
4. Ibid.
5. Ibid.
6. Ibid.
7. Thomas Pinney, *A History of Wine in America: From the Beginnings to Prohibition* (Berkeley: University of California Press, 1989).
8. Hedrick, *Grapes of New York*, 160–63.
9. Pinney, *History of Wine*.
10. Historical Society of Montgomery County, *Historical Sketches: A Collection of Papers Prepared for the Historical Society of Montgomery County, Pennsylvania* (1910), https://archive.org/details/historicalsketch04hist/page/n5.
11. Hedrick, *Grapes of New York*, 160–63.
12. *Cincinnati Enquirer*, June 31, 1990.

Chapter 2

13. "Reading's Pioneers in Grape Culture," *Reading Times*, July 27, 1875.
14. "Excellent Wines," *Reading Times*, November 26, 1867.
15. "Herr Kuechler's Roost," *Times* (Philadelphia, PA), July 31, 1887.
16. "A Gala Day at Reading," *Times* (Philadelphia, PA), May 14, 1890.
17. "Reading's Pioneers in Grape Culture," *Reading Times*, July 27, 1875.
18. Ibid.
19. Ibid.
20. Ibid.
21. Ibid.
22. Ibid.
23. Ibid.
24. "The Grape Crop in Berks," *Reading Times*, July 12, 1871.
25. "Reading's Pioneers in Grape Culture," *Reading Times*, July 27, 1875.
26. Ibid.
27. "Grape Juice," *Reading Times*, September 26, 1876.
28. Ibid.
29. "Herr Kuechler's Roost," *Times* (Philadelphia, PA), July 31, 1887.
30. "Grape Crop in Berks."
31. "Grape Juice."
32 "Grape Crop in Berks.".
33. "Grape Growers of Berks," *Reading Times*, October 19, 1882.
34. "Closed out the Contents of a Wine Cellar," *Reading Times*, November 22, 1881.
35. "Grape Juice."

Chapter 3

36. George M. Meiser IX and Gloria Jean Meiser, "Wine Growers Thrived in Berks," *Passing Scene* 1 (1982).
37. Ibid.
38. "William Young's Vineyard," *Reading Times*, September 1, 1879.
39. "A Promising Vineyard," *Reading Times*, August 8, 1874.
40. "The Grape Crop in Berks," *Reading Times*, July 12, 1871.
41. *Reading Times*, June 22, 1871.
42. "A Summer Resort," *Reading Times*, June 12, 1871.
43. "American Wines," *Reading Times*, December 22, 1864.

44. "Wines," *Reading Times*, July 1, 1862.
45. "Breneiser's Hall," *Reading Times*, March 18, 1869.
46. "Death of Charles T. Rocktashel and August Vollman (sic)," *Reading Times*, July 14, 1886.
47. "Summer Resort."
48. Thomas W. Leidy, "Vineyards of Berks County," *Historical Review of Berks County* 22 (Spring 1957): 48–49, 968.
49. *Reading Times*, September 21, 1900.
50. "'Stone Match on the Mountains,'" *Reading Times*, April 1, 1878.
51. "Wedding Anniversary," *Reading Times*, February 16, 1882.
52. Raymond E. Hollenback, "The Pennsylvania Germans and Grape Culture (Conclusion)," *Morning Call* (Allentown, PA), February 17, 1951.
53. "Is Now Sole Owner," *Reading Times*, March 29, 1911.
54. "Treasures of a Mountain Log Book," *Reading Times*, March 9, 1898.
55. "Reading. Description of the Queen City of the Great Schuylkill," *Times* (Philadelphia, PA), November 27, 1886.
56. "Death of Isaac N. Levan," *Reading Times*, April 25, 1892.

Chapter 4

57. "Herr Kuechler's Roost," *Times* (Philadelphia, PA), July 31, 1887.
58. "City Affairs," *Reading Times*, December 18, 1865.
59. "Excellent Wines," *Reading Times*, November 26, 1867.
60. "Grape Crop in Berks," *Reading Times*, July 12, 1871.
61. "Among the Times' Advertisers," *Reading Times*, December 24, 1874.
62. "Vollmer Wines," *Reading Times*, January 1, 1872.
63. "Reading's Pioneers in Grape Culture," *Reading Times*, July 27, 1875.
64. "Herr Kuechler's Roost."
65. Pinney, *History of Wine*, 142–43.
66. "Excellent," *Reading Times*, April 12, 1866.
67. *Report of the Transactions of the Pennsylvania State Agricultural Society* (Pennsylvania State Agricultural Society, 1872).
68. "Reading Wines," *Reading Times*, February 28, 1859.
69. Pinney, *History of Wine*, 6.
70. Ibid., 159.
71. Ibid., 163–65.
72. "Splendid," *Reading Times*, July 8, 1867.
73. "Promising Vineyard."

74. "The Grape Crop in Berks," *Reading Times*, July 12, 1871.
75. "The Grape Crop," *Reading Times*, July 13, 1869.
76. Pinney, *History of Wine*, 158–59.
77. Ibid.
78. Advertisement, *Lebanon (PA) Daily News*, May 5, 1884.
79. "Mr. Shearer Tells How High Grade Wines Are Made," *Reading Times*, April 4, 1901.
80. Ibid.
81. Roderick Phillips, *Wine: A Social and Cultural History of the Drink that Changed Our Lives* (Infinite Ideas Publishing, 2018).
82. Leidy, "Vineyards of Berks County."
83. "The Housekeeper," *Reading Times*, September 18, 1880.
84. "Berks Wine Makers Get Crushing Blow," *Philadelphia Inquirer*, July 7, 1918.
85. Phillips, *Wine*.
86. "City Affairs."
87. "Blended Whisky. A Disgusted Dealer Tells Some of the Secrets of the Trade," *Times* (Philadelphia, PA), April 6, 1884.
88. Advertisement, *Reading Times*, April 7, 1874.
89. "City Affairs."
90. Advertisement, *Reading Times*, April 7, 1874.
91. "Vollmer Wines," *Reading Times*, January 1, 1872.

Chapter 5

92. "Herr Kuechler's Roost."
93. "Birthday Celebration," *Reading Times*, October 27, 1880.
94. Ibid.
95. Fryer, "Kuechler's Roost," 15–18.
96. "A Pleasant Occasion," *Reading Times*, October 27, 1875.
97. "Celebration of a Birthday," *Reading Times*, October 27, 1879.
98. "New Hotel Proprietors and New Saloons," *Reading Times*, April 24, 1876.
99. Fryer, "Kuechler's Roost," 15–18.
100. "Santa Claus' Greeting," *Reading Times*, December 19, 1878.
101. "Large Purchase of Clinton Wine," *Reading Times*, January 12, 1878.
102. Fryer, "Kuechler's Roost," 15–18.
103. "A New Enterprise by Mr. J.L. Kuechler," *Reading Times*, April 15, 1878.

104. Ibid.
105. "Tribute Is Paid to the Memory of Kuechler," *Reading Times*, February 11, 1909.
106. Ibid.
107. "Kuechler's New 'Roost,'" *Reading Times*, May 19, 1882.
108. Ibid.
109. Ibid.
110. "Aeolian Harp at Kuechler's Roost," *Reading Times*, August 7, 1880.
111. "Kuechler's Alsace Enterprise," *Reading Times*, May 17, 1883.
112. "Herr Kuechler's Roost," *Reading Times*, August 1, 1887.
113. Fryer, "Kuechler's Roost," 15–18.
114. Ibid.
115. Ray Koehler, "In Era of Kuechler's Roost, People Had Time to Enjoy Life," *Reading Times*, October 11, 1962.
116. "Herr Kuechler's Roost," *Times* (Philadelphia, PA), July 31, 1887.
117. Fryer, "Kuechler's Roost," 15–18.
118. "Potato Roast Today," *Reading Times*, September 23, 1899.
119. "Dinner at Kuechler's Roost," *Reading Times*, November 25, 1886.
120. "Ermentrout on Penn Mount," *Times* (Philadelphia, PA), November 25, 1886.
121. "Dinner on the Mountain," *Reading Times*, October 13, 1884.
122. Ibid.
123. Fryer, "Kuechler's Roost," 15–18.
124. "Tribute Is Paid to the Memory of Kuechler," *Reading Times*, February 11, 1909.
125. Ibid.
126. "Pennsylvania Paragraphs," *Times* (Philadelphia, PA), February 18, 1895.
127. Koehler, "In Era of Kuechler's Roost."
128. "Tribute Is Paid."
129. Ibid.

Chapter 6

130. Ibid.
131. "Herr Kuechler's Roost," *Times* (Philadelphia, PA), July 31, 1887.
132. "Tribute Is Paid."
133. "Treasures of a Mountain Log Book," *Reading Times*, December 14, 1897.

134. "Treasures of a Mountain Log Book," *Reading Times*, November 26, 1890.
135. "Treasures of a Mountain Log Book," *Reading Times*, December 14, 1897.
136. "Well-Known 'Mine Host' of 'Kuechler's Roost' Dead," *Reading Times*, January 4, 1904.
137. "Treasures of a Mountain Log Book," *Reading Times*, December 14, 1897.
138. William Woys Weaver, *As American as Shoofly Pie, the Foodlore and Fakelore of Pennsylvania Dutch Cuisine* (Philadelphia: University of Pennsylvania Press, 2013), 111.
139. "Tribute Is Paid."
140. Ibid.
141. "Treasures of a Mountain Log Book," *Reading Times*, December 20, 1897.
142. "Treasures of a Mountain Log Book" *Reading Times*, March 9, 1898.
143. "Treasures of a Mountain Log Book," *Reading Times*, December 14, 1897.
144. "Tribute Is Paid."
145. "Well-Known 'Mine Host' of 'Kuechler's Roost' Dead," *Reading Times*, January 4, 1904.
146. "A Pennsylvania Battle Waged in Ink," *Philadelphia Inquirer*, January 31, 2016.
147. "Pennypacker's Troubles," *St. Louis Republic*, May 27, 1903.
148. "Pennypacker Under a Cloud," *McKean County Miner* (Smethport, PA), August 6, 1903.
149. "A New Poem and Translation," *Reading Times*, March 7, 1885.
150. *Reading Times*, April 26, 1906.

Chapter 7

151. Beneval Weiss, "Out of This World," *Historical Review of Berks County* (January 1952).
152. "A Public Park," *Reading Times*, June 9, 1866.
153. "A Pleasure Road Over Penn's Mount," *Reading Times*, September 3, 1870.
154 . *The Reading Railroad: The History of a Great Trunk Line* (Burk & McFetridge, 1892), 8, babel.hathitrust.org/cgi/pt?id=mdp.39015035051641;view=1up;seq=8.
155. "Gossip of Autumn Resorts," *Dayton (OH) Herald*, November 2, 1889.
156. "On Mt. Penn," *Morning Call* (Allentown, Pennsylvania), June 17, 1890.

157. "Mt. Penn Gravity R.R.," *Reading Times*, September 30, 1889.
158. Ibid.
159. Ibid.
160. George M. Meiser IX and Gloria Jean Meiser, "Mount Penn Gravity Railroad—Part 1," *Passing Scene* 1 (1982).
161. "Mt. Penn Gravity R.R."
162. "Over the Gravity Road," *Reading Times*, March 26, 1890.
163. "Excursionists Coming," *Reading Times*, May 9, 1890.
164. *Morning News* (Wilmington, DE), July 23, 1890.
165. *Morning News* (Wilmington, DE), September 13, 1890.
166. "Visiting Mount Penn," *Times* (Philadelphia, PA), June 13, 1890.
167. "Editors at Reading," *Miners Journal* (Pottsville, PA), June 13, 1890.
168. "The New Switchback," *Lebanon (PA) Daily News*, June 14, 1890.
169. "On Mt. Penn."
170. "The Gravity Railroad," *Reading Times*, June 18, 1890.
171. Ibid.
172. "Editors at Reading."
173. "New Switchback."
174. "Last Night's Open Air Concerts," *Reading Times*, July 10, 1890.
175. "From All About Us," *Morning Call* (Allentown, PA), July 6, 1890.
176. Weiss, "Out of This World."
177. *Mount Penn Gravity Railroad Souvenir Booklet*, Berks History Center Library, 1902.

Chapter 8

178. "Reading as a Summer Resort," *Reading Times*, July 12, 1889.
179. *Reading, Its Representative Business Men, and Its Points of Interest* (Mercantile Illustrating Company, 1893), 13, books.google.com/books?id=Z9AwAQAAMAAJ.
180. "Reading a Beautiful City," *Reading Times*, July 5, 1890.
181. "A-Top Mount Ganser," Reading Times, December 6, 1883
182. *Reading, Its Representative Business Men*, 11–12.
183. "Reading's Attractions," *Reading Times*, June 1, 1891.
184. Ibid.
185. *Reading Railroad*, 86.
186. George M. Meiser IX and Gloria Jean Meiser, Heart Stone Fashioned by Vintner Kiedeisch," *Passing Scene* 1 (1982).

187. Ibid.
188. Ibid.
189. "Many Philadelphia Germans Visit Here," *Reading Times*, June 16, 1913.
190. "Elephant Hurts His Keeper, Then Charges on Mt. Penn," *Philadelphia Inquirer*, August 21, 1899.
191. "Royally Entertained," *Reading Times*, September 7, 1899.
192. George M. Meiser X and Gloria Jean Meiser, "At Steigerwald's," *Passing Scene* 9 (1994).
193. "Celebrated His 65th Birthday," *Reading Times*, December 22, 1896.
194. "The Three New Mountain Resorts," *Reading Times*, April 8, 1891.
195. "Hotel Improvements," *Reading Times*, May 29, 1899.
196. "Obituary," *Reading Times*, February 24, 1903.
197. "Improvements at Centennial Springs," *Reading Times*, May 12, 1893.
198. "Moses K. Graeff's Birthday," *Reading Times*, May 19, 1898.
199. "Notable Resorts of Berks County," *Philadelphia Inquirer*, June 6, 1897.
200. "The Mount Penn Gravity Road," *Times* (Philadelphia, PA), May 22, 1898.
201. I.A. Mekeel, Charles Esterly Severn and Stephen B. Hopkins, *Mekeel's Weekly Stamp News* 29 (Severn-Wylie-Jewett Company, 1915), 293–95.

Chapter 9

202. "At Kuechler's Roost," *Reading Times*, July 30, 1898.
203. Thomas F. Lombardi, *Wallace Stevens and the Pennsylvania Keystone* (Selinsgrove, PA: Susquehanna University Press, 1996), 45.
204. "Well-Known 'Mine Host' of 'Kuechler's Roost' Dead," *Reading Times*, January 4, 1904.
205. "Kuechler's 'Roost,'" *Reading Times*, January 7, 1904.
206. "In Memory of J. Louis Kuechler," *Reading Times*, April 11, 1906.
207. "Identity of Modest Poet Now Revealed," *Reading Times*, July 26, 1911.
208. "Tribute Is Paid."
209. Ibid.
210. Ibid.

Chapter 10

211. "Midnight Fire Ruins Kuechler's Roost," *Reading Times*, July 5, 1919.
212. "New Kuechler's Roost Is Informally Opened," *Reading Times*, August 23, 1907.
213. "Where Cool Breezes Are Softly Blowing," *Reading Times*, July 15, 1910.
214. Ibid.
215. "Delightful Outing." *Reading Times*, July 27, 1910.
216. "'Mine Host' of Kuechler's Roost Dies Suddenly," *Reading Times*, September 11, 1916.
217. Fryer, "Kuechler's Roost," 15–18.
218. "Where Cool Breezes."
219. "'Mine Host' of Kuechler's Roost Dies Suddenly."

Chapter 11

220. David Roland, "The Era of the Mount Penn Gravity Railroad," *Historical Review of Berks County* (January 1952).
221. "Midnight Fire Ruins Kuechler's Roost," *Reading Times*, July 5, 1919.
222. Ibid.
223. "Much Criticism of Resort Fire," *Reading Times*, July 7, 1919.
224. Fryer, "Kuechler's Roost," 15–18.
225. "Business of Gravity Road," *Reading Times*, January 9, 1923.
226. "Mt. Penn Tower Destroyed in Spectacular Night Fire," *Reading Eagle*, April 24, 1923.
227. "Tower Burns," *Reading Times*, April 24, 1923.
228. "May Abandon Gravity Road," *Reading Eagle*, April 26, 1923.
229. "Reading Eagle 150th Anniversary: Fire Destroys the Tower on Mount Penn on April 24, 1923." *Reading Eagle*, April 22, 2018.
230. Edward A. Taggert, "Prohibition! The Failure of the 'Noble Experiment' in Reading & Berks County (1920–1933)," Berks History Center, www.berkshistory.org/multimedia/articles/prohibition.

Chapter 12

231. Sabrina Tavernise, "Reading, Pa., Knew It Was Poor. Now It Knows Just How Poor," *New York Times*, September 26, 2011.

Appendix A

232. *Reading Times*, April 4, 1901.

Appendix B

233. "Treasures of a Mountain Log Book," *Reading Times*, February 19, 1900.

Appendix C

234. *Reading Times*, February 6, 1894.
235. *Reading Times*, March 28, 1894.

Appendix D

236. *Reading Times*, February 6, 1912.
237. *Reading Times*, July 27, 1904.
238. *Reading Times*, February 9, 1912.

Appendix F

239. Corrie Crupi, "The Gravity Railroad," *Historical Review of Berks County* 74, no. 3 (Summer 2009): 125.

Appendix G

240. J. George Frederick, *Pennsylvania Dutch Cook Book* (Courier Corporation, 2012), 49.

Appendix H

241. *Proceedings of the Engineers' Club of Philadelphia*, vols. 7–8, 1890, https://books.google.com/books?id=t7ASAAAAYAAJ.

INDEX

Y

Z

ABOUT THE AUTHOR

Mike Madaio is a food and wine writer based outside of Philadelphia. His career began with the creation of *Main Line Dine*, a popular restaurant and dining blog covering the Philadelphia suburbs, and his writing has appeared in publications such as *Wine Enthusiast*, *VinePair* and *Edible Philly*. He has also achieved Italian Wine Ambassador certification from the Vinitaly International Academy. This is his first book.

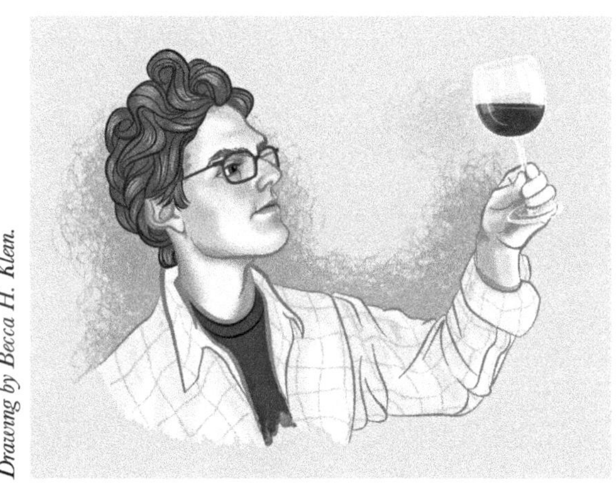

Drawing by Becca H. Klein.

Follow Mike on social @lifeattable.

Visit Mike's website at Lifeattable.com.

www.ingramcontent.com/pod-product-compliance
Lightning Source LLC
LaVergne TN
LVHW052339100826
845147LV00021B/1121

* 9 7 8 1 4 6 7 1 4 1 1 4 7 *